Praise for

DARE TO SPEAK

"*Dare to Speak* is an essential citizen's guide to free speech. Nossel manages to not only illuminate with great insight the complex issues and moral stakes, she also provides a clear path forward."
— **David Grann,** bestselling author of *Killers of the Flower Moon*

"At a moment when Americans seem so unalterably divided and so filled with fury about one another that it seems difficult even to imagine public issues and candidates for office being discussed in a manner that is both civil and serious, *Dare to Speak* offers constructive and potentially achievable ways of thinking about the problem and dealing with it. That's a rare combination of virtues."
— **Floyd Abrams,** author of *The Soul of the First Amendment*

"This timely book not only provides a compelling analysis of free speech's essential role in promoting democracy and human rights, it also serves as a practical 'how-to' manual for every member of our society, explaining how each of us can secure and advance robust free speech rights for all people and all ideas, including the most marginalized. It is an important guidebook for revitalizing liberty, equality, and democracy."
— **Nadine Strossen,** John Marshall Harlan II Professor of Law Emerita at New York Law School and former president of the ACLU

"Free speech is under attack in ways it has never been before in America: from authoritarian populists seeking to constrain an adversarial press, from censorious social media platforms and digital mobs, and from the pernicious misconception that the First Amendment is antagonistic to racial and sexual equality. As CEO of PEN America, Suzanne Nossel has been among our most principled and eloquent frontline defenders of free expression. In her new book, she explores not just the practicalities of speaking freely and effectively in an increasingly illiberal environment but of listening fairly. It's possible to be angry, offended, and passionate while respecting the expressive rights of others. In *Dare to Speak*, she explains how."

— **Jacob Weisberg,** CEO of Pushkin Industries and former editor in chief of the Slate Group

"At a time of declining respect for truth, reason, and decency, *Dare to Speak* offers a framework for promoting the free exchange of ideas in a way that is civil and inclusive. This extraordinarily clever, expertly crafted book is critical reading for anyone who cares about the quality and vitality of our public discourse."

—**Lee C. Bollinger,** president of Columbia University

"Suzanne Nossel writes from the front lines of our political and cultural debates with heart and intelligence, with passion and wisdom. *Dare to Speak* is a vital and urgently needed guide to the numerous threats facing our most cherished rights and a testament to the courage necessary to protect them."

—**Dinaw Mengestu,** award-winning author of
All Our Names and *How To Read the Air*

"In *Dare to Speak,* Suzanne Nossel offers a thoughtful, perceptive, and inspiring set of insights to guide the citizens of our democracy as they struggle to understand and to respect the freedom of speech. Nossel explains why a robust freedom of speech is essential in a free society; the many ways in which the freedom of speech can cause harm, both intended and unintended; and the proper responses to the advocacy of ideas that we loathe and quite naturally want to silence. At a moment in history when these issues are at the forefront of many of our most bitter social and political divisions, *Dare to Speak* makes an essential contribution to our understanding and to our ability to live up to the highest aspirations of our democracy."

—**Geoffrey R. Stone,** coauthor of
Democracy and Equality and *The Free Speech Century*

DARE TO SPEAK

DARE TO SPEAK

DEFENDING FREE SPEECH FOR ALL

SUZANNE NOSSEL

DEY ST.
An Imprint of WILLIAM MORROW

HarperCollins books may be purchased for educational, business, or sales promotional use. For information, please e-mail the Special Markets Department at SPsales@harper collins.com.

FIRST EDITION

Designed by Michelle Crowe

Library of Congress Cataloging-in-Publication Data has been applied for.

ISBN 978-0-06-296603-2

20 21 22 23 24 LSC 10 9 8 7 6 5 4 3 2 1

To my family

CONTENTS

AUTHOR'S NOTE

AFTER GRADUATING FROM COLLEGE IN THE 1990S, I SPENT TWO YEARS IN Johannesburg, South Africa, taking part in efforts to curb deadly political violence during that country's transition from apartheid to democracy. The work involved going to townships to facilitate local peace committees comprising political activists, labor leaders, corporate executives, police, and armed forces seeking ways to forestall violent conflict. This experience—monitoring demonstrations and mediating conflicts—remains the most indelible of my professional life. My colleagues and interlocutors there were among the most dedicated, inspiring, and courageous people I have encountered anywhere. Working at the front lines of community conflict, I gained appreciation for the power of dialogue to bridge divisions, for peaceful protest to force change, and for ideals of freedom, democracy, and equality to inspire. Years later I entered government to represent the United States at the United Nations, helping to forge a global deal to settle the United States' swelling arrearage to the worldwide body. Here my role involved finding common ground across political and ideological schisms, among delegations from nearly two hundred countries. From there I entered the media world, seeing firsthand how essential creative expression and press freedom are to our economy and national identity.

In 2009, I joined the Obama administration, serving at the State Department and focusing on human rights issues at the United Nations. That's where the seeds of this book were planted. One of our priorities was a UN resolution championed by the Organization of the Islamic Conference (now the Organization of Islamic Cooperation), a grouping of Muslim-majority countries. The tract sought to prohibit the so-called defamation of religion, meaning speech that denigrated particular religious beliefs. The premise was that voicing such hostile attitudes—contempt for Muslims, in particular—could fuel discrimination, bigotry, and hate crimes. The push to ban defamation was sparked by a controversy several years earlier over the publication by a Danish newspaper of cartoons that spoofed the Muslim prophet Muhammad. The caricatures triggered peaceful protest but also, several months after the fact, violent reprisals in more than a dozen countries. Western civil society organizations and governments, including the United States, opposed the anti-defamation resolution on the basis that it would impinge on human rights, particularly freedom of expression. Twice a year, in New York and Geneva, we would rally countries to vote against it. Although we always lost, our campaigning was steadily eating away at the majority backing the resolution.

The exercise struck me as absurd. The Islamic Conference countries feared violent bigotry, and sought a worldwide injunction on derogatory speech to curb that harm. Though their preferred solution was wrong, the problem they faced—anti-Muslim prejudice—was real. Meanwhile the biannual diplomatic fight accomplished nothing to either address Islamophobic animus or advance free speech.

Colleagues and I argued for a shift in strategy. We wanted to offer an olive branch, saying that we shared the concerns about discrimination toward Muslims and wanted to work with the Islamic Conference on an alternative resolution centered on practical measures to address it—including dialogue, education, and beefed-up prosecutions for hateful crimes. In return, we would ask the conference to abandon the quest to ban the so-called defamation of religion.

The proposed bargain did not go over well at first. Within the State

Department, many fretted that by showing any willingness to negotiate we would telegraph weakness and end up forfeiting our unstinting defense of free speech. Most Muslim diplomats could not fathom giving up on their treasured resolution. Pakistan was chairing the Islamic Conference, and I fought to make a trip there to formally offer our proposal. It was so difficult to schedule a call with my key interlocutor that I ended up finally being put through during the wee hours of a Sunday morning, speaking from a hotel broom closet so as not to awaken my sleeping family.

When the trip was scheduled, State Department officials could not agree on language for us to present, so a Foreign Service colleague and I had to invent it on the fly, working late on embassy grounds in Islamabad. We explained to the Pakistani officials that prohibitions on speech would not make anti-Muslim sentiment vanish and that they'd be better off with an approach that could attract international consensus rather than an increasingly threadbare majority. They agreed to negotiate. Months later, we had agreement on a new resolution that emphasized global cooperation on practical measures to counter religious intolerance. The Islamic Conference ended its quest for a global ban on criticism of religion. *The Economist* described the outcome as a "diplomatic coup" for the Obama administration and noted that the new approach came as a "relief to both sides." Efforts to implement and fortify the new resolution have now been underway for almost a decade.

This experience led me to the bedrock conviction that the fight against bigotry and intolerance need not—and must not—come at the expense of freedom of speech. This idea has been reinforced over seven years at PEN America, an organization of writers and their allies who come together to celebrate and defend free speech worldwide. We recognize up-and-coming novelists and poets, confer prestigious literary awards, defend persecuted writers around the world, mentor incarcerated writers and others locked out of the literary community, publish reports on pressing free speech issues, and host hundreds of events each year. While we have long worked globally on free expression advocacy in China, Russia, Myanmar, and elsewhere, we have in recent years become alarmed by threats to free speech at home. Although this book is my own work and does not represent organizational policy, my experience at PEN America has shaped my insights and conclusions. Our extensive work on campus free speech has brought me face-to-face with the demands of students to eradicate the stubborn legacy of racial discrimination, and pushed me to explain how free speech precepts are not inimical to that cause but rather can advance it.

During my time at PEN America we have had to address new and virulent threats to free speech, including the spread of fraudulent news, the devaluation of truth in our discourse, the censorious force of online harassment, and the withering away of local news outlets. We confront new questions daily: whether political screeds can amount to incitement, harassment, or other exceptions to the First Amendment; when a protest crosses over from legitimate free speech to silencing the opposing side; whether and how a doctored and misleading video should be shareable on social media; and whether Twitter should ban the president of the United States for violating its terms of service. It feels almost impossible to call this book finished, since every visit to social media or a news platform reveals new speech-related incidents and issues to squeeze into the analysis.

The state of discourse in America today raises a troubling question of whether the principle of free speech can survive intact in our diverse, digitized, and divided culture. Talking about free speech is hard because, inevitably, the speech that gives rise to such conversations is unpopular, offensive, dangerous, or otherwise contestable. In an era when insults can go viral and arguments can be recorded or screenshot to last in perpetuity, the prospect of mixing it up on a contentious issue can be uninviting. When free speech issues arise, it may be easier to follow the crowd, nod along with outraged friends, or change the subject. I am hoping this book makes it easier to resist that temptation and instead enter into dialogue about why free speech matters and how it can be protected without running roughshod over values of equality.

INTRODUCTION

EVERY WEEKDAY I RIDE A PACKED NEW YORK CITY NO. 2/3 SUBWAY TRAIN to and from work. Bodies cling to poles, hands press against the roof for balance, people lean on doors, and elbows, hips, and stomachs abut willy-nilly. Although I ride in Manhattan, the train's full route snakes through the Bronx and out to Brooklyn, uniting a cross section of New Yorkers in which no single race, ethnicity, religion, socioeconomic background, or age group predominates.

Like a gritty ballet, this ritual of diverse riders swaying together in a jammed subway car has a set of protocols that allow it to be performed un-eventfully thousands of times a day. Eye contact is averted. Riders use all their might to prevent the force of the braking train from throwing them into the arms or lap of another passenger. If you jostle or step on a foot, you apologize quietly and are forgiven. No one may take up more than their fair share of space, but those who need more—because of their size or a disability—are mostly accommodated without incident. If an elderly or a pregnant person uses eye contact and positioning to request a seat, someone usually obliges. If somebody encroaches on your space or body, you speak up loudly and those nearby rally. The experience is unpleasant, but the stress of delayed trains, spotty Wi-Fi, shrieking brakes, and the occasional rat on the tracks is—on most days—not compounded by unruly interactions with fellow human beings enduring the same.

A few of the rules—standing clear of the closing doors and avoiding unwanted touches—are reinforced by posted signs. But much of the code that enables more than four million New Yorkers to ride cheek by jowl each day is unwritten. According to 2019 Transit Authority statistics, the system averages one reported crime per every million riders per day. Racism, sexism, belligerence, leering, homophobia, stampeding crowds, and a myriad of other urban ills rear their heads in periodic incidents that inflict trauma and produce headlines. Yet most of the time, most people behave.

Accepted values underpin these norms: the idea that the subway is for all; we have equal entitlements to seats and space; the weak and needy deserve help. If most New Yorkers were not capable of upholding norms that allowed them to self-govern this teeming space, it would need many more rules and far more stringent enforcement.

Coexisting peaceably with fellow New Yorkers on public transportation turns out to be a lot easier than doing so with people from all over the world in public discourse. The subway experience is no model for harmonious living, but it is an example of coexistence that largely avoids out-and-out conflict. Like our society, the subway system is prone to disruptions and sudden jerks. But the people riding it know how to handle those unsettling eruptions. Our encounters on public transport are fleeting, anonymous, and largely silent. Yet without the unwritten guidelines, the subway as we know it would cease to be possible.

In public debates, where meaning, truth, power, and reputation are all at stake, a common set of rules is imperative. Whereas our discourse used to be bounded by geography, social class, language, and the limited reach of media, our global conversation is now a mosh pit of expression where you and your ideas can encounter anyone, anywhere. We need to find ways to self-govern our discourse so that it can remain accessible, open, and freewheeling and that authorities—be they government, institutional, or corporate—are neither tempted nor called on to forcibly intrude. As American society rapidly becomes more demographically diverse, as digitally enabled speech crosses boundaries to reach unintended faraway audiences, and as a polarized political climate tempts us to view others with suspicion or disdain, the potential for misunderstanding and offense multiplies. Big cities are microcosms of society. We need to develop for our discourse an equivalent of the systems and habits that make varied and crowded urban settings livable.

This book suggests guidelines that can protect ideas and opinions from suppression and also widen the circle of those who stand ready to defend free expression. My hope is to offer approaches and principles that can open conversation, tamp down conflict, unearth common ground, and avoid bans or punishments for speech. Rather than formulating mandates for government, technology platforms, universities, or other institutions, this book is focused mostly on the role and responsibility of individuals—all of us—as guardians of free speech. This book is intended for all who seek to voice controversial viewpoints, hear them out from others, and keep their boardrooms, classrooms, dormitories, and dining tables open to fruitful conversations between people whose beliefs differ.

Free speech controversies have become fodder for daily headlines. Hateful speech is on the rise, sometimes linked to hate-fueled crimes, leading some people to question whether freedom of speech is inimical to the values of equality and inclusion. Professors are disciplined or dismissed for offending students. Journalists and celebrities are fired for errant tweets. People argue that articles, poems, and books should be withdrawn from publication because they are offensive, or because the author lacks the life experience to legitimately write them in the first place. Once-obscure legal concepts like defamation and incitement are gaining new vitality. Whether on social media, on TV, or even in everyday conversations, moral denunciation can crowd out thoughtful give-and-take. Online harassment and denigration are rampant. With the harms of expression on daily display, it's easy to question why the framers of the Constitution thought protecting free speech was so important.

Hypocrisy, or at least inconsistency, in defense of free speech runs wild. Lawful protesters are derided for "incivility" for vociferously challenging speakers with whom they disagree. Those who thunder about cops curtailing a boisterous labor picket line may not be so quick to rise to the defense of an anti-abortion demonstrator—or vice versa (as the old taunt goes, "Free speech for me, but not for thee"). And free speech is invoked for partisan purposes—the right wing argues that its speech is under attack, whereas the left downplays free speech concerns in favor of priorities like racial and gender justice. Those who care deeply about *both* free speech *and* equality find themselves pressed to take sides between vaunted principles that sometimes seem to conflict.

These conflicts split along not only ideological but also generational lines. Younger Americans, who lean progressive, place greater weight on diversity and equity encompassing race, religion, gender, sexuality, and other identities. When campaigns on behalf of equality for historically marginalized groups butt up against free speech rights, the younger generation appears more ready to limit freedom of expression. On the flip side, too many free speech champions subordinate very legitimate concerns about racial and gender prejudice, as if they were a secondary set of problems. But the imperatives of realizing an inclusive society are urgent, and young people won't—and shouldn't—agree to subordinate them. We are in the midst of an essential reckoning over the legacy of slavery, racism, and other forms of exclusionary persecution. This process entails critically examining many facets of our society, including our free speech principles. The route to resolve these tensions, I believe, lies in explaining how concerns of diversity and inclusion can—and must—be reconciled with robust protections for speech. The quest for a diverse, inclusive society is in fact fortified by the defense of free speech, and the case for free speech is more credible and more persuasive when it incorporates a defense of equality as well.

The First Amendment: Necessary but Not Sufficient

When you bring up "free speech" to Americans, there's a good chance that, in their response, they'll use the words "First Amendment." It's almost a reflex. Yet many free speech conflicts lie outside the purview of constitutional law. The First Amendment reads, "Congress shall make no law respecting an establishment of religion, or prohibiting the free exercise thereof; or abridging the freedom of speech, or of the press; or the right of the people peaceably to assemble, and to petition the Government for a redress of grievances." Courts have held that it applies not just to "Congress" but also to the executive branch and—through a doctrine known as "incorporation"—state and local governments and institutions like public universities. There are pressing First Amendment battles raging now—involving campaign finance, privacy, and whether the government can compel speech—as there have been for decades.

But because its language is confined to governmental infringements, the First Amendment is silent on many of the free speech conflicts of our time. The First Amendment doesn't offer an answer to the censorious power of online mobs who menace individuals on private Internet platforms. With several narrow exceptions, the First Amendment does not tell us how to curb the detrimental effects of hateful speech. The First Amendment cannot establish which content is too vitriolic, bigoted, deceitful, or misleading to be shared online. It doesn't speak to whether or when a private company can punish an employee for offensive speech, nor whether a private university can deny a platform to a white supremacist or a climate change denier. While First Amendment values shape the conduct of private parties, its influence over them is indirect and often voluntary.

The First Amendment is framed to ensure a "negative right," the right to be free *from* government interference. But free speech also entails an affirmative right to speak out, a liberty that cannot be fully guaranteed in law and must be enabled by society through education and opportunity. When we consider why we value free speech—its truth-finding, democratic, and creative functions—it also becomes clear that the freedom to speak, narrowly construed, isn't enough to guarantee these benefits. That's why at PEN America we often talk of ourselves as not just champions of free speech but also guardians of open discourse. Our role encompasses not just fighting censorship but also combating harassment, disinformation, the denigration of truth, and other forces that can pollute open, reasoned, and fact-based exchange. We work to lower the obstacles to written expression and enable broader participation. If harassment deters individuals from taking part in public debate; if disinformation drowns out truth; and if thinkers dismiss the possibility of reaching audiences of different views, free expression cedes its value. Free speech includes the right to persuade, to galvanize, to seek out truth alongside others, to reach new understandings, and to shape communities and societies. But these benefits can be enjoyed only in a climate that protects open discourse writ large.

In many of these areas, case law and legal theory is still emerging—lagging behind changing technologies, habits, and norms. In other instances, the disputes don't implicate legal rights or responsibilities justiciable by a court. They fall into a zone that we as a society need to organize and moderate on our own, relying on institutions, leadership, reason, and our civic faculties.

We've also fallen into a series of patterns that could justify and prompt the suppression of speech. We have begun to question whether pushing toward a more equal society might necessitate narrower bounds for what can be said. If racial slurs and invective reinforce white dominance and prevent people of color from feeling that they are full participants in social life, might not banning and punishing such rhetoric help uproot these deep-seated inequities? Our climate of political polarization and mistrust fuels the demonization of speech with which we disagree. The imperative of excoriating the content of objectionable opinions can seem far more compelling than the virtue of defending a speaker's right to voice them. Social media can incentivize voicing indignation over a post without taking the time to read it, or parroting a friend's umbrage despite barely knowing what provoked it. We use labels like misogynist, racist, transphobic, socialist, white nationalist, anti-Semite, fascist, traitor, deplorable, Boomer, or snowflake to denigrate the speech of those with whom we disagree, even if a closer look at the intent and context of what they said would reveal something more complex. A popular refrain in today's free speech debates, that "freedom of speech doesn't mean freedom from consequences," unhelpfully lumps all such aftereffects together. In so doing it elides the distinction between reactions to speech that are perfectly lawful and appropriate—such as umbrage or even social ostracism—and those, including government punishments, that eviscerate the freedom itself.

As these controversies multiply, the meaning and importance of free speech is obscured. We lose sight of the role of open exchange as a catalyst for uncovering truth. We overlook the centrality of free speech to enabling individuals to inhabit and demonstrate their own identities. We can forget that without free speech the communications platforms, entertainment options, and scientific advances that enrich our daily lives would be thwarted beyond recognition. We can forget that all social justice movements in U.S. history have relied on free speech protections to push contrarian ideas into the mainstream, and that those of today do the same.

Those on the left accuse their political opponents of using free speech as cover to excuse expressions of bigotry and intimidation. But free speech shouldn't be condemned on the basis of the worst ideas that can claim its protection. Those on the right invoke free speech as a cudgel, calling out their opponents as cowering and unprincipled. In howling over infringements on their right to free speech, they drown out the genuine articulations of discomfort, pain, or outrage that denigrating expression can evoke. The ideal of free speech as a principle that applies universally, a precept that has equal importance to the powerful and the powerless and that transcends questions of race, gender, age, and other identities, is fading.

A note on terms. Freedom of speech generally refers to the right of an individual to voice ideas through any medium. Freedom of expression is a broader concept, encompassing press freedom, artistic freedom, freedom of assembly, religious freedom, and the right to receive and impart information. Courts have even defined it to include such things as attire (wearing an armband), movement (exotic dancing), or burning a cross or flag in protest. The First Amendment, as a matter of plain language and legal interpretation, encompasses all of these liberties. "Freedom of speech" is included in the text of the First Amendment; the International Covenant on Civil and Political Rights talks about "freedom of expression." I use the terms mostly interchangeably in this book.

Training and Equipping a Force of Free Speech Defenders

In drafting the Bill of Rights, the Framers of the U.S. Constitution prioritized First Amendment freedoms for a reason. Free speech has played an indispensable role in the flourishing of science, education, technology, the arts, literature, film, television, news, and the practice of democracy itself. The current strains over free speech represent a severe risk. As debates rage over whether and how individuals should be punished or censured for expressing their views, those who care about free speech need to speak up. As global social media platforms reshape their rules, we need to make sure online discourse doesn't become too constricted, distorted, or wretched to abide. As editors and publishers face pressure to let only people of a certain heritage write about particular populations, free speech defenders need to champion the freedom of the imagination while forcing the gates open wider to allow people of all identities the opportunity to tell their stories. As professors face blowback for raising thorny topics like rape and affirmative action in class, they need advocates to help insist that important subjects cannot be off-limits and to ensure that those needing support to handle such course material receive it through means other than silencing the unsettling speech. When propagators of hatred style themselves as free speech champions, true free speech guardians need to demonstrate that unfettered argument can expose and discredit their invidious lies.

The rules that will govern speech in the twenty-first century are being written right now, formally and informally. European countries are experimenting with new constraints on speech, some of which would be unconstitutional in the United States, and others of which may warrant close scrutiny. Almost daily, social media companies roll out new guidelines and rule changes governing their platforms. Young people are forging new norms for discussing race, sex, and gender identity. Those who remain silent in the face of these debates cede the ground to those with the most extreme views and the most self-serving motivations.

The twenty principles in this book are an attempt to articulate ideas that can help each of us rise to the defense of free speech in ways that avoid simply fueling controversy and instead help rally others to the cause. The principles are divided into four categories, precepts to adhere to:

- When speaking
- When listening
- When debating free speech questions
- When considering free speech–related policies.

The principles offered for consideration *when you speak* revolve around the responsibilities that each of us bear living in a diverse society. They urge cognizance that in the digital age, speech traverses geographic and cultural boundaries, often divorced from context. Speakers therefore have to be conscientious with language, exercise care in speaking, and be willing to apologize where appropriate. But because the consequences of speech can be unpredictable, it is incumbent on speakers to push themselves to express even difficult ideas, and avoid the temptation to shut up because others may complain. Speakers need to back up one another, defending the right to voice unpopular opinions.

Listeners have an equally important charge. Whether a television audience or social media followers, listeners usually issue the demand for speech to be banned or punished. As listeners, we should never lose sight of the intent and context that help frame how expression should be understood. Disproportionate reactions to speech can contribute to a culture of censoriousness. But listeners also bear an obligation to aid in identifying and condemning speech that is hateful and hate-motivated crimes. If those twin menaces continue to spiral, the case for free speech will become even harder to sustain. In protesting objectionable speech, listeners should stop short of efforts to silence it. We should be willing to consider forgiving errant speech, rather than insisting on punishment or holding a grudge forever.

The next set of principles relates to *participation in debates over the boundaries of free speech.* In considering the boundaries of free speech, we must acknowledge the harms that certain speech can inflict: emotional pain, the promulgation of pernicious falsehoods, or (particularly when speech crosses into harassment, intimidation, or other illegal activity) violations of privacy and dignity. While the harms of speech can be speculative, imagined, or exaggerated, they can also be devastating and lasting. Recognizing the harms speech can inflict, moreover, must not mean equating speech with violence. Doing so legitimizes violent reactions to speech, and can convert reasoned debates into physical altercations. Free speech debates also need to take account of systemic inequalities in our society. Not everyone has the same power, stature, or prominence in a community or a classroom. A truly open marketplace for free speech must take into account distortions, based on race, gender, socioeconomic status, and many other factors, and enact steps to ensure that speech rights are truly open to all.

The final set of principles concerns *speech-related policies, including laws, regulations, and social media company practices.* For informed debate over how policies should change, it's essential to understand how protections for free speech function. Before advocating new limitations on speech, we must consider whether existing exceptions to the First Amendment might already apply. It's also important to remember how government and corporate controls on speech can go wrong, and to consider these potential dangers. At the same time, Silicon Valley cannot be let off the hook when it comes to the manifest harms of some types of online speech. Finally, we should remind ourselves why free speech is elemental to a just society, a vital pillar of democracy, an indispensable catalyst for innovation, a wellspring for creativity—and a guarantor of equality much more than a threat to it.

The principles are intended to be understood collectively. In some cases they play off one another. If you exercise conscientiousness in how you speak and apologize for your blunders, you deserve to have listeners heed the context of your words, and to forgive you if you slip. If you're going to effectively defend unpopular speech, you need to acknowledge the offense and even harm some such speech can cause. While the entire book addresses free speech in our digital age, two chapters focus specifically on the Wild West of online expression. The first examines how tech platforms' content-regulation efforts can go awry, and the second insists that, given their outsize influence, we must force tech companies to persevere until better solutions are in place.

Ultimately, I am an optimist. I believe that we can reconcile the tensions between countering bigotry and keeping speech free, and that we will find ways to tame the most virulent harms of online speech. Not all the solutions are in view now, but it is clear that it won't be enough to rely on regulators, lawyers, and courts. If we care about free speech, we need a citizens' movement to safeguard its future against threats, whether from government, the tech platforms, or the censorious outrage of others. This book is an effort to elaborate principles that can guide what needs to be a collective effort at informal self-governance aimed to keep us all talking, and away from one another's throats.

PART I

PRINCIPLES FOR SPEAKING

1.

Be Conscientious with Language

THE OLD ADAGE WAS "WATCH YOUR LANGUAGE." BECAUSE WORDS CAN
sometimes do harm and we live among people of different views and backgrounds, we have long understood the wisdom of taking care with what
we say and how we say it. In today's fraught debates, mindfulness about
speech can help us avoid unwanted controversy. Conscientiousness involves considering the range of people who may hear or read your speech
and how it may strike them. Some conscientiousness is just commonsense
thoughtfulness and decency. If you are speaking to a familiar audience—
your family—you may be able to state sketchy opinions without thinking
twice. If you know that everyone in the room loves the Red Sox, celebrates
Christmas, or reveres the current president of the United States, you can
reflect these beliefs without risk. But maybe your nephew has brought a
college friend to Thanksgiving and she has a different religion, nationality, or political slant. She might appreciate being asked, "Do you have
any plans for the winter holidays?" rather than "Where will you celebrate
Christmas?" If you don't know her politics, you might think twice before
launching into an attack on a candidate for office. Simply taking into
account her presence shouldn't temper the humor or comfort level of the

gathering, but it might influence how questions are asked or points are made.

Using language conscientiously avoids the assumption that your own interpretation of words is universal. When you discover that terms or turns of phrase that you thought innocuous—for example, the use of "mankind" to refer to the human race—are heard as sexist, the conscientious speaker and writer will hear out the concern, rather than responding defensively (for example, by insisting that you've used the phrase your whole life or just heard it on the news). Although not every protestation will be merited, conscientiousness abjures the default belief that just because you've always spoken a certain way and meant no harm, your choice of words is appropriate or ideal. It reflects a measure of concern to ensure that your language does not denigrate others, reinforce stereotypes, or trample on sensitivities. It does not mean stifling provocative or even offensive opinions, but calls for rendering them knowingly and prudently. Conscientiousness with language can also help to rectify imbalances of power by lowering the barriers that certain individuals may face when joining in conversation. By avoiding stereotypes and jargon that are particular to a certain group and can reinforce feelings of inferiority or intimidation among outsiders, the conscientious use of language can enable everyone to speak more freely.

Conscientiousness also means being mindful that, online, we lack control over how our words are forwarded, shared, quoted, cited, or transmitted to remote audiences. In 2013, a sixteen-year-old in Australia was on his way to a concert by the pop artist Pink when he tweeted: "@Pink I'm ready with my Bomb. Time to blow up #RodLaverArena." On arrival at the show he was apprehended by security guards who trailed him from his Twitter profile and encouraged police to arrest him. The shaken teen was released after he explained that he was referring to Pink's hit song "Timebomb" and was simply looking forward to the music and special effects. Experienced travelers know never to joke about hijacking before boarding a plane, no matter how obvious it may be that you are kidding. In an era of school shootings, attacks in public places, and religiously motivated violence, this sort of verbal restraint is well advised.

Unpredictable responses to speech, even if unfair, have become all too predictable, especially online. Trying to reinsert missing context and nuance after a tweet has traveled the world can be impossible. In 2014, the comedian Stephen Colbert joked on-air about Washington Redskins owner Dan Snyder establishing a foundation to benefit Native Americans, even while refusing to change a team name that many found retrograde and offensive. Colbert ironically assumed the persona of the obtuse owner—with a follow-up tweet saying, "I am willing to show #Asian community I care by introducing the Ching-Chong Ding-Dong Foundation for Sensitivity to Orientals or Whatever." The satirical intent that was entirely obvious on-air was lost online where some who viewed the tweet in isolation didn't realize Colbert was mocking Snyder and not Asians. Suey Park, an online activist who launched a campaign to "#CancelColbert," said she did not care about the intent or context of the remark, as she was sick of seeing Asian Americans be the butt of jokes. Colbert weathered the attack, but Park's avowed indifference to intent and context reflects a reality in the digital age: your words can land anywhere in ways you may not anticipate and may be powerless to correct. In turn, Park was targeted by a vicious call-out campaign for failing to get the joke.

Presumption of Heterodoxy

In a diverse society, those speaking publicly should assume their audience includes a full spectrum in terms of age, gender, race, ethnicity, socioeconomic status, political affiliation, religion, and ideology. During the 2005 BET Comedy Awards, comedian Paul Mooney joked about singer Diana Ross being caught drunk driving and about her ex-husband, who had recently died in a mountain-climbing accident. Mooney didn't know that Ross's daughter, Tracee Ellis Ross, was in the audience. Steve Harvey, the next act in the lineup, did, and he acknowledged Ellis Ross, leading a round of applause for her. But Mooney said afterward that knowing she was present would not have changed his routine. He said, "Her mama could've been in [the audience]; that's not the point. . . . When you are a celebrity and you do crazy stuff, that's the game." Mooney concluded that celebrities, who prosper because of public exposure, are always fair game. Right or wrong, he made his remarks about Ross after having considered the risk of even an unlikely offense. Back in 2005, it was easy to imagine a joke reaching an unanticipated listener in a large theater. Now the same is true of anything transmitted digitally. Conscientiousness demands keeping this wide audience in the back of your mind as you decide what to say, even if your decision, ultimately, is to accept the risks of making a potentially offensive or hurtful remark.

A challenge of conscientiousness is that offense is in the eyes of the beholder. Certain well-known slurs and stereotypes are widely recognized as objectionable. But with other terms, it depends who you ask. In 2017, the *New York Times* asked its readers to identify the racially related terms they found most "cringe-worthy." Answers were all over the map, including "racial tolerance" ("we don't wish to be tolerated like petulant children"); Latinx ("I don't think the term Latino or Latina need to be revised"), and "Native" ("borders on the word 'primitive'"). By 2020, undoubtedly, such a list would have evolved, with some once-rankling terms having become widely accepted and other expressions having moved decisively into unacceptable territory. The bounds of what is considered offensive are subjective and shifting; it's impossible to avoid ever offending anyone. Taking some care to consider what might be sensitive and how to word it is the best that most of us can be expected to do.

Be Your Own Editor

Conscientiousness with language requires keeping abreast of changing social mores, subtleties involving particular groups, and the evolution of language. This may seem like a hefty burden—there can be so much to consider before speaking up that it may feel safer to remain silent. With the ability to reach people anywhere at the click of a button comes the responsibility to be aware of that sprawling audience and its sensitivities.

As the Internet and social media have dismantled old hurdles to reaching an audience, their immediacy requires us to internalize some of the traditional functions of editors and publishers. Years ago, the only way to get a book or article into the public domain was to write a proposal or manuscript, maybe secure an agent, and get an editor to review it and a publisher to print it. If you couldn't clear these hurdles, the public wouldn't read your work. The corollary was that before regular readers saw your prose, the draft would have undergone multiple rounds of scrutiny for language, tone, argument, legal pitfalls, and likely audience response.

Today the most influential media platforms like the *New York Times* and *Washington Post,* as well as book publishers, still operate as gatekeepers. But in many venues individuals can express themselves with little or no vetting, and their ideas may win a substantial following. While this is a great boon for free speech, it carries dangers. Writers can't rely on editors and publishers to flag things that could cause unwitting offense. Instead, they need to internalize the scrutiny and forethought of the old-fashioned editorial process. Responsibilities that editors and publishers shouldered alongside sharpening prose—following trends, understanding societal hot buttons, considering alternative viewpoints and the potential for offense—now fall to all who put their ideas out for consumption.

There is no equivalent of Strunk and White's *The Elements of Style* for the conscientious writer or speaker. No single source can tell us the nomenclature to use and avoid for various groups. On the plus side, though, the Internet puts at our fingertips pretty much everything we need to know to avoid blundering into inadvertent offense.

HOW TO BE YOUR OWN EDITOR

- Talk and listen to diverse groups of people
- Read widely
- Before describing them, consider how those with a given identity describe themselves
- If you think something might be offensive, find out if it is
- Use terminology tip sheets that spell out how to avoid stereotyping and offer more inclusive alternative language
- Reread before hitting "send" or "post"

SAMPLE ALTERNATIVE PHRASINGS TO AVOID OFFENSE

- Able-ist language (instead of "stand up for rights," "defend your rights")
- Sexist language (instead of "early man," "prehistoric humans")
- Racist language (instead of "a black professor," "a professor" bringing up race only if relevant)
- Ageist language (instead of "feisty" or "spry," "articulate" or "passionate")
- LGBTQ-friendly language (instead of "sexual preference," "sexual orientation")

The Euphemism Treadmill

When I was growing up, the term "Oriental" was widely used to refer to people and products originating in East Asia. At a certain point, though, "Asian" and "Asian American" entered common parlance and "Oriental" came to be understood as conveying an outdated Western conception of Asia as exotic. When we told my mother that "Oriental" was no longer considered an acceptable term, she balked, demanding to know how a word that had been widely used as long as she could remember had suddenly become offensive. But she came around. Similarly, at PEN America, we sometimes used to refer to a series of programs aimed at fostering writing opportunities for the incarcerated, undocumented immigrants, and day laborers as amplifying "marginalized voices." Though the phrase originated with the academic left, one prospective funder faulted our terminology, saying that the term "marginalization" failed to place the blame squarely enough on mainstream society for favoring the privileged. She urged us to talk about "excluded voices" instead. Chastened, we thought harder about how we could more accurately describe the individuals these programs aimed to elevate.

When people are confronted with an objection to language that others find offensive, they may defend themselves on the basis that no one complained before. With many slights, though, it is fair to assume that the groups most affected might have opposed strenuously years earlier had they believed they could effect change, and not feared reprisals from speaking up. Ignorance, prejudice, and subjugation have long protected certain norms and terms from scrutiny to the point where they are so firmly ingrained that people can find it hard to imagine that they are considered objectionable.

Social psychologist Steven Pinker is skeptical that retiring outmoded terms in favor of new ones that carry less baggage can reshape perceptions. He refers to the constant overhaul of problematic terms as the "euphemism treadmill," whereby new words are embraced but then succumb to the very taint of those they were anointed to replace. For individuals with cognitive challenges, the term "imbecile" was once coined to be neutral sounding and not derisive. It eventually gave way to "retarded," then to "mentally handicapped," and later to "having intellectual disabilities." Journalist Heather Kirn Lanier described the mother of a typically developing child admonishing her misbehaving son to "quit acting like you're special needs" to illustrate how even terms that are adopted in an effort to foster respect can become contaminated by the very same associations they were intended to help erase.

While Pinker is right that neologisms can acquire the very stigma of the words they are intended to replace, that doesn't mean language shouldn't evolve. When a group of people believe that a particular word describing them is a hindrance, society should listen. Lanier has researched the campaign to banish the term "mentally retarded" (originally coined as a clinical-sounding, nonjudgmental label), recounting how it is sometimes referred to as the "r-word" to invoke the offensive punch of the n-word. The Special Olympics mounted a campaign captioned "Spread the Word to End the Word" and, in 2010, President Obama signed Rosa's Law, a bill that excises the term "mentally retarded" from many federal documents. Four years later, the U.S. Supreme Court followed suit, substituting the phrase "intellectual disability." The hope, of course, is that progressively evolving social norms can help to ensure that new terms do not simply get trampled on Pinker's euphemism treadmill. For example, our aspiration should be to ensure that rising recognition of the dignity and worth of individuals with intellectual disabilities will mean that, decades hence, the Supreme Court doesn't need to once again retire an outmoded term that has taken on negative connotations.

Sending Words Out to Pasture

That said, we should be slow to entirely banish words and phrases from usage. In a 2018 opinion piece, University of Connecticut professor Michael M. Ego argued that the phrase "chink in the armor" should be retired because "chink" is a derisive term for Chinese Americans. He asks, "Why should American society continue to use phrases that are hurtful and demeaning to anyone?" Ego draws an analogy with the word "faggot," saying that it was used frequently by the *New York Times* only until 1981, replaced thereafter by the word "queer." But there's a difference between "chink" and "faggot." The latter has been used over the last century pretty much exclusively as an epithet (although it does have another rarely used meaning: a bundle of wood). Those who heard it were right to be offended because there was no plausible use that did not involve some insult. "Chink," on the other hand—as Ego acknowledges—has another meaning that dates back centuries and has remained in usage: a narrow opening in a wall or a weakness or flaw. It is worth recognizing that the phrase "chink in the armor" may bring to mind the slur and be jarring for people to hear; those reactions are genuine and shouldn't be dismissed. A similar problem has arisen with the word "niggardly," which means parsimonious and has an Old English etymology unrelated to the racial slur. But because the words sound similar, individuals who have used the word "niggardly"—often talking about budgets or economic growth—have sparked uproar since the phonetic similarity is so close. (One Washington, D.C., government worker was even fired for using it, although after a backlash he was rehired.) Many words have both ugly and innocuous meanings: "spic and span," "cracker," "nip." When words can be misunderstood or misheard as slurs, it's worth considering an alternative choice to avoid the distraction. But, as long as the term is being used with a legitimate, innocent meaning, misplaced umbrage shouldn't silence a speaker. When offense is taken for benign uses of words, the dustup should be an opportunity to reflect on the richness of language and affirm that no offense was intended. Expunging multidefinitional words entirely would result in a cramped lexicon and detract from the work of combating bigotry.

Sometimes a whole line of questioning takes on objectionable connotations. Asking people of color where they are from, though perhaps intended simply to make conversation, can be heard to assume that the individual is a stranger, not American, or does not belong. The identical question posed to a new white coworker might be received differently. A neutral alternative, like "Tell me more about your background," gives the subject a choice of how to answer, avoids putting someone on the spot, and sounds like a question you might ask anyone.

Rebirth of Onetime Slurs

A thorny facet of conscientiousness is a recognition that the words you can use may depend on who you are. In 2016, Jayne Tsuchiyama, a Honolulu-based doctor of Chinese herbalism, wrote an opinion piece in the *Los Angeles Times* about why the word "Oriental" should not be retired from usage. She argued that it never had negative connotations, and that repudiating it hurt older Asian American businesspeople and Oriental medicine programs. If someone who was not of Asian descent had written a similar piece, it probably would have been construed as offensive, at least by many. But as an Asian American, Tsuchiyama was permitted to make her case.

The U.S. Supreme Court dealt with a related phenomenon in 2017 in the case of *Matal v. Tam*. The dispute involved efforts by Simon Tam, the lead singer of an Asian American rock band, to trademark the name "The Slants." The U.S. Trademark Office rejected the band's application on the basis that "Slants" was derisive toward Asian Americans and banned under a law against registering "disparaging" trademarks. Tam argued that he was seeking to reclaim a onetime slur as an empowering term—as has been done with other words like "queer" or "bitch." The Supreme Court agreed, finding that a blanket ban on disparaging words amounted to viewpoint-based discrimination and that "the proudest boast of our free speech jurisprudence is that we protect the freedom to express 'the thought that we hate.'" That the Slants members were Asian American gave them the moral authority to reclaim the term as an ironic badge of honor.

Vigilance with respect to bigotry can sometimes veer into censorship of individuals with the greatest moral entitlement to determine whether and how certain words are used. When author Walter Mosley spoke the n-word aloud in the writers' room of a television series he was working on, a coworker complained anonymously to the network's human resources department, prompting a call from on high telling Mosley he could not use the word. A shocked Mosley retorted: "I *am* the n-word in the writers' room." Mosley quit the show and wrote an op-ed saying, "There I was being chastised for criticizing the word that oppressed me and mine for centuries. . . . As far as I know, the word is in the dictionary. As far as I know, the Constitution and the Declaration of Independence assure me of both the freedom of speech and the pursuit of happiness. How can I exercise these freedoms when my place of employment tells me that my job is on the line if I say a word that makes somebody, an unknown person, uncomfortable?"

While race- or gender-based rules for who can say what would never pass legal muster, in the more informal world of social interactions, they matter. There are all sorts of things that some of us can say and others can't—for valid reasons. Certain kinds of criticisms and jokes are perfectly acceptable when made by an insider, but would be deeply offensive coming from elsewhere. A Jew may take delight that three of the nine Supreme Court justices are Jewish; a non-Jew who regularly points out the same fact may raise eyebrows. Entire comedic traditions are premised on the ability, and even the need, for groups to be able to laugh at themselves or forge a sense of kinship around a controversial word or stereotype.

Amid a more integrated society, opinions, music, jokes, and tropes that were once enjoyed only within tight circles can reach farther, a generally positive thing. It is easy to share Walter Mosley's ire about being instructed not to use the n-word. But for a network trying to enforce rules evenhandedly, one can see why the slur was considered a categorical no-no. When the human resources department heard Mosley's explanation of his own background and choice to use the word, though, it should have seen the wisdom of relaxing the rule in his case. The best most of us can do is follow the lead of those closest to the debates and, when in doubt, seek out a range of opinions about how members of a given group regard terms in question.

Navigating Neologisms

Many people blanch at newfangled terms that they see as products of political correctness or values they may not share. Moving too aggressively to adopt new terms or hew to the nomenclature employed by an in-group to which you do not belong can also come off as cloying, or trying too hard.

One of the most debated recent evolutions of language involves the adoption of new pronouns to refer to people who identify as neither male nor female. The use of "they," "them," and "their" to refer to single individuals has irritated some strict constructionists, arguing that English is being debased. Some, like the goading psychology professor Jordan Peterson, object to the forced use of gender nonbinary pronouns by the Canadian Human Rights Commission or other institutions. Others simply feel awkward with the newer terms or worry that they will screw up.

On the radio show *Fresh Air*, Penguin Random House copy chief Benjamin Dreyer, a self-described conservative on language usage, explained how he came to accept these locutions. He described his reaction to having a colleague whose preferred pronoun was "they." At first Dreyer did everything possible to avoid using the term, which wasn't yet standard. "I'd refer to the colleague as 'the colleague,'" he said. "I mean, can you hear how dreadfully stilted I'm becoming?" But at a certain point, the word "they" "popped out" of Dreyer's mouth and he said to himself: "Oh, be done with it already. You know, like, just honor your colleague, honor this person that you work with, honor this person you actually like a lot and honor the pronoun choice." In 2019, Merriam-Webster added the nonbinary pronouns "they" and "them" to the dictionary as pronouns in the singular, adapting grammatical conventions to make way for what has become a pronoun of choice for a segment of the population whose identity and rights are winning wider recognition.

No one is obliged to embrace every neologism or be at the vanguard of adopting newfangled designations. Nor does anyone need to perform the verbal equivalent of a citizen's arrest every time someone else uses a disfavored term. Members of minority groups themselves, inevitably, have a range of views about whether they prefer, for example, Native American or Indian, black or African American, or Latino or Latinx. But you should not insist that such new terms are unacceptable or wrong, or hold out once they have come into the mainstream. The basic premise that people should be allowed to decide what they want to be called is an affirmation of free will, autonomy, and, indeed, the freedom to express oneself.

Does linguistic conscientiousness amount to self-censorship? It shouldn't. If you hold highly controversial views, linguistic conscientiousness won't be enough to persuade the masses of your point of view, but it can allow you to argue your case on the merits without the distraction of unintended offenses or misunderstandings. Linguistic conscientiousness should not mean having to hit "pause" before every beat in a conversation. Over time, rather, it becomes a practice like environmental conscientiousness, where littering or wastefulness simply comes to feel gratuitous and undesirable.

HOW TO BE A CONSCIENTIOUS SPEAKER

- Don't assume that your own understanding of the meaning of words and phrases is universally shared
- Unless you have full control over your audience, assume that they may encompass a wide range of experience and viewpoints

- Strive to keep abreast of how language and usage are changing and consider whether your own idioms may need to evolve
- Particularly when they are empowering to others, don't reject new terms simply because they are unfamiliar or defy tradition
- Don't allow linguistic conscientiousness to veer into self-censorship of ideas and opinions; virtually anything can be expressed if you take the time to find the right words

2.

Fulfill a Duty of Care When Speaking

ALTHOUGH THE PHRASE IS ASSOCIATED WITH SPIDER-MAN, CARTOONIST Stan Lee did not invent the idea that "with great power comes great responsibility." But it was a worthy concept to popularize. Those in positions of institutional authority—university leaders, school principals, clergy, elected officials, and corporate executives—owe an added duty of care tied to the leadership roles they hold. While such individuals may technically be free to speak and write in their personal capacity, what they say may reverberate widely and be construed to reflect on their institution. This puts a heavy onus on those in leadership to think before they speak.

Linguistic conscientiousness is not a one-size-fits-all proposition. Its demands hinge on context and setting. If you are relaxing with close friends, conferring with your tight-knit team at work, or joking around the dinner table, you will have more leeway than if you are in front of a classroom, tweeting on a work account, or appearing on national television. We all need sheltered enclaves to explore provocative ideas, relax our guard, and let off steam. We need to be able to raise privately questions and concerns that could get us into hot water if done out in the open. We need cloistered settings where we can freely probe touchy questions of politics, gender, religion, and more. If we lapse, assuming any offense is taken, our friends and family will—we hope—be quick to forgive. But beyond these most intimate settings, a different level of responsibility is required.

The Reasonable Speaker

Tort law—which governs noncriminal acts, intentional or accidental, that result in injury or loss to others—posits the concept of a "reasonable person" and the level of care that individuals need to take to avoid physically harming others. In tort law, before flinging a lasso, dumping a pail of gravel, or driving a car, the "reasonable person" would weigh the foreseeable risk of harm from the action, the likelihood of such harm, and alternative approaches that lessen the danger. If you're exercising an appropriate degree of care—driving within the speed limit, staying in your lane, braking at stop signs—and an accident happens, you generally will not be at fault. But if the driver involved has been negligent—speeding, weaving through traffic, or running a stoplight—culpability is heightened.

Basic care with language resembles this general duty. We owe it to one another to be mindful of what we say, in light of who may hear it. If we willfully dodge that duty—firing off a drunken tweet, failing to reread a mass email before hitting "send," or wading into a public debate on a subject we know little about—we may pay a price. Depending on the situation, conscientiousness may demand more than thinking before you speak or rereading prior to making a Facebook post public. If you've been tapped for a high-profile job, you will need to figure what sensitivities lurk and move gingerly until you have a handle on them. If you plan to speak out on a heated topic, extra care is warranted in preparation and perhaps vetting your draft with knowledgeable friends who can help you skirt minefields.

Social media discourages the exercise of such care. If you want to weigh in on a breaking news event, offer a snappy retort, or be first to tweet a clever pun, speed matters. Think too hard, await a friend's opinion, or run your draft tweet by an editor and the moment passes. The free flow of social media threads is what makes them compelling; we witness real-time reactions, opinions being swayed, collective wisdom coalescing. Social media is also deliberately casual, with space limits favoring abbreviations, slang, and nicknames. Carefully edited language sticks out. It's easy to tell when Donald Trump is venting spontaneously on Twitter and when he's posting scripted official statements. Exercising a duty of care on social media may cut against what makes the platforms most potent, but it can also protect the speaker from a misfire.

The Burdens of Leadership

The law acknowledges that in certain situations, the "reasonable care" of an ordinary person is not good enough. The driver of a huge tour bus needs to be more cautious in changing lanes than that of a small sedan. The bus driver needs more training, vetting, and preparation as well as a different license. When someone's role involves greater potential to cause harm, an additional duty of care applies. Tort law ascribes such an elevated duty of care to parents, teachers, and employers, among other categories.

A similar notion applies to the speech of those in positions of influence. The more weight your words have, the more responsibility you bear to use them with care. Precepts of academic freedom shield university professors from reprisals based on what they write or teach. These protections ensure that the broadest range of ideas can be aired and explored. But professors in the classroom still bear a duty of care in relation to their students. Universities are charged with educating students from a range of countries and backgrounds. The professor must run a classroom where all students can learn without the interference of bigotry, denigration, or harassment. An older man who referred to a woman ahead of him in line at the supermarket as "young lady" might come off as a charming gentleman. But the same designation used by a professor toward a student might come across as condescending or prejudiced. What might be excusable for a reasonable person may be less so for those who owe a heightened duty of care due to the position they hold.

These days, even a single comment that suggests insensitivity toward historically excluded groups can land institutional leaders in hot water. Second chances that most people might enjoy may be construed as impracticable or undeserved for someone entrusted to leadership. In 2005, Harvard University president Lawrence Summers spoke at a conference about why men outperform women in math and science, speculating that the difference may be partly explained by genetic predispositions. Though he had not intended to offend and drew on credible research on the topic, the remark contributed to his eventual ouster as president. His remarks would have been protected from reprisal under academic freedom had they been made by a regular professor, but being a university president involves additional responsibilities. (Summers returned to his position as a tenured faculty member.) In assuming such a leadership role, a faculty member knowingly accepts a duty of care to represent the university responsibly—including not to call into question the innate capabilities of a substantial segment of the Harvard community. Moreover, Summers's remarks reflected a set of preconceptions and biases that pervade society and reinforce the underrepresentation of women in math, science, and technology. Having made the comments in an official capacity, Summers could not argue that they did not reflect on his leadership at Harvard.

Summers is not alone in having a single statement contribute the loss of a prominent position. The former CEO of Papa John's Pizza resigned after talking about someone else who had used the n-word, and the executive chairman of advertising agency Saatchi & Saatchi stepped down after making comments dismissing concerns over barriers for women in the field. While one can debate the merits of these individual cases, it remains clear that institutional leaders have a special obligation not to speak heedlessly.

Size Matters: The Bigger the Platform, the Heavier the Duty

An elevated duty of care also applies to those who command large audiences for a living. Celebrities, prominent journalists, and television hosts enjoy prestige, hefty salaries, and cultural clout. In 2018, NBC talk show host Megyn Kelly did a segment on Halloween costumes in which she questioned why people object to blackface, adding that when she was growing up it was considered "OK" for people to darken their complexions as long as they were dressing up as a character. Kelly was right that there was a time several decades ago when blackface was more common and not universally recognized—at least not by white people—to be patently offensive, as it is today. But as a television star supported by teams of producers, writers, and researchers, Kelly was justifiably held to a strict standard. She was excoriated for failing to recognize that mores had changed and that blackface, if ever acceptable, is now clearly over the line. A series of glum apologies failed to undo the damage and Kelly was off the air. Although flagging ratings and personality conflicts may have contributed to her ouster, her obliviousness about a racially inflammatory issue left her with few defenders.

After comedian and television star Roseanne Barr came under fire for a tweet comparing former White House senior adviser Valerie Jarrett to the offspring of the "Muslim Brotherhood" and "planet of the apes," she offered a raft of excuses. Barr claimed she did not know that Jarrett was black and had tweeted under the influence of sleep medicine Ambien (prompting its manufacturer to tweet, "Racism is not a known side effect [of our drug]"). Few found these excuses persuasive. Barr's history of racially tinged and provocative remarks helped seal the decision to axe her program. ABC called the tweet "abhorrent, repugnant, and inconsistent with our values." Had Barr been a third-tier celebrity committing a first offense, she might have survived. But leeway that is afforded to ordinary people does not apply to someone whose professional stature and market value depend on their appeal.

Information Is Power

The duty of care is also heightened when we venture into contentious subjects outside our expertise. Temple University professor Marc Lamont Hill is a specialist in urban policy, civil rights, and African American studies and has also engaged in general television punditry. In 2018, he gave a speech at a United Nations event to mark a "Day of Solidarity with the Palestinian People." He called for "action that will give us what justice requires and that is a free Palestine from the river to the sea." Many observers, including the Anti-Defamation League, pointed out that the slogan "the river to the sea" is commonly used to imply the destruction of the State of Israel (located between the Jordan River and the Mediterranean Sea). Some critics said Hill's words were anti-Semitic and even an implicit call for violence. Hill found the response "baffling," saying he had not intended "a call to destroy anything or anyone." Temple University's newspaper published a piece exploring the history and uses of the phrase, quoting Middle East expert Sean Yom, who said, "Any language which can be remotely interpreted as questioning either right to exist can be seen as inflammatory and a frontal assault on a people."

Hill eventually apologized, acknowledging that in his words, "many heard a dog-whistle that conjured a long and deep history of violence against Jewish people. Although this was the furthest thing from my intent, those particular words clearly caused confusion, anger, fear, and other forms of harm. For that, I am deeply sorry." Hill was fired from his job as a CNN commentator but Temple University rightly refused calls to discipline him, citing academic freedom. Knowing that he was wading into the fractious debate over Israel-Palestine in a prominent setting like the UN, Hill would have been wise to share his remarks in advance with experts on various sides of the conflict. In general, if you are venturing out publicly on unfamiliar terrain, you owe (not least to yourself) a particular duty of care to chart the fault lines.

Online Is Never Really Off Duty

In theory, employers and schools should distinguish between private comments and official pronouncements. But in practice, social media has blurred the lines, especially for leaders who, it can be argued, are obliged to always uphold a professional public image. In an era of viral videos, hot mikes, and viral distribution, public and personal identities can fuse. First Amendment law recognizes an exception for public employees, who do not have the right to say things that violate their work duties. For example, a police officer cannot tell protesters to flout the law and then raise a First Amendment defense when the department tries to fire him for that speech. Certain private employees hold analogous obligations related to their duties. The dean of Yale's Pierson residential college, June Chu, stepped down after it was revealed that Pierson students had come across nasty restaurant reviews she had posted on Yelp that were insulting to white people and movie theater workers. The posts had nothing to do with her academic research and they compromised her ability to perform her job of advising all students. Compounded by her failure to own up to the scope of her scorching commentaries, Chu's scornfulness toward particular groups undercut her credibility as a steward of an inclusive learning environment at Yale.

But the propensity to police an individual's private speech as a de facto qualification for participation in institutional life can go too far. When Rutgers professor James Livingston posted on Facebook that his Harlem neighborhood was becoming "overrun with little Caucasian a**holes" and that he would "'resign' from [his] race" (he is white), right-leaning news outlets called for his ouster. Though his ill-tempered comments were clearly ironic in tone, online critics questioned his ability to treat white students fairly. Yet there was no indication that any Rutgers students actually believed Livingston was racist or unfair in the classroom. When accusations of racism or other offenses are raised by third-party bystanders and don't garner support from members of the purportedly targeted or vulnerable group, it's fair to question their credence. Rutgers initially told Livingston he had violated the university's discrimination and harassment policy but, after complaints by free speech groups and Rutgers faculty, closed its investigation with no disciplinary action.

The case of Harvard Law School professor Ronald Sullivan had a different result. For ten years Sullivan and his wife served as deans of Winthrop House, a Harvard undergraduate residential college. When Sullivan joined the defense team for the notorious movie mogul Harvey Weinstein, who was accused of sexual harassment and assault, some Winthrop students protested. They claimed that Sullivan's decision to represent Weinstein rendered him unfit to provide mentorship and counsel to students, especially those affected by sexual harassment. Sullivan defended himself, pointing to his work prosecuting sexual assault and also his history of taking on controversial clients, including death row inmates, on the principle that our legal system demands that all defendants have legal representation. Representing Weinstein implied no more indifference to the crime of sexual assault than representing accused killers showed an unconcern about murder. There was no indication that Sullivan had ever been soft on harassment cases on campus. But after protests, sit-ins, accusatory graffiti, and even a lawsuit, Harvard undertook a "climate review" of Winthrop House and, purportedly on the basis of its findings, dropped Sullivan and his wife as deans.

Though Harvard claimed that its decision was prompted by other problems at Winthrop, the timing made plain that it had capitulated to the vocal students. But in this case, Sullivan had not breached any duty of care. He wasn't accused of sexism, of downplaying sexual harassment, or of letting his representation of Weinstein affect his role as dean. As a law professor, he was entitled to take on controversial cases. One reason to have faculty deans for residential colleges is to expose students to the work they do. Fifty-two members of the Harvard Law faculty signed a letter to support him. While student concerns were heartfelt, Harvard should have facilitated dialogue to probe their discomfort, enable Sullivan to explain himself, and resolve the impasse without a de facto punishment for Sullivan's professional decision. A reasonable duty of care cannot dictate that institutional leaders avoid any whiff of controversy. If it does, the result will be leadership by lowest common denominator, whereby only those willing to subordinate their opinions, or who have no strong views in the first place, are qualified to serve.

The duty of care can go too far. If everyone were scrupulous in vetting tweets ahead of time, Twitter would be awfully dull. For speakers, the knowledge that what we say may be held against us can discourage candor, humor, or the voicing of unorthodox views. For the public, lapses in the duty of care can be revealing, as we see political figures and celebrities bare their unfiltered characters. Like many of the principles in this book, the duty of care is not absolute. If most of our leaders, professors, and influentials exercise that duty most of the time, we will be able to afford more space to rare breaches—the occasional off-color joke, edgy tweet, or blunt sound bite that reveals truth. As it is, offensive comments often land hard precisely because they contribute to patterns of misogyny or prejudice that manifest time and again. Through a greater collective level of care, we can earn back the space for greater tolerance for the occasional unscripted moment. Those who have the benefit of protection from reprisals for speech—tenured professors, those with enough professional and financial security to take some risk, and former officials—should take advantage of the protections they enjoy to speak freely, helping to enrich discussions for us all. When top-rated television host Rachel Maddow took her employer, NBC News, to task for its handling of sexual harassment allegations against powerful men in the entertainment industry and at the network, she spoke for many employees of the company who were similarly incensed but felt less empowered to speak out. The rest of us should strive to ensure that exercising a duty of care does not spell the death of risk, impulse, or creativity.

Give Points for Effort

In 2015, Claremont McKenna College dean Mary Spellman replied to an email message from a student belonging to an ethnic group underrepresented on campus. Spellman said that the school had "a lot to do as a college and a community" to support students who "don't fit our CMC mold." She was, by all accounts, an empathic administrator who was popular among students and had never been accused of bias. But the student reacted negatively to being told that she was outside the campus's standard profile. She spread the word about the dean's response, and student protests culminated in Spellman's resignation. A mere five words, amid an email that was clearly intended to convey support, should not have been grounds for Spellman's ouster.

When people try to extend a hand, acknowledge prejudice, or take steps toward inclusivity or equality, they deserve some benefit of the doubt. Although the burden of having to "give points for effort" may fall disproportionately on members of disenfranchised groups, their generosity should pay off in greater understanding—and fewer foul-ups—from conscientious speakers. It makes more sense to encourage people to change their attitudes and actions, even at the risk of screwing up, than it does to suggest that even unintended errors won't be tolerated.

Cultural Appropriation and the Purview of the Imagination

One of the more concrete manifestations of heightened attention to the duty of care, in the literary world, is the phenomenon of sensitivity readers. Authors or publishing houses hire these reviewers to screen manuscripts and flag issues that may ignite controversy or provoke charges of racial, ethnic, gender, or other forms of callousness. The use of these readers is especially common in young adult literature, where harsh online criticism has torpedoed certain books even before they hit store shelves. These episodes reflect a struggle to come to grips with the legacy of prejudice and discrimination that has afflicted the publishing industry along with so many other realms of society. In 2015, PEN America reported on the lack of diversity in children's book publishing, finding glaring gaps in minority representation in the field of publishing and the availability of kids' books by black, Latino, and Native American authors. Organizations such as We Need Diverse Books and Vida have worked to achieve greater equity in publishing, with some success. Statistics collected by the Collaborative Children's Book Center reveal that, after years of near-stagnation, the numbers of books by African American, Latino, Asian, and First Nation authors are now growing steadily. These numbers indicate a rising awareness of the importance of fostering the careers of writers from minority groups and making more varied books available.

The drive to remedy racial underrepresentation in publishing has raised questions about the duty of care that exists for writers who venture beyond their own identity and experience. One line of thinking suggests that no amount of care can overcome the act of usurpation entailed in telling a story about a racial or ethnic group that is not your own. A 2018 tweet by young adult author Kosoko Jackson summed up the perspective of what has since become known as the #ownstories movement: "Stories about the civil rights movement should be written by black people. Stories of suffrage should be written by women. Ergo, stories about boys during horrific and life changing times, like the AIDS EPIDEMIC, should be written by gay men. Why is this so hard to get?" Jackson's call became a rallying cry for a movement premised on the notion "that stories about marginalized people should be written by authors of the same identity group." The goal is to force improved representation in publishing and make storytelling more true to life.

Barely a year after Kosoko Jackson's influential tweet, however, the tables turned. On the eve of publication of his novel *A Place for Wolves,* an online reviewer attacked him for depicting a setting—war-racked Kosovo—without firsthand knowledge. Though his protagonist was black and gay—as Jackson is—his story took place in a time and place that Jackson had only researched and imagined. Jackson withdrew the book from publication and his publisher pulped 55,000 copies. "Live by the sword, die by the sword," one commentator taunted.

Jackson's retraction of his book is one of a spate of cases in which authors and publishers have scuttled books after accusations of racial or other offenses. As attentiveness to issues of appropriation has grown, writers and publishers have relied increasingly on sensitivity readers to inoculate their books. Particularly when venturing into less-familiar subjects, writers are wise to make sure that their books convey the portrayals and messages that they intend. Turning to someone with a background different from one's own—racial, religious, professional, geographic, or otherwise—can yield valuable insights.

But the impulses driving the use of sensitivity readers can have a chilling effect. When Laura Moriarty wrote *American Heart,* a dystopian novel in which Muslims are sent to detention camps, her publisher hired two Muslim sensitivity readers to vet it, and Moriarty made edits accordingly. *Kirkus Reviews* gave the novel a starred review (written by a Muslim woman). But immediately thereafter, the book received so many online complaints (for presenting a "white savior narrative") that the review was taken down, revised, and stripped of its honorific star.

If you believe that those without roots in a given culture have no business writing about it, there will always be fault to find in how they do so. Dhonielle Clayton, a sensitivity reader, COO of We Need Diverse Books, and a leading advocate in this arena, explains that the stakes go beyond just the draft in hand: "The reason I read so many manuscripts this past year is because publishers are giving more book deals to non-black American writers writing about black Americans than to black American content creators." Clayton refers to sensitivity reading as "merely a Band-Aid covering up a deep, bleeding wound. The industry must recognize that real censorship shows up each season in the way new books are bought by editors and find their way into bookstores." The progress now being made toward diversity comes after a long delay, and the gaps in representation loom large over the cultural appropriation debate.

In these skirmishes over authorial prerogatives, individual writers— including some of color—can be the casualties. Fixed rules dictating who is entitled to tell which stories can cramp literary freedom and opportunity, even for writers who are themselves facing barriers. Publishers should not pull books that they have published with conscientiousness and care— especially since online furies reflect the views of only those who join the fray. The power of online indignation to remove books from circulation should worry anyone who believes in free speech. Even if you think a given story was ill-considered or poorly written, what's to say that the next book won't be pulped on political or ideological grounds you would reject?

One purpose of literature is to enable readers to inhabit the inner worlds of characters unlike themselves. If we decide that authors are incapable of such leaps of invention, why would we believe they are possible for readers? And if no one is able to envisage the life of another, the very purpose of fiction—and the very possibility of empathy and compassion across divides—come into question. If authors were confined to writing only about their personal experiences, countless great works of literature could never have been published and the canvas for creativity would be drastically shrunken.

"When I taught creative writing at Princeton [my students] had been told all their lives to write what they knew," wrote the novelist Toni Morrison. "I always began the course by saying 'don't pay any attention to that' . . . Think of somebody you don't know. What about a Mexican waitress in the Rio Grande who can barely speak English? Or what about a Grand Madame in Paris? Things way outside their camp. Imagine it, create it." It is right to expect that authors who venture into unfamiliar subject matter exercise heightened care. But even a writer who has done due diligence cannot be expected to satisfy everyone. While some argue that raw talent can yield such convincing and sensitive portrayals that they evade criticism, the idea that only prize-winning novelists dare write about cultures not their own would set an awfully high bar, even reinforcing the very elitism for which the literary world is often criticized.

As we must exercise care in living daily life, so we should do so when using words. The right level of caution and forethought will depend on the circumstances, with factors such as context, intent, position, and political moment all playing a role in shaping how others will respond to our speech. In coming to expect requisite levels of conscientiousness and care from one another, we should be careful to stop short of imposing a standard whereby innocent lapses and mistakes are considered unforgivable, and no degree of care will be judged sufficient to entitle authors to tell the stories they choose.

HOW TO FULFILL YOUR DUTY OF CARE WHEN SPEAKING

- If you hold a position of influence, consider what additional care is warranted when speaking out on sensitive topics
- When opining on contentious subjects beyond your personal zone of expertise, do your homework first to understand how what you say may be heard by different groups of listeners
- Don't assume speech is private—or will be construed as being voiced in only a personal capacity
- Give points for effort and recognize that when due care is taken, mistakes will still happen
- The duty of care should not be construed to circumscribe the realm of the imagination or dictate who is entitled to tell which stories

3.

Find Ways to Express Difficult Ideas

BEING CONSCIENTIOUS WITH LANGUAGE AND EXERCISING A DUTY OF care cannot mean that difficult, debatable, or heretical ideas are out of bounds. On the contrary, care and conscientiousness should make the expression of those ideas possible, and lower the cost of voicing an opinion. When someone makes the effort to set forth a controversial viewpoint in a reasoned, respectful manner, listeners should credit that effort. If even measured, thoughtful expressions of disputable viewpoints are met with censoriousness, there is little incentive to moderate language, forge common ground, or persist in good-faith public discourse.

History is full of ideas that were at some point considered deviant. The struggles for religious liberty, women's rights, reproductive freedom, civil rights, LGBT rights, and many other forms of progress were thwarted by restrictions on voicing what were once seen as dangerous ideas. For decades laws prevented the dissemination of information about birth control; in 1929, reproductive freedom pioneer Margaret Sanger was arrested after giving a speech advocating women's rights. Not until 1977 did the Supreme Court extend full legal protection to the ideas Sanger was advancing, ruling that the First Amendment prohibited bans on advertising for contraception. Free speech protections have been essential to ensuring that champions of once-revolutionary ideas could make their case.

Defenders of free speech reject the notion that certain ideas are categorically out of bounds. The categories of speech that the First Amendment polices most forcibly, such as child pornography and incitement to imminent violence, are not simply ideas that someone opts to articulate but involve dangerous or abusive actions that physically harm others. Yet there are protected forms of speech whose value seems dubious. When political debate descends into racist slurs or sexist tirades, it can be easy to conclude that the harm caused outweighs any possible benefit. Indeed, the reasons to protect this speech lie not in the merit of the expression itself but in the risk of empowering the state to step in. The question we ask is not whether particular speech is worthy of protection but whether we want to afford our government the leeway to restrict it, knowing that once such power is granted, officials will use it as they see fit. Affording government that authority—even if intended for sparing use only to target avowedly hateful speech—would open the door to the kinds of restraints once used to silence civil rights organizers and feminist activists. We rely instead on taboos, counterspeech, and social and institutional norm enforcement to deter and blunt the damage of speech that is hateful. But this should leave room for reasoned, fact-based discourse on contestable—and even combustible—topics, including religious, racial, and gender differences, the roots of terrorism and inequality, and challenges to scientific consensus on various topics. Amid a "gotcha" culture, supporters of free speech need to make space for discussion of difficult topics, defend those who take part, and model modes of discourse that can keep tough issues on the table.

Tongue-Tying Topics

In January 2018, amid a raft of claims of sexual assault against famous men, *Saturday Night Live* poked fun at the silent hysteria that can set in when trying to broach a delicate topic. The spoof begins with several couples enjoying themselves over dinner when a woman brings up recent allegations against comedian Aziz Ansari, who had been accused of pressuring a woman and making her feel uncomfortable during a date. The assembled fall silent. The restaurant darkens. A male dinner companion hides his face inside his turtleneck as horror-movie music swells. "Think," one woman stammers, "I think some women . . . or rather some men . . . have a proclivity . . . help me." She trails off. Another character tries to articulate a thought: "While I applaud the movement . . ." "Watch it," a dinner companion warns sternly. The conversation descends into one character stabbing his own hand, another willing herself to evaporate, and stock footage of a nuclear bomb detonating. By the end of the skit, the friendly dinner had collapsed into violent trauma.

We are reluctant to wade into touchy topics because it's hard to choose the right words, tensions can erupt quickly, and relationships can cool. Much has been written about our tendency to retreat to enclaves of the like-minded, consorting only with those who share our views. At a recent PEN America event, a young woman stood up to lament that she had recently graduated from an Ivy League university only to realize that in four years there she had never heard out anyone with whom she really disagreed. But for those who want to build an audience, advance a debate, or effect social change, it is essential to be able to communicate with—and even convince—those who do not start on your side. Unless you are bringing new people around to your point of view, your impact will be circumscribed. Only through give-and-take with opponents can you persuade, in the process honing your own views and arguments to better account for valid points on the other side. By giving in to the instinct to silence a contestable viewpoint—someone else's or perhaps even your own—you risk narrowing the field for what opinions can be voiced. While it may be instinctive to clam up when you suspect your opinions put you in the minority, the robust defense of free speech demands speaking up at precisely these moments.

Several elements can help make it easier to marshal a charged argument. One is compelling storytelling. Author Ta-Nehisi Coates's article in *The Atlantic*, "The Case for Reparations," catalyzed a national debate over a policy idea—paying reparations to the descendants of slaves—that had not been seriously entertained in a long time. Coates brought what was once considered a radical idea into the center of public discourse by describing the serial injustices inflicted throughout the life of Mississippi-born Chicago resident Clyde Ross—properties stolen, educational opportunities denied, mortgages withheld. This story formed the basis for Coates's case that the privations of slavery did not end with abolition, but were compounded by policies, practices, and norms that have kept African Americans from accumulating wealth over generations. Coates's skill as a raconteur, meticulous research, and personal conviction pulsed from the page, rendering his piece a call to action that has led to congressional hearings and mounting support for a commission to study the question of reparations.

Research and rigorous argumentation can render a controversial case harder to dismiss. When you are taking on the conventional wisdom, you need to be prepared to show your work. Paul Bloom, a professor of psychology and cognitive science at Yale, published a 2016 book, *Against Empathy: The Case for Rational Compassion,* in which he argues that empathy does more harm than good. What saved the book from being more than a mere provocation was that Bloom marshaled his case methodically, drawing on scientific and psychological literature to argue, for example, that empathy involves an uncontrolled propensity to internalize the suffering of others, making the more detached variation—compassion—a healthier social currency. Credibility, facts, and expertise are essential for persuasive discussion on touchy topics.

Anticipating and Addressing the Antithesis

The most persuasive arguments anticipate and respectfully address their counterpoints, rather than deriding or ignoring them. Persuasion requires taking the time to understand the other side, absorbing the best arguments from an opposing point of view, considering how things might appear differently depending on your vantage point, and anticipating what rebuttals might be proffered to your points. Ideally you should understand the opposing case as well as you do your own. In so doing you can generally narrow the zone of disagreement and win a measure of credence from the other side.

In a March 2019 piece in *New York* magazine, journalist Andrew Sullivan took on the loaded topic of Israel's lobbying power in Washington. Disarming an obvious criticism, he opened by saying he wanted to "get out of the way first" an acknowledgment that invocations of historic tropes involving Jews as money-grubbing or disloyal to the United States were anti-Semitic. He then laid down a challenge for himself: "Is it possible to write honestly about the Israel lobby's power in D.C. without using any anti-Semitic 'tropes' at all?" Sullivan went on to declare "the zeal of many Jewish Americans for Israel" "completely understandable" and to underscore that amid a rising tide of global anti-Semitism, "defending Israel is a core interest of not only Jews but all of us in what's left of the West." He goes on to examine a question of "proportion" and to argue that Israel receives exponentially more aid than other close U.S. allies. He also argues that U.S. generosity toward the Jewish state should translate into greater Israeli respect for American policies, including, for example, the Obama administration's opposition to new and expanded settlements in the West Bank. Sullivan's up-front, unstinting acknowledgment of central points made by the opposing side of the debate makes it harder for doubters to simply reject his argument, and virtually impossible for them to discredit him as anti-Semitic.

Among the most combustible topics in our public discourse are genetic differences based on ancestry. Given the history of noxious race-based theories used to justify slavery, conquest, barbaric human "experiments," torture, and systemic mistreatment, it is easy to understand wanting to avoid thinking in such terms. Moreover, scientists have conclusively debunked race-based theories of genetics, focusing instead on how ancestry and population movements account for certain physiological differences. The *New York Times*' Amy Harmon has detailed the reticence of the scientific community with respect to debates over ancestry and genetics, noting that the field's history includes infamous chapters. Yet as white nationalists have begun once more to invoke genetic science to claim superiority, scientists have felt compelled to speak out.

There are ways to engage even the most sensitive topics responsibly. Anticipating misinterpretations of a study he helped conduct of worldwide variations in the presence of genes associated with elevated education attainment, Danish scientist Fernando Racimo created a "frequently asked questions" document aimed at laypeople. He uses it to put to rest anxieties that his findings suggest that East Asians are smarter than other people or that academic performance is genetically predetermined. Other scientists have gone online to refute right-leaning websites that distort their findings to support racist conclusions.

Harvard geneticist David Reich has advanced a different rationale for researching population-based genetic distinctions, namely the advancement of medicine. He argues that genetic differences must be probed to help understand and treat diseases such as multiple sclerosis, kidney failure, and prostate cancer. Judging that there exists credible research linking genetics to educational attainment, he calls for a "candid and scientifically up-to-date way of discussing any such differences, instead of sticking our heads in the sand and being caught unprepared when they are found." A group of sixty-seven scholars published an open letter in *Vox* rejecting Reich's conclusions on the basis that the racial categories he referenced were more fluid and overlapping than he acknowledged. But their respectful tone suggested that the geneticist had accomplished at least part of what he'd set out to do: open the door to reasoned discussion of a delicate topic without giving succor to racists.

On the flip side of the debate over the role and limits of genetics, a major study released in August 2019 found no single genetic determinant of homosexuality (no "gay gene," in other words). The scientific finding that environmental factors contribute substantially to sexual orientation is controversial in some circles. There are fears that such evidence could play into the hands of those who denigrate homosexuality as a deviant life choice or revive the discredited practice of conversion therapy. But the study itself was thorough, methodical, and credible. Moreover, it did not exclude the role of genetics in sexual orientation but simply found that five different genes could collectively account for roughly a quarter of the influence over whether someone engages in same-sex sexual activity. As author, LGBT activist, and former PEN America president Andrew Solomon put it when sharing the results in a Facebook post, "This study will be controversial, but on balance, I think it's better to know more than it is to tell researchers not to do their research. The truth will set you free, etc."

Dealing in Differences

Media outlets, nonprofit organizations, and publications can create essential space for rational debate on contentious issues. One of the most impressive such engines I have witnessed is a Manhattan-based youth organization called the New York Urban Debate League. Both my kids are avid debaters and have benefited greatly from participating in the league. The debates bring together schools from every stratum of city life, from the priciest private academies to neighborhood schools in poor sections of the five boroughs. Kids aged ten to eighteen debate timely topics including whether to ban the Confederate flag, eliminate the statute of limitations for sexual assault, or repeal the Second Amendment. They work in small teams and must prepare both sides of each argument. Only twenty

SAMPLE OF ORGANIZATIONS AND PUBLICATIONS MAKING SPACE FOR RATIONAL DEBATE

Intelligence Squared has staged more than 160 debates on provocative topics, broadcasting the forums on television, radio, and podcast

Boston Review's forum presents an essay on a timely topic, alongside a series of responses from divergent voices

Reddit's "Change My View" explicitly aims to reshape contributors' opinions on hot-button topics

The Conversation US enlists academics to write for the public in their areas of expertise, bringing deeply researched insights to topical issues

minutes before each debate round starts do they learn which side they are assigned to argue. The process instills an understanding that there are plausible, defendable arguments on each side of virtually any debate. Kids learn how to rebut counterarguments, rebuild their own case, cast doubt on one another's evidence, and crystallize and weigh a debate down to its most essential elements. I have often thought that if the kinds of intramural teams and competitions available for adults in various sports existed for debate, it might help build a more civil, less combative society.

When people show the courage to buck the party line, whether you agree with them or not, supporting their courage can help ensure that they aren't burned by the experience and don't revert to silence. It also helps signal others that speaking up doesn't mean being left out to dry. If the price of a dissenting view is too high, certain speakers will be relegated to silence, and listeners are then confined to a narrower set of ideas and viewpoints to take in.

HOW TO FOSTER THE EXPRESSION OF DIFFICULT IDEAS

- When expressing a controversial viewpoint, take the time to respectfully hear out the objections and address them
- Marshal facts, evidence, and expertise in support of your case
- Anticipate how your point of view may be misunderstood and try to preempt that
- Make space in your information diet for alternative viewpoints and news sources
- Create and support forums that expose audiences to divergent views

4.

Defend the Right to Voice Unpopular Speech

"I DISAPPROVE OF WHAT YOU SAY, BUT I WILL DEFEND TO THE DEATH YOUR right to say it" is a saying commonly attributed to the French philosopher Voltaire, who died in 1778. Most Voltaire scholars think the famous words were actually written by his biographer, Evelyn Beatrice Hall. The phrase caught on because it pithily denotes an essential precept underpinning liberal conceptions of freedom of speech: that the law, institutions, and even the citizenry must be prepared to defend and protect speech that is unpopular, distasteful, offensive, and even menacing. It is the idea that sanctioned suppression of speech is more dangerous than even the most risky speech itself. After all, we don't need legal protections for sentiments that are uncontroversial. No one's going to stop you from saying "happy birthday" or posting a cat video. The whole premise of shielding speech from government intrusion or other forms of censoriousness is to rein in the impulse of those with power to silence critical, provocative, and threatening ideas.

The freedom to offend is not a license to offend, nor an assurance of protection from consequences. Strong taboos stigmatizing slurs are not inconsistent with robust protections for free speech. Certain speech is so harmful and has such little redeeming value that no one should want to hear it. Outside of fringe publications, overtly racist, anti-Semitic, or anti-Muslim cartoons rarely make it into print in the United States, for example. Some of the exceptions to the First Amendment explicitly carve out types of expression—including, under certain conditions, cross burning and hanging nooses in trees—that cross the line from political speech into deliberate intimidation.

But much of the time, no such definitive judgment is possible. Offensiveness is not always objectively determinable. A large majority of Americans polled in April 2019 believe their fellow citizens are "too easily offended these days." Given the subjectivity and elasticity of the concept of offense, losing the freedom to offend would mean forfeiting a great deal of freedom of speech.

The case for defending offensive speech is commonly made with reference to John Stuart Mill's classic 1859 treatise, *On Liberty*. Mill cites the imperative of free speech as a route to uncovering truth, and articulates profound skepticism about the right of any authority to judge what speech is abhorrent and can justifiably be silenced. Contemporary theorists have updated Mill's argument. Human rights lawyer Nani Jansen Reventlow offers three reasons to defend offensive speech:

1. views on what is offensive "will inevitably change according to who is judging" (for example, President Donald Trump has called journalists enemies of the American people, political opponents "traitors," and accused critics of "hat[ing] our country");
2. allowing offensive ideas to be spoken and written "serves as an important safety valve against the expression of such ideas by means of physical violence" (people who feel forcibly silenced may be prone to lashing out);
3. that "in order to move forward as a society, we need dissenting voices; even ones that express their views in a way that may be offensive or shocking to others." (Martin Luther King was once considered by critics to be a dangerous radical who deserved to be locked up.)

One argument against protecting offensive speech from government bans centers on the fact that disempowered minorities bear the brunt of the exercise of such offenses and that their entitlement to equality is incompatible with a right to denigrate at will. It is unquestionably true that offensive speech often targets members of less powerful groups and can inflict harm. But the corollary—that government prohibitions on speech can effectively protect such populations—is false. If anything, minority voices are more likely to be stifled by tighter curbs on speech imposed by those in power. Danish free speech expert Jacob Mchangama has marshaled a list of global examples of the suppression of minority voices by the guardians of religious orthodoxy, sexism, and nationalism in places where free speech protections are weak. These include the persecution of Christians and Ahmadi Muslims under Pakistani blasphemy laws and the arrest of the Russian activist punk band Pussy Riot, who were sentenced to prison in 2012 for committing "hooliganism" motivated by "religious hatred." Mchangama concludes that restricting free speech to "secure the well-being of minorities is both false and dangerous," noting that while "Christians, Muslims, atheists, liberals, and feminists are brutally persecuted in countries where these freedoms are denied, they are able to live peacefully with each other in liberal democracies where these rights are guaranteed."

One of the most prominent exemplars of the right to offend is novelist Salman Rushdie. He spent years in hiding beginning in 1989 after Iranian supreme leader Ayatollah Khomeini issued a worldwide call to Muslims to murder Rushdie in retaliation for a novel, *The Satanic Verses,* deemed blasphemous. During his ordeal, Rushdie was supported by PEN as well as by many readers, publishers, bookstore owners, and writers who lent practical assistance and kept his books on the shelves despite threats and acts of lethal violence. Rushdie, who served as president of PEN America in the early 2000s, has characterized the left's demand for free speech curbs as a form of Marxian false consciousness whereby people cleave toward a solution that will actually only worsen the ills from which they suffer.

The complication, of course, is that the ability for diverse groups to live peacefully together is challenged when hateful and discriminatory attitudes pervade. To be clear, the right to offend does not imply an obligation to offend or to celebrate offensive speech. It doesn't mean that willful offense is acceptable, much less desirable. Rather, it interlaces with other principles, including the need to use language conscientiously, to exercise a duty of care, and to be cognizant of the harms that speech can inflict. As President Barack Obama has said, "Modern, complicated, diverse societies" require "civility and restraint and judgment," and when we "defend the legal right of a person to insult another's religion, we're equally obligated to use our free speech to condemn such insults and stand shoulder to shoulder with religious communities, particularly religious minorities who are the targets of such attacks." While some critics charged the president with going too far by citing a duty to condemn insults to religion, his point about the value of showing solidarity with those subjected to hateful speech is vital. This dual obligation to defend the right to offend even while convincingly condemning the offense itself is difficult to get right but crucial to preserving free speech today.

Salman Rushdie has reflected on how to keep debate open while minimizing offense to individuals: "You are never rude to the person, but you can be savagely rude about what the person thinks. That seems to me a crucial distinction: People must be protected from discrimination by virtue of their race, but you cannot ring-fence their ideas. The moment you say that any idea system is sacred, whether it's a belief system or a secular ideology, the moment you declare a set of ideas to be immune from criticism, satire, derision, or contempt, freedom of thought becomes impossible."

The risks of speaking out on a controversial subject are compounded if you don't believe anyone will have your back. If you can rely on the aid of your allies, editors, publisher, or institution—even if they disagree with the substance of your views—arguing a contestable point becomes less daunting. For individuals reluctant to defend free expression, learning how to speak up in support of an embattled speaker, even one whose views you reject, is key. In the fall of 2019, after the Houston Rockets basketball team general manager Daryl Morey tweeted support for prodemocracy protesters in Hong Kong, the Chinese government went ballistic. Beijing demanded that Morey be fired and threatened the league with financial penalties. After an initial equivocation in which he judged the incident "regrettable," National Basketball Association commissioner Adam Silver found his footing as a strong voice in support of Morey. When the Chinese demanded Morey's ouster, Silver said, he told them "there's no chance that's happening. . . . There's no chance we'll even discipline him."

Universities have a special obligation to speak up for faculty, administrators, and students. Entire systems for the protection of academic freedom, including tenure, exist to safeguard the academy from intellectual conformity. Universities should be places where novel, provocative, and even revolutionary ideas can be incubated and where students encounter views that challenge, confound, and even anger them. Because universities are imbued with prestige, dissenting ideas that germinate in the academy have been viewed by governments as uniquely threatening. Purges of independent-minded academics during the Soviet Union, the Chinese Cultural Revolution, the Red Scare, and in modern Turkey offer searing reminders of what can happen when disfavored views are left exposed.

Yet today many educational institutions seem prone to waver. In fall 2015, a Yale University Committee on Intercultural Affairs issued a guidance memo to the full student body on Halloween costumes, pointing out that certain historical, ethnic, or cultural costumes (blackface or sombreros) could be offensive. It was a reasonable advisory to circulate, since youth from different backgrounds might not realize how their dress might come across to others. In response, Erika Christakis, a Yale lecturer on child development who also served alongside her husband, Nicholas Christakis, a tenured professor, as a leader of one of Yale's residential colleges, sent her own response to the students in her college. Christakis had heard from students who felt infantilized by the Halloween directive. In her note she questioned the wisdom of administrators propounding parameters for dress-up. She took issue with the Intercultural Committee email as an overreaching "exercise of implied control" over the students, criticized its de facto prohibition on cross-cultural costumes, and asked, "is there no room anymore for a child or young person to be a little bit obnoxious . . . a little bit inappropriate or provocative or, yes, offensive?"

Christakis's email, though it took a different stance from the committee's, made a reasonable point about letting students find their own way and learn from one another. Unlike Yale residential dean June Chu's crude, racialized reviews on Yelp, Christakis's was a considered argument that drew on her academic knowledge. But it provoked a firestorm of student protest, including insults, epithets, an open letter signed by 740 students, alumni, and administrators, and calls by some students for both Christakises to be fired from their residential roles. National media attention and alumni petitions both for and against the couple followed. A video, which went viral online, captured a crowd of students, mostly of color, in an extended confrontation with Nicholas Christakis as other administrators looked on. Erika Christakis apologized in a public letter but, at the end of the academic year, she and her husband nonetheless resigned their posts as leaders of the residential college. Erika also resigned from teaching at Yale.

When PEN America researched the Yale Halloween conflagration, we found that the fracas was fueled, as is often true in similar cases, by a wider context of student frustration with the university's perceived failure to stanch currents of racism. Yale's leadership was rightly mindful of student dissatisfaction with a range of perceived racial offenses at the university, including a residential college named after avowed white supremacist John Calhoun (the name of which the college has subsequently been changed), allegations of excessive force and racial profiling by campus police against black students, and purported incidences of bigotry by Yale fraternities.

Although university officials ultimately affirmed Erika Christakis's right to her opinion, they were more full-throated in supporting the rights of students to ostracize her and demand her and her husband's removal. The dean of Yale College sent a campus-wide email expressing full support for the costume guidance that Christakis had critiqued, calling it "exactly right," at least in its "intents." His email was silent on Christakis's right to voice her contrary opinion, and the calls to punish her for doing so. He lauded the brouhaha as "one big free speech happening," downplaying the intimidating and censorious impact on Christakis. Another email from both the president and dean affirmed free speech principles, but stopped short of saying that the Christakises would be protected from reprisals. Only after external free speech advocates pointed out the "conspicuous omission" did the president add reassurance. Yale's leadership seemed torn between the rightful desire to extend empathy toward offended students and the equally necessary obligation to defend speech with which Yale's leadership disagreed. Yet institutions can and must do both.

As Erika Christakis recounted in a *Washington Post* op-ed a year later, surprisingly few people on campus spoke up in her defense. "And who can blame them?" she wrote. "Numerous professors, including those at Yale's top-rated law school, contacted us personally to say that it was too risky to speak their minds. Others who generously supported us publicly were admonished by colleagues for vouching for our characters. Many students met with us confidentially to describe intimidation and accusations of being a 'race traitor' when they deviated from the ascendant campus account that I had grievously injured the community."

The Yale administration should have clearly defended Christakis's right to speak out and bluntly repudiated calls for her to be punished. People have every *right*, of course, to demand retaliation for offensive speech, but the impact of such demands can nonetheless be chilling. Calls to punish speech put pressure on officials and make such punishment more likely. In the future, residential advisers might refrain from issuing a reasoned policy memo on a matter of college life for fear that it could generate controversy and jeopardize their job. By strongly defending Christakis's right to thoughtfully dissent, even while disagreeing with the content of her views, the university's leadership could have created space for disagreement and enabled an even more robust "free speech happening."

In 2018, when former first lady Barbara Bush passed away, Fresno State University creative writing professor Randa Jarrar tweeted that the Bush family matriarch had been an "amazing racist" who "raised a war criminal." She further wrote, "I'm happy the witch is dead. Can't wait for the rest of her family to fall to their demise the way 1.5 million Iraqis have. Byyyeeeeeee." As her tweet went viral, Jarrar was pilloried for her screed against a dead woman during a family's mourning period. Eighty thousand people signed a petition for her ouster. In response university president Joseph Castro said he was "shocked, upset, appalled just like everybody else," as he was within his rights to do. But he also said that "this was beyond free speech" and that Jarrar's tenure was under review as a result, in clear violation of a public university's mandate to protect its faculty from reprisals for speech. PEN America and other groups wrote to Castro reminding him of his legal obligations and commitment to academic freedom, after which the campus backpedaled and confirmed that Jarrar's position was secure.

Standing by a Speaker Accused of Offense

Dilemmas inherent in defending offensive speech are not confined to the college campus. In March 2018, *The Atlantic* announced it had hired Kevin Williamson, a conservative journalist. Editor in chief Jeff Goldberg declared Williamson a writer "whose force of intellect and acuity of insight reflect our ambition." Goldberg acknowledged Williamson's tendency to troll ideological antagonists and his history of racist and insensitive comments. (While working for *The National Review,* he had likened a black child to a "primate," compared trans people to voodoo practitioners, and tweeted that abortion was akin to "premeditated homicide.") But Goldberg extolled Williamson as an "excellent reporter" and avowed his commitment to making the magazine "a big tent for ideas and argument." He further wrote that a person's "worst tweets, or assertions, in isolation" should not override consideration of the totality of his work and stated his belief in "giv(ing) people second chances and the opportunity to change."

Those calibrated words did not prevent a frenzy of criticism. Within weeks, the magazine had second thoughts about its commitment to second chances and Williamson was fired. Goldberg justified the reversal citing "new information," namely a podcast in which Williamson had doubled down on calling abortion premeditated murder. But this supposedly intervening evidence only confirmed a viewpoint that was already well known. This approach—citing some new piece of information to justify backtracking on support for an exponent of controversial views—is familiar. The new podcast seemed a way to skirt the appearance of having capitulated to a mob. Oftentimes such decisions are motivated by a combination of outside pressures and internal misgivings over hard-to-defend speech. *The Atlantic* made a debatable but principled decision to hire Williamson, but then appeared to fold once the outcry became too furious.

Several months later, a similar situation arose when the *New York Times* hired Sarah Jeong as a technology editorial writer. Jeong was targeted by conservatives who dug through her Twitter history and discovered posts reading "#CancelWhitePeople" and other incendiary messages that mirrored hyperbolic, racist, and misogynistic attacks that had been directed toward her. Andrew Sullivan, writing in *New York* magazine, attacked Jeong as a racist with genocidal ambitions who propagated "eliminationist rhetoric" against ostensibly "subhuman" white people. Jeong responded by screen-capping racist threats directed toward her, writing that "I have faced torrents of online hate. . . . I engaged in what I thought of at the time as counter-trolling. While it was intended as satire, I deeply regret that I mimicked the language of my harassers." Jeong's ability to offer some mitigating context for her outlandish tweets was likely decisive in the *Times'* decision to stand by her. The paper issued a statement saying it had reviewed her social media output prior to making their offer and had told her that such rhetoric was unacceptable at the paper. The *Times'* response to the Jeong controversy offers one model for the defense of controversial and unpopular speech.

Campus Speakers in the Crosshairs

Some of the most visible free-speech-related controversies in recent years have involved controversial speakers being invited to university campuses, prompting protests and uproar, sometimes to the point where planned lectures are canceled or disrupted. These incidents raise a series of related questions about who deserves an invitation to campus, how to foster a broad range of ideas at the university without courting unrest, and whether there are ever grounds to rescind a speaking invitation.

It helps to look at the approach that most universities take to speaking invitations. Typically, academic departments, research centers, administrative offices, publications, and student clubs are free to invite whomever they wish. The College Republicans can host right-wing journalists and the Democratic Socialists can welcome progressive activists. To expose students to many perspectives, it makes sense to allow just about any accredited entity on campus to book a room and extend a speaking invitation. If university administrators had to put an official stamp of approval on every invitation, the result would be a much narrower range of vetted speakers.

This doesn't mean that speaking invitations should be extended willy-nilly or that everyone who may desire a forum on campus has a right to one. Those who issue speaking invitations should do so conscientiously. Care and diligence are warranted to determine if a planned speaker is likely to provoke blowback. It is crucial, however, that those doing the inviting not treat all controversy as a negative. If campuses ruled out all potential speakers who had attracted a backlash for their views, college would be a dull place and its discourse limited. But potential repercussions should be evaluated and planned for ahead of time. Event sponsors should be ready to articulate why an invitation was issued: perhaps because the speaker has an important book, has put forward significant research findings, or is shaping public debate. As Columbia journalism professor Jelani Cobb has put it: "No chemistry department would extend an invitation to an alchemist, no reputable department of psychology would entertain a lecture espousing phrenology." There needs to be some cognizable rationale as to why a speaker merits a forum on campus.

But when an invitation has been properly issued by an authorized campus entity, administrators should rarely, if ever, override that decision. For a public university to decide that a potential speaker is unwelcome on campus based on what they have said, or are likely to say, it would mean that they were unlawfully discriminating on the basis of viewpoint. Although high security costs are sometimes invoked as grounds to call off a speaker, such rationales are unlikely to pass constitutional muster, since anticipated protests are themselves a reaction to a particular set of opinions. Private universities have the legal authority to veto speakers, but doing so compromises virtues of a decentralized system for issuing invitations.

Some of the toughest calls involve self-styled provocateurs known for little more than ginning up controversy. In 2016, former Breitbart journalist Milo Yiannopoulos embarked on a self-styled "Dangerous Faggot" campus tour aimed to goad his antagonists into shutting him down. Before an invited appearance at the University of California, Berkeley, more than 150 masked, black-clad Antifa demonstrators confronted police with fireworks, rocks, and Molotov cocktails, resulting in a half-dozen injuries and significant property damage. The university canceled Yiannopoulos's speech two hours before it was set to begin, prompting him to tweet: "One thing we do know for sure: The Left is absolutely terrified of free speech and will do literally anything to shut it down." Critics assailed Berkeley for betraying its storied commitment to free speech. Four Bay Area residents who had come to hear Yiannopoulos sued the university for failing to protect their safety.

Berkeley learned its lesson. Later that year, when Yiannopoulos announced plans for a comeback featuring former Trump administration aide Steve Bannon and other prominent conservatives, the university let the event proceed. Provost Carol Christ made plain that the university considered many of Yiannopoulos's ideas inimical to the values of the campus community. She affirmed that students' protest rights would be protected "with vigor." Her dual message—that the university scorned Yiannopoulos's ideas yet would uphold his right to voice them—conveyed solidarity with agitated students and fealty to free speech. As she later put it, "We called his bluff, the charade collapsed and his student hosts cancelled the event." Yiannopoulos came to campus alone, generating what Dan Mogulof, assistant vice chancellor at Berkeley, called "the most expensive photo op in the university's history": $800,000 in security for a speech of less than twenty minutes. Although the money could certainly have been better spent, the one-time cost of allowing such a spectacle to run its course may be preferable to playing Whac-A-Mole with a speaker who hopes to be silenced in order to be able to cry foul. After Yiannopoulos's underwhelming second visit to Berkeley, the wind began to come out of the sails of his national crusade, suggesting that the costs associated with standing up to such a provocateur may not be recurring.

When Cornell Law School professor William Jacobson was invited to Vassar to deliver a lecture titled "Hate Speech Is Free Speech, Even After Charlottesville," protesters pushed Vassar president Elizabeth Bradley to disinvite him. Coming within months of the deadly Charlottesville melee in 2017, emotions ran high and students professed fear that the talk could spark violence. Instead of spurning Jacobson, Bradley announced that at the same time as the speech, other organizations would sponsor a "community gathering . . . that will be a place of healing and peace" and with "adequate emotional support staff." While some critics mocked such measures as an overindulgence of an imagined emotional fragility on the part of students—the talk, after all, wasn't mandatory—they helped the speech come off without a hitch, and allowed Bradley to retain the confidence of both the libertarians that invited Jacobson and those who objected to his visit.

In October 2017, Bard College's Hannah Arendt Center for Politics and the Humanities came under fire for including Marc Jongen, a prominent thinker and politician from Germany's far-right Alternative für Deutschland (AfD) political party, in the lineup for a conference titled "Crises of Democracy: Thinking in Dark Times." The AfD had recently captured the third-largest number of seats in the German Bundestag. Arendt Center director Roger Berkowitz believed that hearing from Jongen would facilitate informed discussion on rising global authoritarianism. Bard-based political theorist Ian Buruma was asked to respond to and challenge Jongen.

When the Arendt Center tweeted out some of Jongen's remarks, critics accused Bard of legitimizing a racist ideologue. Fifty scholars published a letter in the *Chronicle of Higher Education* pointing out that the AfD had boasted of the invitation on its Facebook page. Bard was criticized for failing to issue "an unequivocal, principled statement distancing itself from the anti-immigrant, anti-refugee, and Islamophobic agenda of Jongen and the AfD." Berkowitz replied that none of the critics had attended the conference and that no one who was present had joined the protest. He said, "The AfD is a real-world example of the crisis facing wobbling liberal democracies. The only way to respond to this crisis is to listen to, engage, and reject these arguments." Bard president Leon Botstein faulted the protest as emulating "the public denouncements of the Soviet era . . . [that] put terror in the hearts of young musicians and writers."

The incident illustrated the challenge of airing and reckoning with problematic ideas without lending them legitimacy. Inescapably, when someone is given a public forum, some measure of the attendant prestige redounds to that individual. The Arendt Center compounded the issue by tweeting out Jongen's quotes, amplifying his message in a form divorced from the context.

Not all campus engagements are created equal: a faculty appointment, commencement address, or fellowship is a weightier token of esteem than being on a long agenda of speakers at a policy conference. The problem, of course, is that when comments are tweeted out or a photo behind a lectern appears on Facebook, the difference between an esteemed lectureship and an appearance like Jongen's—meant to facilitate a critical reckoning with fascism—can be lost.

The quest to avoid legitimizing a noxious set of opinions should not be grounds to exclude a speaker if there is a strong justification for her participation. An academic conference attended by scholars, experts, and students doing relevant course work was the right setting to engage Jongen's views. An appearance in the campus stadium or even in a lecture hall of self-selected students would have been a different matter. Novelist Francine Prose, a writer in residence at Bard, wrote in the *Guardian* that she brought her class to hear Jongen. They were, she explained, "proud to be associated with a school that trusted their ability to weigh unpopular ideas. . . . They felt that hearing Jongen had been part of their education."

At times, offering a platform to a controversial or less than credible speaker can be revelatory or even catalytic. When former New York City mayor and Trump attorney Rudolph Giuliani became known for dissembling during news interviews, some commentators criticized the networks for continuing to book him on their shows. But it was during a September 2019 interview with CNN's Chris Cuomo that Giuliani admitted to having asked Ukraine to investigate former vice president Joseph Biden, setting off an inquiry into whether President Trump had committed an impeachable offense.

AT PEN AMERICA, our mandate frequently requires defending speech with which we disagree. We have affirmed Milo Yiannopoulos's and avowed white supremacist Richard Spencer's rights to speak on campuses where they have been duly invited, while at the same time denouncing the hateful content of their rhetoric. Though we have a long-standing policy of opposition to academic and cultural boycotts as inimical to the free flow of ideas, when Omar Barghouti, head of the Boycott, Divest, and Sanction movement against Israel, was denied a visa to travel to the United States for a speaking tour, we spoke out. In that case, our disagreement with Barghouti's agenda and our insistence that he had the right to expound his views had an identical premise: by excluding Barghouti on ideological grounds, U.S. immigration authorities were blocking the right to exchange ideas.

WHY AND HOW TO DEFEND UNPOPULAR SPEECH

- Historically the suppression of disfavored ideas has served to reinforce power structures and suppress dissent
- Engaging with objectionable viewpoints can help refine and strengthen the arguments against them
- When providing a forum for offensive viewpoints to be aired, take care to minimize the opportunity for the speaker to portray such engagement as an endorsement
- Separate the content of the speech from the speakers' right to express themselves—where appropriate reject the former while defending the latter
- Those in leadership roles may need to simultaneously affirm institutional values, show empathy toward those affronted by speech, and affirm the rights of the speaker

5.

Apologize When You've Said Something Wrong

APOLOGIES HAVE COME TO BE SEEN AS A SIGN OF WEAKNESS. IN 2016, President Barack Obama traveled to Hiroshima to lay a wreath for the 140,000 residents who perished there seventy-one years earlier. Though Obama never suggested that dropping the atomic bomb was a mistake, critics nevertheless derided his visit as an "apology tour." Despite widespread belief that the 1991 Senate Judiciary Committee hearings in which Anita Hill testified against Supreme Court nominee Clarence Thomas were one-sided and unfair to Hill, former vice president Joseph Biden, who chaired the committee proceedings, has stopped short of apologizing to her, instead simply sharing "his regret for what she endured." He clearly feels remorse and seeks forgiveness, yet somehow an outright apology seems like a bridge too far. "Does being President Trump still mean never having to say you're sorry?" asked an NBC News headline, over a story quoting a White House adviser who said, "His general philosophy is you get no credit for an apology, so don't do it."

Hard for Me to Say I'm Sorry

Apologies may be fraught, but they're essential, especially in a diverse and raucous society like ours. Many verbal offenses can be resolved with a simple apology. Microaggressions like mixing up the names of two Jewish women who both teach in the philosophy department, asking a fellow party guest if she's pregnant when she isn't, or failing to realize that the young Latino man in scrubs is the neurosurgeon deserve a prompt, straightforward, genuine apology. If the lapse is isolated, there's a good chance any hard feelings will dissipate. But without a basic apology, bad feelings can linger.

When speech offends more deeply, apology can mean the difference between an uneasy encounter and a career- or life-altering conflict. As important as knowing when to apologize is knowing how. Expressions of regret often come across as grudging, self-serving, tone deaf, or even accusatory and end up stoking rather than relieving resentment. The right kind of apology can prevent the sting of offensive speech from burrowing more deeply into the skin of those aggrieved. It can preserve the reputation of a speaker and help repair relationships and even communities fractured by contentious speech.

GOOD APOLOGIES

- **Self-reflective:** Show you understand what you did wrong and why
- **Encompassing of all related wrongful conduct:** When in doubt, be overly inclusive
- **Sincere:** Use language and tone that show genuine concern
- **Take full responsibility:** Don't deflect blame or emphasize an excuse
- **Focus on regret for actions committed:** Rather than saying you're sorry for how someone felt or another result of your actions, say you're sorry for what you did
- **Prompt:** Don't let things fester

In March 2019, Democratic presidential candidate Beto O'Rourke unleashed an elaborate apology for a remark made three days earlier on the campaign trail in Iowa. He had joked that his wife, Amy, was raising their three children "sometimes with [his] help." Even though he had ostensibly been poking fun at himself, his statement infuriated feminist activists and commentators. They pointed out that female candidates could never get away with such a hands-off approach to parenting and that, instead, women often have to set aside their ambitions for the benefit of their male partners.

O'Rourke acknowledged that the criticisms were "right on" and that he should have noted that his wife's disproportionate load stemmed from long-standing societal discrimination. "I have been in some instances part of the problem," he added. O'Rourke acknowledged how he had benefited from his race, gender, and wealth, linking his position of privilege in his marriage to benefits he enjoys as a white man.

As apologies go, O'Rourke's ticked most of the boxes. His mea culpa was prompt. He took full responsibility for the offending comment. He did not blame listeners for misunderstanding him, nor invoke his wife's support to minimize the offense. His comments about broader patterns of thought and behavior made the regret seem more introspective and encompassing. Its length and format—a live interview in which he spoke without notes— reinforced his sincerity, demonstrating that he was not expediently mouthing talking points.

Above all, he avoided what psychiatrist Aaron Lazare has called a "pseudo-apology"—an unconvincing, halfhearted stab at penitence marked by vagueness, the passive voice (constructions like "I apologize if offense was taken"), conditionality, minimization, and sidestepping.

In December 2018, comedian Kevin Hart was announced as the host of the 2019 Academy Awards ceremony. A day later, tweets and tapes surfaced of homophobic remarks he had made, including a comment that "one of my biggest fears is my son growing up and being gay." Hart undertook an apology tour, to no avail—because his was a pseudo-apology. He began with a counterattack, blaming those who were disturbed by his comments. First, on Instagram, he said, "My team calls me, 'Oh my God, Kevin, everyone's upset about the tweets you did years ago. Guys, I'm almost 40 years old. If you don't believe that people change, grow, evolve as they get older, I don't know what to tell you." When the Academy of Motion Picture Arts and Sciences warned Hart to apologize or be dropped as host, he declined, insisting that he'd done so already. Years earlier Hart had indeed offered a self-reflective look at his past comments, saying "It's about my fear. . . . The funny thing within that joke is it's me getting mad at my son because of my own insecurities—I panicked." But he was unwilling to repeat this admission when under fire. His hesitation cost him the backing of the Academy, which faced exposure for having failed to do its homework before selecting him.

Having lost the Oscars gig, Hart finally offered up some truly apologetic words, saying, "I sincerely apologize to the LGBTQ community for my insensitive words from my past," and, "I'm sorry that I hurt people."

"PSEUDO" APOLOGIES

- **Self-serving:** "I apologize if you were offended"
- **Incomplete:** "To the extent that you were not fully included, I am sorry"
- **Accusatory:** "I regret that when you put me on the spot, I reacted poorly"
- **Defensive:** "While I don't believe I am the only one who owes an apology . . ."
- **Focuses on how actions were received:** "Our statement elicited strong reactions, which we regret"
- **Significantly delayed:** "Having heard from many of you that our actions were not well received"
- **Minimizes the offense:** "I hope this episode can be appreciated in the larger context of our efforts"
- **Uses the passive voice:** "If you were hurt, I am sorry"
- **Scripted:** "In consultation with our trustees and staff, I wish to convey . . ."

But a month later, he turned defensive again, telling talk show host Ellen DeGeneres that the resurfacing of the remarks was an "attack," and faulting news outlets and the public for failing to note his previous apologies. This was a pseudo-apology. While playing offense may work when charges are being rejected as false, accepting blame for having done something wrong while in the same breath turning the tables on your accusers is hard to pull off. Had he aimed to satisfy critics, he might have done well to consult LGBTQ contacts for help finding the words to win back trust. CNN talk show host Don Lemon, who is gay, commented, "To many . . . [it seems] that he has somehow turned himself into a victim instead of acknowledging the real victims of violent and sometimes deadly homophobia."

In some instances, a revelation is so incendiary that the impulse to apologize can overtake facts and reason. When the story broke that Virginia governor Ralph Northam had been pictured years before in a medical school yearbook in blackface, standing next to someone dressed in Ku Klux Klan robes, the governor hurried to the podium to apologize for "the decision I made to appear as I did in this photo and for the hurt that decision caused." A day later his message changed. He said that after conferring with classmates he realized it wasn't him in the photo, although he had once worn blackface when dressed as Michael Jackson. The apology was cringe-inducing, including an awkward reference to how difficult it is to remove shoe polish from skin and an offer to demonstrate Jackson's moonwalk. Yet Northam weathered the calls for his resignation, and polls showed most voters—including black voters—wanted him to stay in office. Why did Northam survive? Voters seemed to place his youthful use of blackface in the context of his long progressive record on civil rights. It may also have helped that his instinct was to express contrition, however ham-handedly. He never sought to minimize the wrongness of wearing blackface or blame the media.

When his own forays into blackface costumes were exposed in September 2019, Canadian prime minister Justin Trudeau had Northam's experience to draw on. Seeking to convey candor and acceptance of responsibility, he strode to a scrum of microphones on his plane and launched into a plaintive description of the costumes he had worn, acknowledging having done so more than once. He admitted that he "should've known better, but I didn't." When asked if he thought the disclosure, which came amid a hotly contested reelection campaign, was a political hit, Trudeau refused the bait, keeping the focus squarely on his own regret, saying, "It's not about timing but about having done something I shouldn't have done." Trudeau also survived, winning a second term a month later.

Unapologetic, but Still Attentive and Empathic

Not everything merits an apology. No one would like a world of constant self-abasement in the service of placating critics. Apologizing too quickly or rotely can devalue the currency of regret. But even when an apology isn't needed, a show of empathy and self-reflection can help defuse conflict. Denny Bonavita, a columnist at Pennsylvania's *Currier Express,* was called out by readers of Welsh extraction for describing Donald Trump as a welsher, a term that means swindler. Bonavita researched the etymology of the word and found that its origins are not anti-Welsh and the confluence between the words is coincidental. He expressed regret for the offense he caused, but deliberately stopped short of apologizing since the word he used was not actually anti-Welsh. His explanatory piece offers a concise model of how to deescalate a speech-related controversy by acknowledging the basis of a different point of view while stopping short of crediting or endorsing it.

In January 2019, University of Chicago law professor Geoffrey Stone uttered the n-word aloud in a constitutional law class, as he had done for many years. He did so while recounting an anecdote to illustrate the legal doctrine of "fighting words." The story involved a class years earlier in which a black student questioned whether words could actually trigger violence. That student's doubts prompted a white classmate to conduct a natural experiment, calling him the n-word to his face. In response, as Stone described it, "the black student immediately lunged at the white student, illustrating that the doctrine was indeed still relevant." That instinctive physical response proved Stone's point about the power of words. While Stone had told the story many times before with little apparent reaction, the latest retelling elicited an angry response. The university paper published an op-ed proclaiming, "Racism lives at the University of Chicago Law School," and accused Stone of trivializing his black students' experiences, reinforcing racist stereotypes and white dominance. The piece called for Stone to be suspended unless he agreed to stop using the word.

At first, Stone defended himself, saying that "the point of the story is not to offend or insult anyone" and that "in a course on the First Amendment, it is essential to identify and to confront the very speech that defines the limits of free expression." After meeting with concerned students, though, Stone had a change of heart. He said, "I had a very thoughtful conversation with a group of African American students yesterday and they gave me a much clearer sense of how hurtful, upsetting, and distracting they find the use of this word even when it is not used in a manner meant to be insulting or demeaning." Declaring himself "impressed by the depth of their feelings and reactions," he decided to forgo further use of the anecdote in class. Stone praised the courage of the students who sat down to share their views—itself a demonstration of the power and import of free expression. While stopping short of an apology, Stone conveyed concern for his students and a willingness to reconsider his behavior. In so doing, he displayed enough openness and empathy to quiet the controversy.

In our diverse and digital society, the risk of offending someone through speech is multiplied as different cultures, generations, and speaking styles bump up against one another. By recognizing that the need to apologize is an unavoidable by-product of being on social media or otherwise speaking out, the stigma is reduced and the ability to efficiently move past conflict is enhanced.

HOW TO APOLOGIZE

- Accept that when taking part in fast-moving discourse, some mistakes are inevitable and apologies, necessary
- Think before apologizing so that you can get the message right the first time
- Err on the side of expansiveness in apologizing
- Avoid pseudo-apologies that are vague, conditional, and transfer blame to others
- Even when an apology is not in order, find ways to show empathy and attentiveness to concerns raised

PART II

PRINCIPLES FOR LISTENING

6.

Consider Intent and Context When Reacting to Speech

"HE NEEDS TO OWN HIS IMPACT," SAID A UNIVERSITY OF MARYLAND graduate student of a professor who had offended those in his classroom by using the n-word. Voicing the word during a lecture on the topic of racial slurs, the faculty member sought to convey the affront of the notorious epithet, but not to inflict injury. "He may not have intended it," the student continued, "but if you rear-end someone's car and smash their bumper, you pay up whether you meant to do it or not."

The decoupling of speech from considerations of intent and context has scrambled our discourse. Words mean different things to different people and in distinct settings, especially in a diverse society. But we often forget that words and statements are polysemic. Terms like "faggot," "dyke," or even "cunt" are sometimes reappropriated with pride or, as here, brought up to make a point about language. To understand a word's meaning, you need to know who is saying it and what the intended message is. In the digital arena, where nearly all speech can be cut, pasted, screenshot, reposted, and otherwise transmitted without regard to how the speaker had situated the remarks, context disappears. A quote, video snippet, picture, or meme is often all that an online audience sees. Research shows that the more outrageous it is, the farther and faster it travels. To paraphrase Jonathan Swift's adage about lies and the truth, an offensive snippet can often make it halfway around the world before the context gets its boots on.

Free speech advocates should urge us to consider intent and context in judging whether a statement crosses legal, moral, or social lines. Before calling something offensive, it's worth asking whether the insult was willful. An absence of malice may not absolve a speaker, but it's relevant to weighing culpability and consequences. Speakers have an obligation to be conscientious and consider whether they owe a heightened duty of care. The corollary is that speech that is careless—even if not intentionally malign—should be treated more harshly than a remark made with reasonable forethought that still landed poorly. Seemingly offensive speech may be belligerent, blundering, or utterly benign. That a speaker states that she meant no harm is not definitive evidence that ill will was neither intended nor courted. When we're criticized for our words, it can be almost reflexive to claim that we meant no offense. The avowal may be true, or a self-serving attempt to win leniency. An assessment of intent and context needs to reach beyond subjective accounts of what was in the speaker's mind.

Because of its shock value, outdated, sexist, racist, homophobic, politically pointed, and otherwise outlandish speech tends to travel well online. Posters and tweeters can win likes and followers, bolstering their social clout. Studies have demonstrated that marks of approval on social media can trigger chemical reactions in the brain that leave us craving more. But for those who wish to resist both formal and informal censorship, the impulse to trumpet your ire over the latest outrage should be tempered by recognition that unless you're sure of your facts, you may reinforce false narratives or fuel unjust outcomes.

In 2010, right-wing Web entrepreneur Andrew Breitbart posted a video of U.S. Department of Agriculture official Shirley Sherrod speaking before an NAACP audience. The video showed Sherrod telling of working with a white man to save his farm. She recalled her ambivalence about helping him when many black people were losing their land and said she "didn't give him the full force of what I could do." She also recounted bringing him to a white lawyer so that "his own kind would take care of him." Fox News pounced on the implication that Sherrod had mistreated the white farmer. The story roared through the blogosphere to the media. Soon government officials forced Sherrod's resignation and even the NAACP's president condemned Sherrod's remarks.

Only after Sherrod's reputation had been shredded did the full context of her remarks emerge. Her speech was actually about moving beyond race and recognizing poverty as the key factor in rural development. The fuller account made clear that Sherrod had diligently assisted the white farmer, and in fact become good friends with him such that he spoke out in her defense. The NAACP retracted its denunciation and criticized those who had doctored the video. The secretary of agriculture apologized to Sherrod and offered her a new job; even President Obama called to apologize. In the end, those who failed to verify whether Sherrod had been fairly accused ended up with nearly as much to apologize for as those who had slandered her.

Author Chimamanda Ngozi Adichie pressed the case for considering context and intent in recounting how a woman who was introducing her once botched her name, calling her "chimichanga," a deep-fried burrito. A friend of Adichie's told her she should have been livid about the flub, which seemed to indicate a Western confusion about all things foreign. But Adichie knew the woman had practiced the pronunciation ahead of time and just "ended up with an utterly human mistake that was the result of anxiety." For the Nigerian American author, "The point of this story is that intent matters. Someone might very well call me chimichanga out of a malicious desire to mock my name, and that I would certainly not laugh about. But there is a difference between malice and a mistake." She urged others to "think of people as people, not as abstractions who have to conform to bloodless logic but as people—fragile, imperfect." Indeed the value of looking empathically at those who may offend us applies to many principles in this book.

The incentive structure of online discourse cuts against giving the benefit of the doubt or searching for mitigating context. Human nature conditions us to jump to conclusions and seek confirmation for our beliefs. In March 2013, tech blogger Adria Richards overheard two men at a computer programming conference joking about "dongles" and "fork-ing," both technical terms (a dongle connects a computer to a network; forking means branching off in a software development process). Richards assumed they bore sexual innuendo. She tweeted a photograph of the men to her nine thousand followers quoting the two words as emblemizing "the toxic, male-dominated corporate culture" of tech. One of the men was fired. The ensuing online combustion ended up costing Richards her job as well.

In June 2018, *New Yorker* fact checker Talia Lavin posted photos on Twitter and suggested that an Immigration and Customs Enforcement (ICE) agent had a tattoo depicting a Nazi iron cross. But the fact checker hadn't checked her facts. Commenters pointed out that the cross image didn't really resemble the notorious Nazi emblem; in fact it was a sym-bol from the officer's platoon, which had fought in Afghanistan. Within fifteen minutes, Lavin deleted the tweet. But her peremptory judgment of the agent got her labeled an Internet scoundrel. ICE defended its agent. *The New Yorker* disavowed her tweet, and Lavin apologized profusely and resigned from her job. Nearly a year later she was still dogged by criticism and threats.

Lavin and Richards could have spared themselves anguish and career repercussions by ensuring that they understood what they had heard and seen before reacting. The threats, trolling, and abuse they endured were clearly disproportionate and undeserved. But both acted rashly to elicit an impassioned reaction from an online audience—a dangerous impulse. For avid social media users, misinterpretation and viral pile-ons are known occupational hazards. Those who engage online should do so with aware-ness of the perils of the platform and recognize the risks they assume.

In the gotcha culture of politics, taking an opponent's remarks out of context may be considered fair game, or at least common enough to be unremarkable. But when ostensibly neutral journalists do so, intentionally or not, they disserve their audiences. Donald Trump has surely provided no shortage of valid reasons for outrage. But at times overly eager journal-ists have circulated out-of-context remarks that sound worse than they ac-tually were. In May 2018, when Trump called members of the murderous MS-13 gang "animals," the *New York Times*' headline read: "Trump Calls

Some Unauthorized Immigrants 'Animals' in Rant." Trump's language may have been out of line, but the substitution of "Some Unauthorized Immigrants" for "Gang Members" misled readers. A meme then circulated online comparing Trump's statement to a line falsely attributed to Hitler: "Jews are not people; they are animals." For the *Times*' headline writer, confirmation bias—the tendency to interpret new information in ways that reinforce what we already believe—was clearly at work. After Trump clarified that he intended to refer only to gang members, the *Times* issued a new story titled, "Trump Defends 'Animals' Remark, Saying it Only Referred to MS-13 Gang Members." CNN likewise apologized.

In a landscape where incorrect or incomplete accounts can spread virally, the media hold special responsibilities. Rather than accepting at face value an interpretation of some context-free snippet, or using an out-of-context quote to drive clicks, credible outlets are expected to independently verify what they report. When information crosses over from an unconfirmed dispatch on social media to the subject of a mainstream news report, it assumes an aura of accuracy that is harder to rebut. Unfortunately, the frenetic news cycle and commercial pressures weigh against such vigilance.

Context Can Be Complex and Culture-Specific

Sometimes understanding context involves a deeper dive. In 2015, PEN America gave its annual Freedom of Expression Courage Award to the surviving staff of *Charlie Hebdo,* the satirical French magazine, twelve of whose staffers had been murdered in a terrorist attack in retaliation for *Charlie Hebdo*'s publishing cartoons of the Muslim prophet Muhammad. We believed that by poking fun at political leaders, religious commissars, and other purveyors of piety, *Charlie Hebdo* stood as a dauntless force, keeping the outer bounds of discourse and satire open to all. A week before the annual gala where the award would be presented, six distinguished writers announced plans to boycott the event to protest *Charlie Hebdo*'s alleged racism. The dispute became a major global story, with dozens of pieces published arguing for and against the award. While PEN America and most of our members stood firmly behind the award, I came to understand why some in our community vehemently opposed the honor.

A key discussion point was how to properly interpret the *Charlie Hebdo* cartoons. Some argued that caricatures of Muhammad were inherently offensive since some devout Muslims believe that, as a religious matter, he should not be depicted at all. Others felt the nature of the drawings, with hooked noses and wacky grins, were derogatory. Supporters pointed out that *Charlie Hebdo* regularly skewered priests, political leaders, and Hasidic rabbis—not attacking the vulnerable but rather aligning with them to challenge power structures bent on keeping them down. We hastily convened an event in New York that included two *Charlie Hebdo* staffers alongside experts in the traditions of French satire who could interpret a form foreign to most Americans.

The most vivid illustration of the importance of context to understanding *Charlie Hebdo* came in the form of a 2014 magazine cover image. The cover depicted a black woman in lipstick and earrings illustrated as a gorilla, complete with a furry body, paws, and a tail. The image of a black person shown as an ape goes back centuries and is flagrantly racist, suggesting that black people are subhuman. Looking at that cartoon, I reacted initially with shock and horror. But as I learned and looked more closely, I came to see it differently. Next to the figure is a small blue and red flame, the symbol of France's far-right National Front political party. The caption above the image reads "Rassemblement Bleu Raciste" (translated as Racist Blue Union), a play on the name Rassemblement Bleu Marine, the moniker of a right-wing French coalition. The cover ran shortly after a National Front politician had posted a photoshopped image of French justice minister Christiane Taubira, who was born in French Guyana, portrayed as a monkey. He was quoted on television saying that Taubira belonged "in a tree swinging from the branches rather than in government." The *Charlie Hebdo* cartoon, taking the form of a political poster, was intended to lambast the far-right's naked racism.

Tellingly, Christiane Taubira herself weighed in at the funeral of the cartoonist Bernard Verlhac, known as Tignous, who drew the image and was murdered in the 2015 attack. Her eulogy extolled him for seeking "the drawing that makes people laugh but not only that; the drawing that makes people think but not only that; the drawing, too, that makes people ashamed of having laughed over a solemn fact or situation." She championed artists who "kept watch over democracy to make sure it didn't fall asleep." That Taubira publicly memorialized Tignous was a powerful lesson in the centrality of context. As the figure depicted in that jarring cartoon, she of all people understood what it meant.

To be effective, satire must skate close to the line. The shock value of what looked like an appallingly racist depiction was part of what gave Tignous's image its force. Asking him to tone it down to avoid the risk of misinterpretation would have thwarted the effort, rendering it so innocuous as to be impotent. As journalist Caleb Crain put it, "Some of the *Charlie Hebdo* cartoons do look pretty awful at first glance to an American eye." But he notes that even in the most shocking among them, "the object of the satire always turns out, upon research, to be the racist tropes and ideology that the cartoonist believes are lurking just below the surface."

It is not hard to grasp why some audiences saw the decontextualized *Charlie Hebdo* cartoons as deeply objectionable. It is also true that some Muslims in France disapproved of the Muhammad cartoons regardless of what the *Charlie Hebdo* satirists intended (others did not). It may be that some images and tropes are so incendiary that their power as satire is inevitably outweighed by the feelings of offense that they evoke. But, where there is ambiguity, it is essential to take context and intention into account, even when that means taking the time to learn more.

Don't Apply Strict Liability to Speech

The student mentioned at the start of this chapter who wanted her professor to be held accountable for using the n-word, regardless of pedagogic context and intent, brings to mind a concept from tort law: strict liability. Strict liability renders an individual legally culpable for the consequences of his actions, even if he took due care. Strict liability applies to inherently dangerous activities like speeding (saying you didn't know the speed limit won't get you out of a ticket) or using explosives. Even if all proper precautions are taken, if a construction blast injures a pedestrian, strict liability faults the builder.

The Maryland student is not alone in believing we should apply strict liability to speech, as a social if not a legal matter. The n-word, Nazi imagery, and blatantly racist tropes are examples of speech that people ought to recognize as inherently incendiary, no matter the circumstances or intentions. Had *New Yorker* fact checker Talia Lavin thought twice about accusing a stranger of Nazi sympathies (as opposed to a more garden-variety offense), she might have hesitated to hit "tweet." But while it's important to educate people about the piercing impact that these particularly bigoted tropes can wield, imposing an equivalent of strict liability would yield perverse results.

In February 2018, Ben Frisch, a math teacher at New York City's Friends Seminary School taught a geometry lesson. He lifted a straightened right arm to demonstrate an obtuse angle. Doing so brought to his mind the Nazi salute and Frisch blurted "Heil Hitler." Lowering his arm, he explained that it used to be common to mock Hitler. A few students gasped. When word of the incident made it back to parents, complaints ensued. Several parents reportedly threatened to withdraw their children if he was not dismissed. Ultimately, Frisch was given an ultimatum to resign or be fired. He chose to be fired and then challenged the school for wrongful termination.

No one seriously doubted that Frisch's gesture had been unwitting and implied no animus. None of his students thought he was anti-Semitic. The Quaker son of a Jewish father and two great-grandmothers who were killed in Auschwitz, Frisch gave every reason to believe that the incident was just a botched attempt at levity. But for months the school resisted student protests on his behalf and fought Frisch's claims for reinstatement. As Friends senior Benjamin Levine put it in his 2018 commencement address, "It's so much easier and simpler to decide someone is racist or ignorant or naïve—or anti-Semitic—than to engage in the messy work of trying to communicate and understand when conflicts arise." An arbitrator eventually ruled for Frisch, concluding that while his behavior was "inappropriate," there was nary a "scintilla of evidence" of anti-Semitic or Nazi sympathies. Even in the case of saying "Heil Hitler" in a classroom, context and intent are essential to interpretation and meaning.

Can a Slur Ever Be but a Slur?

In recent years I have heard from several university faculty members caught by surprise by ferocious reactions to the n-word. Several professors have learned the hard way that referencing the n-word in pedagogy, a practice once fairly widespread, is now regarded by some students as tantamount to using the slur. In 2018, a Princeton professor who used the word in a class on hate speech faced a walkout that prompted the cancellation of his entire course. At Augsburg University in Minnesota, a professor used the word while discussing author James Baldwin, who uses the word repeatedly in his writing. The professor painstakingly explained the long-recognized "use-mention distinction" between employing the word as an epithet and simply uttering it as part of a quote or historic reference. The university suspended him anyway.

The debate over intent and context regarding this inflammatory word remains unresolved. In 2002, Harvard Law School professor Randall Kennedy wrote a book on the subject with the word in its title and with the subtitle *The Strange Career of a Troublesome Word*. Kennedy, who is African American, judged the n-word the "paradigmatic racial slur," more demeaning and deadly than any other. But he also noted that the word was sometimes invoked to mimic or condemn racist usages, such as in Mark Twain's *Huckleberry Finn* or Richard Wright's *Black Boy*—a bad word's power deployed for good ends. Rejecting the "eradicationist" view that the word should be banished, Kennedy affirmed certain uses, including in comedy or a friendly salutation. While denoting its use "presumptively wrong," he argued that the presumption could be rebutted if the usage was informed and not racist. He rejected the notion that white people should completely disavow the use of the word, arguing that such a premise could reinforce racial divides. This remains Kennedy's position—he deplored Augsburg's punishment of the professor. Kennedy is not alone. New School scholar Rich Blint, who specializes in James Baldwin, refuses

to expunge the use of the word in talking about Baldwin's work and scholarship, believing that to do so would be a form of posthumous censorship,
since Baldwin used the word to force his audiences to face up to its cruel
legacy.

Yet nowadays there is a widespread sentiment among black college
students and many others that white people's use of the word is never
tolerable. A 2018 poll in the *International Journal of Society, Language and
Culture* found that 76 percent of students at historically black colleges
in the Deep South thought it unacceptable for a white person to use the
word with anyone, anywhere. Strong feelings surrounding the word have
led school systems, librarians, and classroom teachers to avoid books that
use it, including *Huck Finn*. The view among younger Americans that the
n-word is always beyond the pale poses a dilemma for teachers who believe
articulating it in full has value, whether to be faithful to a literary passage
or historical incident or to illustrate the explosive quality of speech. Yet
the flare-ups have become so frequent that faculty cannot credibly plead
naïveté if their use of the word upsets students. While the "use versus
mention" contrast is clear as an intellectual matter, when students opt not
to recognize such distinctions, faculty can be put on the defensive.

Free speech champions rightly blanch at any narrowing of the boundaries of acceptable speech—and the idea that popular attitudes should
outweigh objective questions of intent and meaning in the import of a
word. Likewise, many people rightly uphold the academy as a place where
even the most vexing ideas—and words—must be open to dispassionate examination. In deciding whether changing student mores warrants
pedagogical restraint, several factors come into play.

WHEN A WORD OR PHRASE MAY CAUSE OFFENSE

- How likely is it that offense will be taken?
- Can the context make unmistakably clear that the word or
  phrase is arising not as a slur or similar?

- Can the risk of offense be mitigated through preparation, explanation, and discussion?
- Can an alternative locution be used to make the point, and how much—if anything—would be lost by using it instead?

Opting against using the n-word is not quite the same as refusing to give voice to an idea; it doesn't exclude a whole concept from debate. Nor does the n-word have to be actually heard for its meaning and force to be grasped. The admittedly awkward euphemism "n-word" is itself so unusual that it evokes the taboo. But not saying the n-word out loud should not mean avoiding discussion of its historical significance, the linguistic import of the use-mention distinction, or the case that Kennedy and others make about when and why it can be used legitimately. As stewards of learning, professors should be conscious of where a rising generation draws its red lines. Universities should never punish anyone for merely mentioning a word without any inflection of bigotry. Yet individual instructors need not turn their backs on academic freedom to reappraise the pedagogical value of speaking the word in full amid the risk that it will be heard as a slur.

A willingness to attend to considerations of intent and context implies an appreciation that the purpose of speech is to enlighten, exchange, and understand. Words are signifiers, and without paying attention to intent and context those signals can be misread. But our modern discourse of callouts, gotcha, and online outrage can sideline this primary objective of promoting understanding. By pointing out nuances, defenders of free speech can help break the censorious cycle of online mobs and hit jobs, insisting that speech be evaluated not for shock value, but for its meaning.

TAKE INTO ACCOUNT INTENT AND
CONTEXT WHEN JUDGING SPEECH

- Don't respond to speech until you've considered the intent and context surrounding it
- If there is ambiguity, take the time to investigate and understand the circumstances before criticizing speech
- As a member of the media, recognize that you bear a special responsibility to examine questions of context and intent and bring them to the attention of audiences
- Resist the notion of "strict liability" for offensive speech, recognizing that even what seems most offensive may look different in context
- Where necessary, take the time to truly interrogate the context of speech, including the culture and setting in which it was spoken, and thereby avoid misinterpretation

7.

Call Out with Caution

"CALLING OUT" DISTASTEFUL SPEECH CAN SIGNAL SUPPORT FOR TARGETED or marginalized groups and raise the cost of noxious speech without suppressing or punishing it. A "callout" is itself, of course, a form of protected speech. We're free to criticize whomever we wish. Yet our callout culture, wherein offensive remarks, infelicitous phrasings, and misstatements can get someone lambasted online and even make their way into news coverage, is remaking the landscape for speech in ways both good and bad. On the plus side, we're all more aware that we may be held accountable for what we say, not by the government or even an institution like our employer or university, but by anyone who hears or reads our words. Yet callout culture also has a toxic and censorious side.

In early 2018, journalist Bari Weiss was impressed with the performance of Mirai Nagasu, who landed the first-ever triple axel by an American figure skater in Olympic competition. Weiss invoked a famous line from Lin-Manuel Miranda's *Hamilton* musical to tweet "Immigrants: they get the job done." But Nagasu, though of Japanese ancestry, is not an immigrant. She was born in California. Weiss had wrongly assumed, based on Nagasu's ethnicity, that she wasn't born in the United States.

Her tweet implied that Nagasu's background and race were atypical for an American skater. Weiss defended her tweet as a well-intentioned attempt to celebrate Nagasu but then deleted it amid what she described as a raft of online abusers telling her she was "a racist, a ghoul and that I deserve to die."

When attorney Aaron Schlossberg was caught on video making nativist and xenophobic remarks at a Manhattan deli and threatening to report employees to Immigration and Customs Enforcement, the Internet exploded with rage. Many thousands tweeted outrage and trashed his law practice on Yelp. Ten thousand people signed a petition calling for his disbarment, a former client sued him for malpractice (arguing that his reputation was sullied by association), and his landlord evicted him from his office. It's hard to summon sympathy for Schlossberg, but he wasn't the only one to get called out. The journalist Julia Ioffe, who condemned Schlossberg as a "vicious racist," added that as a refugee from the Soviet Union she found "the mob unsettling even if it's a mob whose motives I agree with." This mild comment was itself met with hundreds of attacks as a result. "Thank you, mob," she tweeted, "for proving my point."

While your basic "callout" is a straightforward expression of free speech, in the digital world, it is easy for callouts to metastasize, delivering a punishment vastly disproportionate to the underlying offense. By calling people out publicly online, critics invite an echo chamber to resound in approval. That can turn a warranted, measured takedown into an avalanche of bullying that can cross into the physical realm. The podcast *Invisibilia* recounted the story of a feminist musician named Emily who was active in the Richmond, Virginia, punk scene. An acquaintance called her out for having, years earlier, mocked an online nude photo of a high school classmate. The callout went viral. Emily owned up to having been "a high school bully and a slut-shamer," and apologized personally to the girl in the photo, who accepted the apology. But it was too late. Nasty tweets, posts, and messages spouted forth. Emily was banned from Richmond punk circles, stopped going out in public, and became a social pariah. Richard Wrangham, an expert on social ostracism at Harvard, has compared such an ordeal to the physical pain of being flogged.

In his 2015 book, *So You've Been Publicly Shamed*, author Jon Ronson recounts what has become the emblematic tale of Justine Sacco, a thirty-year-old communications executive who was on a plane for South Africa when she tweeted to her 170 followers, "Going to Africa. Hope I don't get AIDS. Just kidding. I'm white!" She meant the tweet as a sardonic commentary on racial disparities in health care, a jab at her own white privilege. But Twitter took her post as racist, and when she landed eleven hours later the hashtag #hasjustinelandedyet was trending. Incommunicado and unable to explain herself or apologize, she had been unable to stanch the furor. Enraged tweeters tagged her employer, costing Sacco her job. The disconnect between a lone, ill-considered, but innocently intended tweet and a global controversy involving thousands of irate strangers is stark. The gratification derived by those who gleefully savage the wrongdoer reflects a vindictive impulse that takes root amid the sterile remove of online discourse. Accusers never had to look Emily or Sacco in the eye. They could delight in a punitive ritual from afar.

Calling In or Calling Out

Some commentators have begun to urge that instead of, or before, "calling out" troublesome speech, objecting listeners should instead "call in," meaning to raise concerns privately or in a low-key, gentle way aimed to minimize embarrassment. Promoting a culture of "calling in" could instill greater conscientiousness without the side effect of censoriousness. If you are confident that friends, colleagues, or online associates will reach out to you privately if you blunder into offense, the risk calculation becomes more favorable for speech.

As a defender of free speech, there are times to call out and times to call in:

YOU SHOULD CALL IN WHEN ALL OR SOME OF THE CRITERIA BELOW ARE MET

- The offense seems inadvertent or unintended.
- The speaker seems open to correction.
- The offending post, or speech, can be revised before propagating.
- The potential harm of the speech can be prevented or ameliorated.
- You are in a trusted relationship with the speaker.

YOU SHOULD CALL OUT WHEN ALL OR SOME OF THE CRITERIA BELOW ARE MET

- Behind-the-scenes efforts have failed.
- The speaker intends to cause offense.
- The speaker has a track record of deliberate provocation.
- The offense is highly public and thus demands a public response.
- The offending remark has already caused offense or distress.
- A show of solidarity with those most affected may mitigate the negative effects of the speech.
- A taboo has been breached and warrants reinforcement.
- You bear some responsibility for the discourse at issue (for example, a classroom teacher or panel moderator who may be seen to approve unless they say otherwise).
- The callouts delivered or forthcoming from others seem insufficient.

As feminist activist Loretta Ross has put it, "Call-outs are justified to challenge provocateurs who deliberately hurt others, or for powerful people beyond our reach . . . But most public shaming is horizontal and done by those who believe they have greater integrity or more sophisticated analyses. They become the self-appointed guardians of political purity." When Harvard president Larry Summers publicly questioned whether women actually face significant discrimination in the sciences and math, women on the faculty had reason to doubt whether they could get a fair shake at the university. A private tap on the shoulder by a trustee would not have done enough to convey both to Summers and to others that such views are unacceptable. Instead, Summers was called out far and wide, including by Harvard faculty, the Harvard Corporation (though it responded only after being prodded by the faculty), and in a joint statement by the presidents of Stanford, Princeton, and the Massachusetts Institute of Technology.

HOW TO ACCOMPLISH A CALL-IN

1. *Acknowledge* that you recognize no offense was intended.
2. *Explain* why the speech could cause offense.
3. *Emphasize* the potential impact of the speech on those affected.
4. *Reassure* the speaker that you know they have good intentions.
5. *Anticipate* they will adjust their language going forward.

When calling in, couching the reproach in between two messages that affirm the individual can make it easier for the speaker to take the criticism to heart. Rather than stressing the wrongfulness of what was said, the emphasis should be on the impact on those affected—how the invocation of a stereotype about women being weaker in the sciences may make a female student less confident speaking in class or walking into an exam. A "call-in" can take the form of a quiet conversation between friends, a personal letter from students to a professor, or a dialogue between an employee and boss. People are likely to respond better when approached gently and privately, even if they feel ashamed or blindsided. Raising a problem in a closed setting allows people time to reflect before reacting publicly. They can let down their guard, won't be tempted to lash out, and will likely appreciate the pains taken to avoid humiliation.

A former classmate of mine illustrated this with a politely reproachful email to a National Public Radio host. She wrote: "Dear X: On two consecutive days this week I have now heard you use the adjective 'lame' to describe yourself. . . . My understanding is that these days, 'lame' has become offensive to the disability rights movement, for obvious reasons, and I wonder whether you could try using more acceptable alternatives such as 'dorky,' 'embarrassing,' or even the Gen Z favorite, 'cringey.' Sincerely, Y." She received an immediate reply from the host thanking her for pointing out the possibility of offense and vowing to use a different word henceforward. No shame, and no ill will.

Calling Out Compassionately

It's also possible to call out publicly without fueling a culture of "gotcha" finger-pointing. Of course, there are some situations—inexcusable transgressions by people in seats of power or expressions of avowed bigotry like the 2017 white supremacist rally in Charlottesville—in which the potency of the offensive expression needs to be matched with forceful, unsparing condemnation. There are moments when only an instinctive, punchy retort will pack the requisite wallop and when norms of civility can justifiably give way to naked expressions of outrage and pain.

PRINCIPLE OF PROPORTIONALITY

The ferocity of the callout matches the degree of offense intended and inflicted.

But such true outrages are not a daily occurrence. Under normal circumstances, the aim of a "callout" should be to stick up for yourself or for those who have been targeted and to put speaker and listeners on notice of why the expression was objectionable. Other goals—like signaling your own virtue before an audience, building up an online following, getting credit for a witty retort or unleashing an avalanche of shame—risk contributing to a pile-on.

When motives are in question, it is important to give the people under fire a chance to explain themselves. By avoiding hyperbole, personal attacks, and imputations of motives, it is possible to call out offensive speech without calling out the dogs. A reasoned analysis of where the speaker went wrong is fair. Supermodel Chrissy Teigen found a way to gently educate in a tweet about Bari Weiss's misguided huzzah to Mirai Nagasu: "It's called perpetual otherism or perpetual foreigner syndrome. No one is ashamed of the word immigrant but it's tiring being treated as foreigners all the time. You made a mistake. It's okay. But people are really giving you calm, great insight. Just learn and breathe. All good." When callouts impute bad motives and invite venom, outsiders can gently call out the critics by pointing out that the target has apologized, that the offending message has been deleted, or that the callout has been heard.

Cue to Cancel

During the summer of 2019, the Merriam-Webster dictionary tentatively proposed a new definition for the word "cancel." The entry defined "canceling" and "cancel culture" as "removing support of public figures on the basis of their objectionable opinions or actions. This can include boycotts or refusal to promote their work." To "cancel" means to sever the relationship between a celebrity and their fans, a writer and their readers, a politician and their supporters. Intermediary institutions—networks, publishers, agents—who were often instrumental in brokering such relationships in the first place can play a catalytic role in cutting ties to the target and signaling others to do the same.

Recent examples of the phenomenon include calls to cancel pop artists Cardi B and Nicki Minaj for purportedly homophobic and transphobic remarks, rapper Kanye West for offensive tweets about slavery, and singer

Shania Twain for saying she would have voted for Donald Trump if she were an American citizen. Individuals, of course, are free to patronize or avoid artists however they see fit. A consumer backlash will influence the marketability of a star or contributor. But pressuring all publishers, movie studios, or museums to shun or blacklist an artist deprives others the freedom to make decisions for themselves. In its extreme form, cancellation becomes a cultural embargo—a decision to cut someone off from opportunities, audiences, prestige, and influence with the implication that those who break the boycott are themselves doing something wrong.

Not all calls to "cancel" relate to speech. A raft of celebrities have been canceled—fired from positions, dropped by publishers, and professionally and socially shunned—because of accusations of sexual misdeeds. Given the severity and credibility of the charges against them, the cancellations of Harvey Weinstein and Bill Cosby seem well warranted; it's hard to fathom anyone wanting to work with them again. In cases of lesser infractions, though, society faces difficult collective decisions about how long and wide an embargo should stretch. Such cases can impinge on free speech when disputes arise over whether works by disgraced artists can still be viewed and appreciated. Even in the case of the worst offenders, we should not cede the power to cancellers to unilaterally dictate what movies can be seen, paintings viewed, or books read. The prospect of trying to expunge someone's influence from the culture based on misdeeds is futile and whiffs of the totalitarian impulse to rewrite the past. If individuals have fallen from grace, consumers should still be able to choose whether they want to listen to their music, read their books, or see their paintings. If the sight of the Dr. Cliff Huxtable in light of what we now know is too distracting to allow a viewer to enjoy reruns of *The Cosby Show,* so be it. That does not mean we should shun those who watch *Shakespeare in Love* or *The English Patient* just because Harvey Weinstein—along with a great many others—had a hand in them. At PEN America, while we support the right to call for such boycotts, our long-standing policy is to oppose all cultural and academic boycotts as an impingement on the flow of speech. With less formal types of sanction, a similar logic holds.

Cancellations based purely on speech raise special concerns. There are some cases—comedian Roseanne Barr's history of outlandish statements topped off by a racist tweet and a dubious apology—when some form of cancellation seems to fit the infractions. No one is entitled to have an eponymous television show, and the decision to take it off the air struck even many of Barr's fans as defensible. But, in general, cancellation, particularly for isolated speech offenses, is a blunt blow with harmful ripple effects for free speech. In 2018, *New York Review of Books* editor Ian Buruma published an article by Canadian journalist Jian Ghomeshi about accusations that Ghomeshi had assaulted more than twenty women. (Ghomeshi was acquitted in a court of law, but evidence of wrongdoing was strong.) The topic of the piece, ironically, was life after cancellation. Ghomeshi described having lost his job and become a social outcast, suggesting that it had led to self-awareness and a path toward redemption. Critics assailed the piece as indulgent, self-serving, and an insult both to the women Ghomeshi had attacked and to the wider #MeToo movement. The dispute divided the *Review* staff, turning a substantial portion against Buruma, who, in an interview, inartfully defended his original decision to publish the piece and overstated the degree to which he had consulted colleagues and had their support. Within days, Buruma resigned under pressure.

A group of 109 contributing writers to the *Review,* including luminaries such as Colm Tóibín, Joyce Carol Oates, and Ian McEwan, sent an open letter to the periodical's board. They wrote that they found it "very troubling that the public reaction to a single article . . . repellent though some of us may have found this article—should have been the occasion for Ian Buruma's forced resignation. . . . Given the principles of open intellectual debate on which the NYRB was founded, his dismissal in these circumstances strikes us as an abandonment of the central mission of the Review, which is the free exploration of ideas." Renowned First Amendment attorney Floyd Abrams went further, accusing the publication's leadership of behaving "as if they resided in some sort of cultural re-education camp." As often happens, Buruma's cancellation went beyond his ouster from the *Review.* Publications to which he had been a longtime contributor told him that his submissions would not be run for fear of antagonizing readers. While it might have been fair to criticize or even reprimand Buruma for a questionable editorial call and blundering response, his summary ouster and cancellation sounds an ominous note for editors who take risks.

One of the major problems with cancel culture is its indeterminacy. As Buruma wrote, "A prison sentence has limits. Public disgrace is open-ended." Kenyan freelance writer Garnett Achieng wrote about the effect that "cancel culture" is having on writers. She says she is so fearful that something she has tweeted might come back to haunt her, making her the "problematic fave of the day," that she finds it "hard to share my opinions on social media." She argues that while people should take responsibility for past actions, "call-out culture does not give individuals being called out room to do so. Instead, the incriminating evidence equates to a person being 'canceled' and any apologies they offer are dismissed." Above all, though, she decries "cancel culture" for destroying the possibility of dialogue. "Instead of calling out people by insulting and shaming them, we would do better to take time to explain *why* what they said was hurtful or problematic."

One consolation in a culture where free expression pervades is that cancellation is less absolute than its proponents might wish or than its victims sometimes claim. Ian Buruma remains on the faculty of Bard College, published a long and self-reflecting piece on the *Review* debacle in the *Financial Times,* and, as of the summer of 2019, had begun to publish again. Collectively, our goal should be to reap the benefits of a culture wherein bigotry and willful offenses are considered unacceptable, but we don't need to live in fear that a misstatement or oversight will unleash an unending maelstrom of reproach.

HOW TO CALL OUT WITH A CONSCIENCE

- Consider whether to "call in" privately or "call out" publicly based on the circumstances
- When calling out, do so without exaggerating the offense or demonizing the offender

- Seek to ensure that the potency and tone of the callout are proportionate to the offense
- Consider the chilling effect of callouts and cancellations for those other than the target, and ways to avoid deterring future speech and debate
- Avoid mindlessly joining the bandwagon of a callout or a cancellation; make sure to grasp the facts and render your own judgment

8.

Fight Hateful Speech and Hate Crimes

IN AUGUST 2019, POLICE IN YOUNGSTOWN, OHIO, INDICTED TWENTY-year-old James Reardon for posting a video in which he held an assault rifle in firing positions, accompanied by audio of gunshots, sirens, and screams. The caption read, "Police identified the Youngstown Jewish Family Community shooter as local white nationalist Seamus O'Reardon" (a variation on Reardon's name). The post tagged Youngstown's Jewish Community Center. Local prosecutors charged Reardon with making unlawful threats that required local Jewish institutions to increase security precautions. In making public the complaint against Reardon, United States Attorney Justin Herndon delivered a message to white supremacists broadly:

> The Constitution protects your right to speak. . . . If you want to waste the blessings of liberty by going down a path of hatred and failed ideologies that is your choice. Democracy allows you to test those ideas in the public forum. . . . What you don't have, though, is the right to take out your frustration at failure in the political arena by resorting to violence. You don't have any right to threaten the lives and well-being of our neighbors.

Herndon warned violent extremists that they would not escape the arm of the law, saying, "You can't set your alarm clock early enough to beat us out of bed. The men and women of law enforcement don't wake up. We never went to sleep . . . we will do everything we can to be there to stop you." Herndon's hybrid message went viral: his commitment to the protections of the Constitution was unflinching, but his contempt for the forces of hatred, bigotry, and violence is equally potent.

The most prominent argument today for increased government controls on speech is the sense that hate speech is running rampant in our society, yielding a cascade of ills, including a jump in violent hate crimes. The emergence of white supremacist activists, rising online vitriol, and a tolerance for bigotry by certain political leaders have fueled fear that venom is coursing through the nation's veins. For some, new laws and punishments seem like a reasonable price to curb hatred. Because free speech advocates generally oppose tighter constraints on expression, it may also seem that they are insufficiently concerned about bigoted invective and bias crimes. But to have doubts about new government restrictions on hate speech does not imply callousness toward loathsome invective. It is possible—and also necessary—to persuade those who are legitimately anguished over the rise of hateful speech that free speech is not their enemy. But to avoid resorting to censorship, active, effective resistance to hateful speech and crimes is essential.

For those who disfavor tighter government controls on discourse, it is not enough to stress how such measures would backfire and leave it to others to figure out what to do instead. To fend off new curbs on speech, it is essential to demonstrate that there exist viable, constitutional measures to combat hateful speech and prevent hate crimes. There is, of course, no silver-bullet solution to societal hatreds. In the wake of deadly bias incidents of recent years, it is apparent that the tools we have—including awareness-raising, social media restrictions on bigotry, and law enforcement tracking of extremism—often fall short. But through more aggressive, comprehensive efforts to counter hateful speech and crimes, we stand a better chance of winning the argument that our current free speech protections can be sustained without allowing an intolerable level of hateful speech—and action—to persist.

A note on language. While "hate speech," is commonly used, its meaning is highly elastic. People use the term "hate speech" to discuss a mess of unrelated issues, from white supremacists to government pronouncements on immigrants to anti-vaccination trolls to the use of slurs. The term "hate speech" is so malleable as to be almost useless, conflating more than it clarifies.

CATEGORIES OF HATEFUL SPEECH

What is hate speech? It is an unhelpfully elastic term applied to speech that falls into the following categories:

1. Unlawful throughout the United States and most of the world (for example, direct calls to violence)
2. Legally protected in the United States and most of the world (for example, garden-variety insults based on gender, race, or religion)
3. Illegal in some countries, but not others (for example, Holocaust denial)

Another problem with the concept of "hate speech" is that it does not distinguish between hateful intent and hateful effect. Cartoons, crude pictures, political humor, and dashed-off social media posts can manifest as hatred, regardless of the motives behind them. But not all speech that offends or degrades is *willful* hate speech. It may be merely insensitive or ill thought out, or have an entirely different context-specific meaning.

Hateful Speech and Hate Crimes

In the digital era, the relationship between hateful speech and hate-motivated criminal acts has become more obvious and alarming. Traditionally, free speech advocates have questioned the strength of the link, partly out of concern that if you believe hateful speech leads directly to hateful acts, there's a stronger case to ban it. Most people who spew hateful speech never verge into physical acts of violence or intimidation. The vast bulk of hateful speech—harsh tweets, noxious graffiti, or extremist blog posts—does not prompt anyone to take criminal action. Most hateful speech is just that—speech—with no resulting action at all. Still, while the association is neither one of equivalence nor strict cause and effect, hateful speech and hate-motivated crimes are related.

The Federal Bureau of Investigation (FBI) defines a hate crime as "a traditional offense like murder, arson, or vandalism with an added element of bias." The bureau counts as hate crimes those "motivated in whole or in part by an offender's bias against a race, religion, disability, sexual orientation, ethnicity, gender, or gender identity." The Anti-Defamation League notes that bigotry is almost always the "but-for" trigger for the hate crime: "In the vast majority of these crimes, but for the victim's personal characteristic, no crime would occur at all."

The legal boundary between hateful speech protected by the First Amendment and hate-fueled acts that can be prosecuted as crimes is quite firm. Hate crimes involve either speech tied to a clear-cut criminal act (an assault or vandalism, for example) or speech that itself crosses the line into action (a death threat or harassment, for example). Without an act that meets the legal definition of a crime, even virulent hateful speech and sentiment does not violate the law. As the FBI notes, "Hate itself is not a crime—and the FBI is mindful of protecting freedom of speech and other civil liberties." But when crimes are committed, the Supreme Court has upheld laws that stiffen penalties when it can be proven that the defendant targeted the victim based on a protected characteristic like race, ethnicity, identity, or beliefs.

While most hateful speech may not cross over into action, many perpetrators of recent prominent hateful crimes have drawn inspiration from online hate. Recent examples include:

- Attacks on refugees in Germany tied to xenophobic Facebook posts in 2018

- Charleston church shooter in 2015 who killed nine after consuming white supremacist dogma online
- Pittsburgh synagogue murderer who killed eleven in 2018 after espousing anti-Semitic theories online
- Perpetrator of the El Paso, Texas, Walmart mass shooting in August 2019 who killed twenty-two and was directly inspired by the livestreamed Christchurch, New Zealand, mosque shootings earlier that year

We cannot be sure that the prevalence of online hate speech was a prime catalyst for these crimes. The perpetrators' bigotry and propensity toward violence almost certainly predated—and motivated—their search for corresponding online content. But whether causal or not, the correlation between hateful speech and hate crimes has made it hard to dismiss the role of hateful speech in contributing to polarization, radicalization, and extreme acts.

Hate-monitoring organizations have been working overtime to document the relationship between hateful attitudes and hate-inspired actions, documenting a spike in hate speech and hate-driven crimes over the last four years:

1. Southern Poverty Law Center 2016 study:
    - Survey of 10,000 educators
    - FINDING: "verbal harassment, the use of slurs and derogatory language, and disturbing incidents involving swastikas, Nazi salutes and Confederate flags" in schools all became more commonplace after the 2016 U.S. presidential campaign

2. Lawyers' Committee for Civil Rights Under Law and the Lead Fund, 2019 report
    - Surveyed 69 universities
    - FINDINGS: Hate incidents, including white leafletting and slurs on dormitory walls rose in 2018 for the third straight year (both the FBI and the ADL also documented increases in hateful incidents on campus during the same period)

3. Two studies from January 2018 by law professors Griffin Sims
   Edwards and Stephen Rushin of the University of Alabama and
   Chicago Loyola University
   • FINDINGS: Trump's election in 2016 "was associated with a
     statistically significant surge in reported hate crimes across
     the United States, even when controlling for alternative
     explanations."

4. National Consortium for the Study of Terrorism and Responses
   to Terrorism, 2018 study:
   • FINDINGS: In 2016, the Internet and social media platforms,
     including Facebook, WhatsApp, Instagram, and YouTube,
     played a part in radicalizing and motivating about
     90 percent of lone actors in terrorist incidents

5. University of Cardiff HateLab 2019 study:
   • FOUND THAT: Over an eight-month period in London as the
     number of "hate tweets"—those judged hostile in terms
     of race, ethnicity, or religion—from a particular location
     increased, as did the number of racially and religiously
     aggravated crimes in the same area.

Though they remain a tiny proportion of all crimes committed, hate-
fueled crimes have an outsize effect on society. Like terrorist attacks
aimed to sow fear, hate crimes (which can constitute acts of terrorism)
not only injure immediate victims but also communicate messages at several levels: They signal those who share characteristics with the victims—
even if they are unrelated and live across the country—that they too
may be unsafe. They inflict lasting pain on communities, inflecting the
meaning of words and the significance of places. They can kindle interest in extremist causes, signal ideological sympathizers that the shared
agenda is worthy of sacrifice, and yield notoriety. They may provoke retaliation, egg on competition, inspire copycats, or prompt reactive social
and policy changes.

Speech and More Speech

The response to hateful speech most favored in the law is counterspeech. In his concurring opinion in *Whitney v. California* (1927), Justice Louis Brandeis famously wrote, "If there be time to expose through discussion the falsehood and fallacies, to avert the evil by the process of education, the remedy to be applied is more speech, not enforced silence."

Legal scholar and activist Nadine Strossen, author of *Hate Speech: Why We Should Resist It with Free Speech, Not Censorship*, defines counterspeech as "any speech that counters a message with which one disagrees." Strossen cites a 2015 study commissioned by Facebook that found that the "crowd-sourced response" to hate speech was "faster, more flexible and responsive" than censorship. Strossen is bullish on counterspeech, noting, "We have witnessed a remarkable and bipartisan outpouring of speech and peaceful demonstrations that have denounced hateful ideologies." She cites examples including the exodus of corporate titans from two White House advisory councils after President Trump's equivocation over white supremacist marchers in Charlottesville and the "unmuting" of black college students who are more vocally opposing racism.

Counterspeech can, however, veer into what might fit a layperson's definition of trolling or harassment. In the book Strossen cites online calls for the firing of talk show hosts for slurs and vulgarity as effective manifestations of counterspeech but does not reflect on instances in which mild offenses are met with thunderous fury, lost jobs, and destroyed reputations—counterspeech run amok. As a law professor, she focused on proving that counterspeech can help render legal bans and punishments for hateful speech unnecessary. She is correct. But free speech advocates should also recognize that informal forms of censoriousness—including online mob persecution—can themselves undercut free speech in practice.

A 2016 STUDY by the Dangerous Speech Project (DSP), an organization focused on mobilizing more effective responses to the most menacing speech, has sought to ascertain whether counterspeech can be effective in diminishing hateful speech or its effects.

The researchers examined the use of counterspeech on Twitter, noting that it can assume a wide variety of forms, including:

- pointing out facts to dispute misstatements or misperceptions
- spotlighting hypocrisy or contradictions
- warning of the consequences of speech
- relating personally to the speaker or the target
- opposing the speech rather than the person who said it
- denunciations
- humor
- empathy

The study further documents five categories of response to counterspeech, some good and some bad, including:

- apologies and recantations
- deletions
- further hateful speech
- a sustained and respectful dialogue
- the eliciting of additional counterspeech from bystanders

Though hardly foolproof, the study finds that counterspeech sometimes prompts individuals to abandon hatred—a phenomenon the DSP dubs "golden conversations." Most such encounters occur between two people, rather than larger groups, and they often involve "extended exchanges" in which the counter-speaker persists despite "apparently implacable resistance and a stream of hateful tweets." They observe, "Where someone seems firmly committed not only to hateful ideology but to declaring it publicly, we would not expect counterspeech to sway that person. Yet in some cases, it apparently has—and has even helped to bring about lasting change in beliefs."

The project's "Practical Guide" to dangerous speech details criteria to judge when speech crosses the line from offensive to truly perilous.

FACTORS FOR DETERMINING WHEN
SPEECH IS DANGEROUS

- A dehumanizing point of view
- Telling people they face a mortal threat from a disfavored or minority group
- Identity and influence of the speaker
- Susceptibility of the audience to the message
- Communication medium
- Political and social context

In addition to spotlighting when speech ought to set off warning bells, the DSP analysis can also help identify the opposite: speech that isn't dangerous. If we are more confident in distinguishing speech that is truly alarming, we'll be better able to react proportionately to speech that is merely nasty or unpleasant.

Notably, the DSP does not favor government-enforced prohibitions on expression. The project supports free speech "because it is a fundamental human right—and also because silencing people can make them more likely to resort to violence, if they have no peaceful way of expressing and resolving their grievances." But it is not enough to cite the best answer to hateful speech as "more speech" and expect society to oblige. Institutions committed to the defense of free speech—universities, foundations, and free speech organizations—should seek to maximize the potential of counterspeech as an alternative to speech-suppressive strategies. This would entail research about what makes counterspeech most influential, which strategies work best, and how to amplify counterspeech efforts.

Voices of Authority

Counterspeech is especially important when it comes from officialdom. When leaders and powerful figures speak out against denigrating speech, the impact can be five-fold:

1. authoritatively refuting invidious claims;
2. conveying that toxic messages are rejected writ large;
3. isolating and stigmatizing the speaker;
4. offering a unifying rallying cry for those who oppose the message; and
5. supporting those who feel targeted.

IN 2017, WHITE SUPREMACIST Richard Spencer made plans to visit the University of Florida. Under the First Amendment, the university, a public institution, couldn't deny him the right to rent a hall and advertise an event. However, when Spencer claimed that university president Ken Fuchs "stood behind" him, Fuchs tweeted, "I don't stand behind racist Richard Spencer. I stand with those who reject and condemn Spencer's vile and despicable message." Fuchs urged students to avoid the speech and even the protests to deny Spencer the spotlight he sought. Fuchs used the hashtags #TogetherUF and #GatorsNotHaters to share videos and positive messages about race relations. Thanks in part to the university's firm posture, Spencer spoke before a half-full auditorium, mostly without incident. Fuchs's handling of the incident won praise as a model for how universities can uphold their First Amendment obligations while deploring bigotry.

Lots of leaders have similarly risen to the occasion. Among the most poignant in recent years was President Barack Obama's singing of "Amazing Grace" at the funeral of South Carolina state senator Clementa Pinckney, a pastor killed along with eight others in an attack on a Charleston church in 2015. Obama sang in a black-church style, communicating solidarity and comfort that words alone could not have conveyed. In 2010, when Florida pastor Terry Jones threatened to burn a Koran, Obama, Secretary of Defense Robert Gates, and Secretary of State Hillary Clinton denounced his plans. Though Jones's action constituted protected expression under the First Amendment, previous Koran torchings had triggered deadly riots in Muslim-majority countries. While Jones went ahead with his stunt a year later, the messages from top U.S. officials signaled to Muslims that the United States government stood with them against hatred.

Responding to Online Harassment

According to a 2019 survey by the ADL, more than half of Americans reported having been subject to hateful speech or harassment online in 2018. Some 37 percent described the attacks as severe, including sexual

SAMPLING FROM PEN AMERICA'S ONLINE HARASSMENT FIELD MANUAL

- Assessing the threat level (is the troll threatening to turn up at your house, or just calling you a pesky nickname?)
- Documenting the misconduct through screenshots to build a record in case you need to press charges
- Utilizing social media platform tools to report, block trolls, and "mute" particular words and phrases
- Carefully confronting your trolls where desired and appropriate
- Condemning the content of the harassment, rather than the harasser
- Talking about the personal impact of the speech
- Showing empathy (if you can muster it)
- Mobilizing online allies so that your counterspeech reverberates
- Activating your employer for support and protection
- Turning to law enforcement when online abuse crosses the line into harassment or threats

harassment and stalking. Tracking this rising trend and its impact on women writers and writers of color in particular, PEN America developed a comprehensive tool, the Online Harassment Field Manual, aimed to equip individuals and institutions to fight trolls.

Though most of PEN America's advice is geared toward safety, some have successfully turned the tables on their trolls. Comedian Sarah Silverman became an online sensation in 2018 when she confronted a sexist Twitter troll with compassion, saying that she recognized his rage as "thinly veiled pain," and even going so far as to assist him with a health problem. Some hate-mongers are dogged by emotional problems and traumas that propel them to lash out. While many trolls are unrepentant and some are truly dangerous, those who can be brought to acknowledge the source of their anger and find new ways of dealing with it can sometimes abandon trolldom for more constructive forms of social engagement.

Education and Dialogue

In the long run, the best solution to hatred is to root it out. That requires education, dialogue, and exposure to diverse groups and populations. Bias is learned, not innate. Interventions from early childhood up through adulthood can help prevent bigoted attitudes from taking hold.

The ADL advocates comprehensive anti-bias programs in schools, including curricula, staff and faculty professional development, student leadership training, community forums, and forceful response to bias incidents. Training for students, teachers, and employees in bias and diversity, equity, and inclusion has become a staple for school systems, campuses, and workplaces. When incidents of bias occur, school and community leaders need to react immediately and energetically to support victims; examine underlying drivers of hatred; and educate the population at large about what happened, its impact, and how to prevent the same in future. (Importantly, this must not mean overreacting to isolated incidents involving biased speech. Factors like intent and context, the potential to call out conscionably, and the prospects for apology and forgiveness should be considered in calibrating an appropriate response.)

DOES ANTI-BIAS EDUCATION WORK?

1. Swedish political scientists Per Adman and Per Strömblad, in *Comparative Migration Studies* (2018), found that amid a sharp spike in hate crimes in Sweden, tolerance education can play an essential role in promoting the "recognition of political rights among immigrants."

2. Christopher Roth and Sudarno Sumarto published a study indicating that educational programs focused on national unity increased interethnic and interreligious tolerance in Indonesia.

3. A 2015 study, out of Russia, found that social practices like sports, combined with tolerance education, led to more open-minded and accepting attitudes among students.

One of the most effective ways to counter bias is through direct human encounters that replace stereotypes and fears of "the other" with interactions that spark empathy. Interracial dialogues, interfaith efforts, LGBT-straight alliances, and a range of other formats provide for this sort of face-to-face contact aimed to break down barriers and foster cooperation across divides. More so than any other technique, education and dialogue offer the potential to attack hateful speech at its source—in the minds of individuals.

Stronger Hate Crime Reporting and Law Enforcement

Hate crimes are notoriously underreported. While recent attention to the spread of hateful speech and crimes is thought to be boosting reporting, gaps in knowledge and understanding obscure a full picture of the prevalence of hate crimes.

The ADL recommends that ordinary citizens and civil society organizations help remedy these lacunae by familiarizing themselves with hate symbols, reporting hate incidents, and supporting groups that fight prejudice. Hate-monitoring organizations stress that the public should be better informed about what constitutes a hate crime and how to report it. For instance, the city of Philadelphia released an action guide that teaches citizens that race-based threats are a criminal act and explains how to alert authorities.

Anti-hate organizations stress that law enforcement and prosecutors need more robust tools to prosecute hate crimes, which happens mostly at the state level. Five states (Wyoming, Indiana, Arkansas, Georgia, and South Carolina) have no hate crime legislation on their books at all. Hate crime laws have a deterrent effect through their enhanced penalties and also send a signal of official intolerance of bigotry. Many other states have not updated their statutes to include sexual orientation, gender, or disability-related crimes or to require police training or mandated data collection.

A 2019 report by the International Association of Chiefs of Police and the Lawyers' Committee for Civil Rights Under Law recommended a series of measures to mitigate hate crimes, including beefed-up training for law enforcement and community activists, more rigorous data collection and analysis, and augmented collaboration among police, prosecutors, and community organizations. Communities undergoing demographic shifts and with growing immigrant populations are particularly vulnerable to the rise of hate. The study also spotlighted the need for updated approaches to weighing contemporary forms of evidence of bias in crime investigations, including digital evidence. Free speech advocates who want to ensure a robust approach to hate crimes should advocate at the state level to fill these crucial gaps and bolster the confidence of affected populations that the spread of hate can be countered.

WHY AND HOW TO FIGHT HATEFUL
SPEECH AND HATE CRIMES

- Effectively countering hateful speech and hate crimes is essential to fend off calls for prohibitions on speech as a solution to these scourges
- Free speech proponents need to support effective approaches to address hateful speech and hate crimes
- Counterspeech is among the most effective responses to hateful speech and warrants further research and investment to make it even more potent
- Education and awareness-raising are critical to addressing the underlying attitudes that drive hateful speech and hate crimes
- Numerous legal and policy steps have been identified and should be supported in order to prevent and mitigate hate crimes

9.

Protesting Without Silencing

ABRAHAM LINCOLN IS OFTEN QUOTED HAVING SAID, "IT IS A SIN TO BE silent when it is your duty to protest." When objectionable speech is public, there can be a justifiable inclination—even a duty—to meet it with an equally public protest. Bold, resounding protests can rally attention and force the speaker to reckon with potent critiques. Mass mobilizations including the Women's March, airport protests against the Muslim immigration ban, the March for Our Lives to protest gun violence, students' Climate Strike, and vigils for immigrants' rights have been catalysts for activism and policy change. The right to peaceful protest is protected by the First Amendment, and governments are rightfully constrained in how they can control demonstrations.

Though the right to protest is sacrosanct, some forms of protest can themselves inhibit free speech. When protests are so vociferous that the intended speaker cannot be heard, the outcome is a defeat for free speech. If protesters were to imagine a speech they agreed with being shouted down, it becomes easy to understand the problem. Censorious protests can feel triumphant to their participants, but they interfere with the speech rights of the targeted speaker and of listeners who wish to hear the message. By shouting down speech, protesters put their opinions ahead of all others. They assign the power to decide who gets to speak to those with the greatest numbers or loudest voices, traducing norms designed to give everyone a chance to be heard.

The University of Chicago law professor Harry Kalven and others have dubbed this phenomenon the "heckler's veto." Journalist Nat Hentoff wrote in the *Village Voice* in 2006 that "First Amendment law is clear that everyone has the right to picket a speaker, and to go inside the hall and heckle him or her—but not to drown out the speaker, let alone rush the stage and stop the speech before it starts." The heckler's veto can also operate when protests become so boisterous and disorderly that a sponsor or authority feels impelled to shut speech down to avert mayhem.

THE HECKLER'S VETO

When protesters prevent a speaker from being heard and block willing listeners from hearing out speech. They may do so through physical barricades, drowning out speech with loud noise, or creating a level of disorder that forces authority figures to shut down the event.

In 2010, when Israeli ambassador to the United States Michael Oren gave a lecture at the University of California, Irvine, a group of students arranged to successively shout him down, rising one by one as security removed each from the room. Erwin Chemerinsky, then the dean at Irvine Law, explained that after eleven protesters were arrested, he received complaints saying they had done nothing wrong, and only been exercising their free speech rights. He exposes the fallacy of this argument: "A person who comes into my classroom and shouts so that I cannot teach surely can be punished without offending the 1st Amendment. . . . Freedom of speech, on campuses and elsewhere, is rendered meaningless if speakers can be shouted down by those who disagree. . . . There is simply no 1st Amendment right to go into an auditorium and prevent a speaker from being heard, no matter who the speaker is or how strongly one disagrees with his or her message."

The phenomenon is not limited to college campuses. In early 2017, several Town Hall events hosted by Republican congressmen descended into chaos as rowdy protesters sought to shout down their representatives. Nor are such disruptions unique to the left. In 2017 when California's Whittier College hosted state attorney general Xavier Becerra, right-leaning hecklers made it impossible for listeners to hear the discussion.

When conservative scholar Charles Murray was invited by Middlebury College's American Enterprise Club to deliver a lecture in March 2017, he was met with thunderous protests. Murray's 1994 book, *The Bell Curve,* had advanced discredited theories of racial disparity with regard to intelligence. Although Murray was on campus to discuss a newer, less controversial book, his very presence sparked fierce opposition. The disruption meant that his planned talk before an audience of four hundred had to be delivered via livestream instead. After the talk, about twenty enraged protesters (some masked) swarmed Murray's car. One protester delivered a serious concussion and neck injury to political science professor Allison Stanger, Murray's interlocutor in the conversation. These protesters' actions not only infringed on Murray's right to speak but inexcusably crossed the line into violence.

Protests can be effective without impinging on free speech rights. When Russian musical director Valery Gergiev, closely allied with Russian president Vladimir Putin, visited the United States to play at New York's Carnegie Hall, protesters turned out to call attention to a repressive anti-LGBTQ law Putin had passed. The critics sought to embarrass both Gergiev and music venues like Carnegie Hall and the Metropolitan Opera House for turning a blind eye to Putin's bigotry. They created posters with satirical messages to mock the planned appearances and got them published on classical music blogs and media outlets. Outside the event, demonstrators unfurled a rainbow banner and attracted coverage from the *New York Times, Wall Street Journal,* and other media—and certainly caught the attention of concertgoers and the performance venues. Apart from a few boos inside the hall, these protests drove home a message but didn't interfere with the performance.

In February 2018, more than one hundred students at the University of Pennsylvania protested the visit of conservative activist Heather Mac Donald. In a silent protest outside, students held signs with slogans such as "Diversity = 21st century. Join us!" and "Beauty Tip: don't be a white supremacist." Inside the lecture hall, students wore black to show unity and posed tough questions to Mac Donald after her remarks. At the University of Notre Dame in 2017, students walked out of their own commencement ceremony to protest a speech by Vice President Mike Pence. The demonstration was a captivating rebuke that was captured on a video that went viral but did not interfere with Pence's remarks.

By mounting protests that do not unreasonably interfere with the speech in question, demonstrators can claim a high ground. In March 2019, education secretary Betsy DeVos spoke at Harvard University's Kennedy School of Government. She met with vocal protest from hundreds of demonstrators gathered outside—and mostly silent disapproval from students indoors. Despite periodic shouts from the crowd, the inside protest consisted mainly of large posters with slogans including "White Supremacist" and "Our Students Are Not For Sale." A Harvard dean opened the program by stating that anyone who prevented DeVos from speaking would be escorted from the room. Protests need not be entirely polite. Some measure of interruption is fair game. But protesters must stop short of preventing their antagonists from being heard.

When protests do turn censorious, sponsoring institutions must step in. Whether that involves removing students from the room or relocating a talk, the speech must go on. By preparing ahead of time and consulting with both event and protest organizers, authorities can usually avoid being caught flat-footed. Some college students may not fully understand the extent of their rights and responsibilities, and accordingly, education and dialogue, rather than punishment, may be the appropriate response to a first offense. Colleges should avoid being seen to exact too high a price for the misplaced or overreaching peaceful exercise of counterspeech rights.

Protests Seeking Reprisals for Speech

Not all protests involve signs, posters, or chants. They can take the form of letter-writing campaigns, petitions, articles, and social media outreach. Such protests are not censorious in and of themselves. But if they call to ban or punish speech—to cancel a lecture based on its anticipated content, fire a professor for something she said, or withdraw a novel from circulation at the library—they nonetheless constitute a challenge to free speech. Unlike censorious protests in a lecture hall, demands to block speech or for official retaliation against it are themselves protected by the First Amendment. Individuals have every right to call for a speaking invitation to be rescinded, demand that a comedian be pulled off the air, or ask that police arrest someone for a racial slur.

But just because such calls are permissible doesn't make them a good idea. In calling for speech to be banned or punished, protesters encourage authorities—university administrators, employers, publishers—to police speech based on viewpoint. Popular support for such reprisals can legitimize the use of power to infringe on speech rights.

Calling for speech to be banned or punished also forecloses the possibility of dialogue or persuasion. It assumes that the claims in question cannot be debated, disproven, or modified. It deprives those seeking to counter the message the chance to hear out the opposition and hone their

WAYS TO PROTEST WITHOUT SILENCING

Walking out	Silent gestures
Turning your back	Posing tough questions
Signs and banners	Intermittent heckles
Protesting loudly and boisterously outside the hall	Satirical costumes or images

arguments. Calls to prohibit or punish speech also threaten to preemptively chill the speech of anyone else who might contemplate saying something edgy, controversial, or new. Refraining from calls to ban and punish
speech does not mean avoiding impassioned protest. You can expose, rebut, or excoriate and even shame someone for what they say without suggesting that he be penalized or prevented from speaking out again.

In 2019, a group of students at Philadelphia's University of the Arts
demanded the removal from the faculty of scholar Camille Paglia because
of her controversial opinions on sex, gender identity, and sexual assault.
Calling her ideas "dangerous," a thousand objectors demanded her firing
or, barring that, insisted that she be prohibited from selling her books and
delivering public lectures on campus. Students registered a claim with the
school's Title IX office, which deals with incidents of gender discrimination, alleging that a lecture on campus by Paglia would trample their
civil rights. In response, the university's president issued an uncompro-
mising defense of free speech. "Across our nation it is all too common that
opinions expressed that differ from one another's—especially those that
are controversial—can spark passion and even outrage, often resulting in
calls to suppress that speech," he said. "That simply cannot be allowed to
happen."

Though protesters failed to silence Paglia, their demands cast a chill.
"My students seemed to feel as though they were crossing something of
a picket line just to be attending the event without the intent of shouting
Camille down," one teacher said. "That an opinion differing from the majority's, even at a place of supposed open mindedness and tolerance, can
so readily be codified as 'harmful' and/or 'violent' is deeply concerning
to me." An *Atlantic* reporter found few faculty members willing to speak
on the record about the incident, for fear of reprisals. Though the students may have fancied themselves relatively powerless, they had enough
influence to intimidate classmates and faculty members. Protesting responsibly involves recognizing the potency of counterspeech and using
it judiciously. The impulse of protesters to not simply rebut or denounce
Paglia's ideas but to insist that she be denied the opportunity to express
them crosses into censoriousness. Repudiating the speech's content while

granting her right to voice it, on the other hand, honors the expressive rights of listeners and ensures that the substantive struggle against ideas considered objectionable is legitimately waged.

Are There Any Red Lines?

Is shutting down a speech *ever* justifiable? Our law acknowledges that incitement to imminent violence and true threats fall outside First Amendment protection. If someone is ranting at a podium, urging the assembled to commit an act of vandalism or violence, the police can lawfully shut them down. But if no police can be summoned, can individuals shout down the speaker in the name of preventing a riot? If protesters had been able to shout down the Rwandan genocidaires' radio broadcasts in 1994, would that not have been a good thing? It is hard to argue that citizens' censorship to thwart mass murder would not be justified. In a wartime situation, seizing the opponents' means of communication would be considered a legitimate tactic.

But even where there may be clear grounds to shut down speech that stands outside First Amendment protection, there are good reasons to entrust that task to officials rather than citizens. Under most circumstances, if police come to a house and demand that a burning cross be doused, they would do so in an orderly way, with the means to invoke force if necessary. The equivalent of a citizen's arrest in the same situation poses an obvious danger to safety. In situations of mistrust between police and the citizenry, the equation becomes fraught and combustible. There may be no one in a position to defuse incendiary speech and restore calm. If speech is suppressed, those silenced may redouble their efforts to get their message across no matter what it takes.

A second challenge is that whether speech crosses a line may be in the ear of the listener. During the civil rights era, peaceful protests in the South known as Freedom Rides aimed to compel federal enforcement of laws mandating the integration of interstate buses. The demonstrating black and white passengers were greeted at local depots by unrepentant segregationists, who beat the Freedom Riders and torched the vehicles. These southerners considered the Freedom Rides so threatening that they believed they were justified in taking matters into their own hands. Police officers sympathetic to the counterprotesters either arrested the Freedom Riders or simply stood idly by. When considering whether citizens should be allowed to silence one another, the self-righteous cruelty of staunch segregationists sounds a cautionary note. Once citizens are emboldened to shut each other down, that silencing will not be confined to those on the side of justice.

The moral character of objectionable speech shapes what methods of protest we think are justified. But because we each evaluate speech through our distinct ideological lenses, and because norms evolve over time and across cultures, disagreements arise. Some students argued that Camille Paglia's ruminations about gender dysphoria could endanger transgender students by heightening their risk of suicide. To others, the suggestion that Paglia's scholarship and analyses could be "dangerous" is absurd on its face.

Some argue that arguments including climate change denial and Holocaust denial are so baseless and nefarious that they should be disqualified from discussion. But, as British free speech scholar Kenan Malik has put it, there is a problem "that arises from the claim that 'some questions are beyond contention.' Who decides which questions are beyond contention? . . . What is 'beyond contention' depends upon your starting perspective. Should every question that everyone decides is 'beyond contention' be deemed to be so? In which case we effectively create a silent society. Or should only certain people decide what is beyond contention? And if so who?" The quest for truth in public discourse is best served not by official diktats prohibiting certain views from being discussed, but rather through robust debate and reasoned dialogue pushing in the direction of facts and persuasive arguments. While no one should be forced to hear out discredited arguments, those who espouse them are more effectively rebutted by argument, dismissiveness, or even simply being ignored than by censoriousness that clouds the moral authority of their opponents.

At a time of pitched battles over free speech, some protests can lead to the suppression of speech even inadvertently. In April 2019, the *New*

York Times published in its international edition a syndicated cartoon that depicted Israeli president Benjamin Netanyahu as a dachshund with a Jewish Star collar, and included various other imagery widely judged as anti-Semitic. The outcry was fierce. The *Times'* own editorial board dubbed the cartoon "appalling." Publishing the cartoon was an epic gaffe that exposed flaws in the paper's editorial controls and rising ignorance or tolerance of anti-Semitic bigotry. But it initially seemed like a learning moment for both the paper and its readers.

Within two months, though, the *Times* announced it would no longer run cartoons in its international edition, a step it had taken in the U.S. edition years prior. In this case, insofar as I am aware, no one had called for such a drastic step. Although editors said other considerations contributed to the decision, they did not deny that the anti-Semitic cartoon was the catalyst. PEN America lamented the announcement, writing that "free speech and open discourse demands an understanding that mistakes and offenses will occur, and a determination that these not be answered by shutting down expression to avert future lapses. In an age of fast-evolving social mores and heightened awareness of offense, political cartooning has become a risky business. But if outlets like the *New York Times* retreat from this uniquely potent form of political commentary, it may hasten the death of a form that has contributed immensely to our political conversation over time." At a time when speech seems so controversial that one of the world's leading media outlets decides that running editorial cartoons is no longer worth the grief, each of us has the potential to either contribute toward or fight against a climate of censoriousness.

WHY TO PROTEST WITHOUT SILENCING

- Protests that drown out a speaker deny not only that individual's expressive rights but also those of would-be listeners
- Censorious protests obviate dialogue and a search for common ground
- Protests can be highly effective and condemnatory without veering into censoriousness
- Though calls for speech to be punished are themselves protected speech, they lead to censorious consequences
- What is considered speech beyond the pale is often in the eye of the beholder; to sanction the silencing of views you dispute is to open the door to the muzzling of views you support

10.

Consider When to Forgive Speech-Related Transgressions

IN A 1957 SERMON, MARTIN LUTHER KING JR. PREACHED, "WE MUST DE-velop and maintain the capacity to forgive. He who is devoid of the power to forgive is devoid of the power to love. There is some good in the worst of us and some evil in the best of us. When we discover this, we are less prone to hate our enemies." To keep speech free in our cacophonous modern public square, we need the capacity to forgive those who antagonize and offend. Otherwise, there can be little incentive to apologize for an offense or try to mitigate its harm.

Speech-related offenses that evoke censure, stigma, and even "cancellation" from the culture are never formally adjudicated. There is no due process, prosecutor, or defense attorney, nor a jury to deliberate innocence or guilt or judge to impose a sentence. Rather it is in the hands of society to determine an unofficial punishment and resolve what, if any, penance warrants reintegration into society's good graces. Whereas Europe has enshrined a "right to be forgotten" whereby, on request, certain types of misdeeds must be expunged from the online record, the American system offers no such legal entitlement to absolution. Instead, online reputational

Interpersonal forgiveness comes about as a result of changes in motivation whereby one becomes

a. less motivated to retaliate against an offending relationship partner,

b. less motivated to maintain estrangement from the offender, and

c. more motivated by conciliation and goodwill for the offender, despite the offender's hurtful actions.

damage—whether fair or not—can linger indefinitely. Individuals and institutions choose whether to engage with a transgressor, and society as a whole determines whom to support and shun.

Helping to rehabilitate someone can be risky. The people blackballing a malefactor can turn on those who breach the implicit boycott. There may be little upside to being the first person to reach out a hand and pull someone back into favor. But if we don't forge paths to forgiveness for errant speech, we will live in a culture where even a single unfortunate statement can damage your career, ruin your social life, or irrevocably tarnish your reputation. Such an approach is at odds with the insurmountable human tendency to make mistakes. Given the ignorant, unintentional, or otherwise less than fully culpable verbal slights that happen constantly, holding ourselves to a standard whereby passing transgressions are etched in a permanent record raises the costs and risks of speech too high.

The Path to Forgiveness

There is no official playbook to repent for a speech-related infraction, nor set of criteria as to when forgiveness is due. Much depends on specifics: the seriousness of the offense, and the intent, context, and consequences of particular speech. The uncertainty means those called out or canceled are consigned to a murky fate. At what point can a professor who has insulted his students be trusted in the classroom? Should a single offensive slip by a television anchor mean that the person goes off the air permanently? Does a journalist who trafficked in stereotypes deserve another byline?

Several recent instances help provide a road map for how individuals who have committed speech-related transgressions can redeem themselves. Three elements emerge as key:

PREREQUISITE #1:
Persuasive Contrition

To set the stage for forgiveness, an apology should voice a measure of acceptance of the consequences of the misdeed so that the expression of regret does not come off as a self-serving attempt to avoid reprisals. In 2018, Hollywood director James Gunn of Disney's Guardians of the Galaxy movie franchise was fired after the disclosure of a series of offensive jokes and comments about rape and pedophilia that he had posted online nearly a decade earlier. The posts were spotlighted by right-wing conspiracy theorist Mike Cernovich in a clear attempt at character assassination. But Gunn owned up in a penitent public statement. "I have regretted them for many years since—not just because they were stupid, not at all funny, wildly insensitive, and certainly not provocative like I had hoped, but also because they don't reflect the person I am today or have been for some time. Regardless of how much time has passed, I understand and accept the business decisions taken today. Even these many years later, I take full responsibility for the way I conducted myself then."

PREREQUISITE #2:
Character Witnesses

Character witnesses can help contextualize an infraction amid an individual's personality and track record. After a homophobic riff onstage, comedian Tracy Morgan received support from fellow comic Tina Fey, who said, "I'm glad to hear that Tracy apologized for his comments . . . the violent imagery of Tracy's rant was disturbing to me. . . . It also doesn't line up with the Tracy Morgan I know, who is not a hateful man and is generally much too sleepy and self-centered to ever hurt another person." Fey's reputation, her acknowledgment of Morgan's wrongdoing, vocal support for those injured by his comments, and wry character reference signaled that he had prominent backing based on a preexisting reservoir of goodwill. When Disney's James Gunn was fired, cast members, journalists, and Hollywood influentials rallied behind a well-liked colleague; a crowd-funded billboard outside company headquarters advertised RehireJamesGunn.com. When someone is taking fire for a speech-related offense, those who can offer genuine character references should do so, not to excuse the speech itself but to contextualize it in accordance with King's admonition that "there is some evil in the best of us." Unless you believe the person is beyond redemption, bringing to light the positive qualities—even amid criticism—of someone who is under attack can help plant the seeds of eventual rehabilitation.

PREREQUISITE #3:
Earning, Rather than Expecting, Absolution

While some public figures have gotten away with pugnacious insistence that their speech-related misdeeds were just a big misunderstanding, the better path to forgiveness avoids voicing entitlement to mercy, focusing instead on *earning* absolution. Those who have achieved expiation have often taken the initiative to engage substantively with those they have offended, working to win their trust. This involves going beyond the specific misdeed at hand and demonstrating a willingness to learn about and help remediate the broader forces—racism, misogyny, homophobia—that can underpin such an offense. After his homophobic outburst Tracy Morgan met with representatives of LGBTQ organizations, recorded an anti-bullying ad, and spearheaded an episode of his regular television show, *30 Rock,* that fictionalized his transgression and made fun of his apology.

Does Time Heal Wounds?

When a wrongdoer is closely associated with an institution, that entity can become tainted with the stigma unless it convincingly distances itself from the offense. At the same time, since many verbal and even written offenses are less than fully intentional, institutions are often rightly reluctant to throw a valued employee, much less a major revenue generator, under the bus. Loyalty, reputational considerations, commercial imperatives, audience and stakeholder sensitivities, and legal and moral issues all affect how an organization responds.

In May 2017, comedian Kathy Griffin tweeted a picture of herself with a bloody, severed head meant to look like Donald Trump's. Griffin was fired from CNN's New Year's Eve show, saw her other professional opportunities dry up, and was put on a federal watch list. She spent more than a year working overseas, and then embarked on a U.S. comeback tour. Her success at mounting self-sponsored gigs helped pave the way for her to gradually begin to be hired again by entertainment companies who could see that her personal brand was no longer toxic. In the case of James Gunn, Disney reportedly waited several months after making its own internal decision to reinstate Gunn before announcing it publicly.

When a serious lapse has occurred, a swift and convincing institutional disavowal and apology can lay the groundwork to move past the infraction. The day after Gunn's derogatory tweets surfaced, Disney stated: "The offensive attitudes and statements discovered on James' Twitter feed are indefensible and inconsistent with our studio's values, and we have severed our business relationship with him." In the Morgan case, Bob Greenblatt, the head of NBC Entertainment, issued a statement that read in part, "Unfortunately, Tracy's comments reflect negatively on both *30 Rock* and NBC—two very all-inclusive and diverse organizations— and we have made it clear to him that this kind of behavior will not be tolerated." When that initial statement is judged by key audiences to fall short, it can force the institution to take a stronger stand to avoid being seen to downplay the breach.

Institutional apologies must also be sufficiently encompassing. It may not be enough to condemn a single employee for the contravention of norms. If the infraction forms part of a pattern of discriminatory or offensive treatment, that needs to be acknowledged. If that context is left out, others affected may point out that the lapse was not isolated, accusing the institution of turning a blind eye to a larger problem. When Netflix CEO Reed Hastings fired the company's communications chief for using the n-word twice, he circulated a lengthy memo discussing the specific incidents in question but also reflecting on the wider challenges of an organization that had not yet fully embraced inclusivity, saying, "We seek to be great at inclusion, across many dimensions, and these incidents show we are uneven at best. We have already started to engage outside experts to help us learn faster."

When rehabilitating an employee or associate, institutions need to be convinced of the individual's contrition and intent to do better, as well as to demonstrate publicly that they have good reason to forgive the trespass. When it was revealed that South Carolina high school football coach Bud Walpole's players were in the habit of drawing racially stereotyped caricatures of black faces on watermelons and smashing them while making "ape-like" chants, the community was divided. The coach was in the midst of a championship season and told the local NAACP president that he did not recognize the customs as racist. Walpole was initially suspended from his duties and later reinstated. In restoring him, Superintendent Nancy McGinlay stated that she had obtained a "written statement of commitment" from Walpole pledging to respect differences, take part in sensitivity training, and counsel students to be "extra vigilant" in dealing with racial or ethnic issues. The specificity of these promises helped to quell concern that the team's practices had been brushed under the rug.

Employers may also need to air out the concerns of internal stakeholders—students, fellow employees, and particularly those most directly affected by the infraction. Unless the institution shores up internal support, reintegration can trigger a divisive backlash. Forgiveness is not just a benefit to the transgressor. By letting go of a grievance and repairing a relationship, individuals and institutions have an opportunity to retire a grudge and move on from a fraught moment. Forgiveness does not mean forgetting that an offense ever happened, dropping objections registered against a misdeed, or lessening empathy with those harmed.

Of course, not all speech-related transgressions are fleeting or unintentional. Those responsible for expressions of bigotry, harassment, or hateful speech pose a threat to free expression rights by intimidating others and making free speech seem like nothing but a veil that shields vile behavior or ideas. But even for those who have used speech to harm others, paths toward forgiveness should not be closed. In 2011, a group of former extremists came together to form Life After Hate, a Chicago-based nonprofit organization that aims to foster deradicalization, fortify cities and towns to resist the influence of white supremacists, and assist individuals who seek to leave behind extremist movements. Leaving open social and moral space for individuals who turn away from extremist views and seek to reintegrate into mainstream society can help point toward a future in which such viewpoints retreat.

It's also true that the work of forgiveness can fall disproportionately on those who already bear the weight of harm from speech. Even if individual transgressors are forgivable, the social patterns they form a part of may not be. At PEN America, a staff member on one occasion felt that an outside vendor had treated her poorly during a meeting, dismissing her input on account of her race. He apologized and it seemed to me that he ought to be forgiven for the passing slight of breezing over her comments. In my mind it was impossible to ascribe his behavior as reflecting racism; it was too fleeting and indeterminate. The staffer then made the point that the treatment she had experienced from him was something she'd encountered her entire life as a petite woman of color; for her the evidence of racism came less from him than from the pattern to which his conduct conformed. Her point forced me to look at the situation differently. We could ask her to forgive the incident at hand, but could not wish away the forces that made her feel victimized in the first place. Forgiveness must not be treated as an expectation or an entitlement, but rather earned through sincere engagement and expiation.

HOW TO PAVE THE WAY TO FORGIVENESS
FOR SPEECH-RELATED TRANSGRESSIONS

- Be open to forgiving speech-related transgressions
- When eventual forgiveness is warranted, help set the stage through ample apology and the mobilization of character witnesses
- When seeking forgiveness, convey that you recognize it must be earned and is not an entitlement
- As an institutional leader, if an offense occurs, go on record to recognize it, offer empathy to those hurt, and set out remedial actions
- When seeking to reintegrate someone who has offended others back into institutional good graces, consult affected stakeholders and provide evidence to allay concerns about the offense being repeated

PART III

PRINCIPLES TO FOLLOW WHEN DEBATING FREE SPEECH QUESTIONS

11.

Understand the Harms of Speech

A COMMONPLACE SCHOOLYARD RETORT DATING BACK TO THE NINETEENTH century was "sticks and stones may break my bones but words can never hurt me." The taunt was intended to render the verbal bully powerless. But it also affirmed the principle of free speech. After all, if obnoxious words can do no harm, there would be no reason to banish them. A similar logic has sometimes led defenders of free speech to question or downplay the harm that speech causes, for fear that acknowledging it would invite restrictions.

But words can do harm, as U.S. courts have long recognized. We can think of these harms as falling into three categories: *injurious, instigating,* and *intercommunal.* Injurious harm involves words that give rise to feelings of scapegoating, intimidation, inferiority, or stigma. Instigating harm from speech involves words and statements that stimulate, legitimize, or provoke violent or criminal actions. Intercommunal harm derives from speech that has a wider social effect either by misleading, stoking divisions, or undercutting the security or well-being of the larger community.

Types of Harm from Speech: Injurious, Instigating, and Intercommunal

Injurious harm is felt by targeted individuals or groups, akin to a psychological wounding. Slurs, insults, stereotypes, bigoted symbols, and group-based theories of inferiority can inflict injurious harm. Our law recognizes several types of injurious harm—including threats, harassment, and some forms of intimidation—and allows for their prohibition. Nadine Strossen points out that these legal doctrines already address much of what we think of as "hate speech," obviating the need for new, tighter prohibitions. She maintains, for example, that a note on a door saying "Gas Jews Die" would constitute a threat or harassment. Strossen argues that our current laws deal adequately with the harms of injurious speech and only need be enforced. Libel, defamation, and slander also address injurious harm, focusing on reputation.

In recent years, the instigating harm of speech has become more obvious and alarming. I use the concept of "instigating" harm to refer to speech that can catalyze negative action—for example, anti-Semitic slurs and epithets at a Nazi rally or an individual riling up demonstrators to insult or demean racial minorities. The legal doctrine of incitement—the inducement to unlawful behavior—is intended to address the instigating harm of speech. But because U.S. law defines incitement very narrowly, the full scope of instigating harm is not addressed.

Intercommunal harms are the concern of many key Supreme Court cases delineating the bounds of the First Amendment. Whether dealing with seditious speech thought to threaten national security or flag burning as an affront to patriotism, courts have analyzed whether speech poses such risk to the country or society that restrictions are warranted. It is this kind of group harm that was contemplated by the famous reference in Justice Oliver Wendell Holmes's opinion in *Schenck v. United States* (1919) that "falsely shouting fire in a theatre and causing a panic" would be punishable notwithstanding the First Amendment.

Until the 1950s, the Supreme Court held that speech could be banned or punished if it simply had a "bad" or harmful tendency—a vague standard that allowed for punishment of disfavored ideas, including draft resistance or communism. More recently, the court found that speech must be so dangerous that it would cause specific, imminent, and unavoidable harm. The court relies on the concepts of "clear and present danger" and "imminent lawless action" to apply this strict standard. Directly urging violence—whether by directing terrorist acts or instructing how to carry out specific, near-term gang violence—would meet these tests.

In recent years, the relationship between political speech and hate-fueled crimes has come under greater scrutiny. President Donald Trump's indulgence of white supremacist and xenophobic rhetoric coincided with a 17 percent jump in documented incidents of hate crimes between 2016 and 2017. A *Washington Post* study documented a more than 200 percent increase in hate crimes in counties where Donald Trump held a campaign rally in 2016, compared to similar counties. The president and his administration have created an enabling environment for vitriolic speech and, in so doing, been seen to offer at least tacit succor to those resorting to hate-fueled violence. By repeatedly deriding journalists as public enemies and assailing individual reporters by name, the president has offered encouragement for supporters who jeer at and even attack reporters and camerapeople covering Trump rallies. A series of violent incidents has forced news organizations covering the president to hire bodyguards and take other security precautions. Individuals professing inspiration from the president have attacked migrants, Muslims, and members of minority groups that Trump has denigrated. In the summer of 2019, a shooter in El Paso who killed twenty-two people published a manifesto parroting President Trump's talk of a "Hispanic invasion" of Texas. Given the outsize voice of the president, even oblique statements that might seem fairly innocuous in ordinary life—for example, insults toward journalists or political opponents—can prompt death threats and other dramatic ripple effects, particularly given the president's impassioned online following.

The First Amendment offers no remedy for the president's rhetoric or its ill consequences. U.S. law defines incitement narrowly, but a greater range of offenses are prosecutable in Europe and Canada. In 2016, the Dutch politician Geert Wilders was convicted for inciting discrimination with an anti-Moroccan chant at a political rally. Such a chant would be legal in the United States under First Amendment law. Indeed, to expand the definition of illegal incitement in the United States could give rise to pitched conflicts over all kinds of speech—sexist jokes, arguments about affirmative action, anti-cop rhetoric. Our narrower notion of incitement, though prudent, puts the onus on leaders, civic institutions, and citizens to acknowledge the instigating harms of speech and to address them through means including vociferous counterspeech and support for victims.

The digital age has intensified the potential of speech to cause intercommunal harms. The Internet and social media have made it cheap and easy to spread murderous hatred, recruit extremist supporters, and plot nefarious acts. Instructions for bomb-making that would once have had to be written down and photocopied can now be shared globally by video. The injurious harm of a slur can readily turn into an echoing refrain of debasement against an entire community. The algorithms of certain social media sites are structured to funnel users toward ever more inflammatory content, be it harassment of women, ostracism of immigrants, or vilification of journalists.

Not All Harms Are Created Equal

The question of when and how speech can inflict actual harm and how heavily to weigh such wounds is vexing. If denigrating messages are repeated and pervasive, they can cause psychological damage. But the bruising power of speech hinges on the context, the speaker, and the listener. The same exact comment could inflict a lasting hurt or be laughed off as a joke, depending on the circumstances. The damage depends on intonation; setting; imputations of motive on the part of the speaker; the listener's susceptibility to feelings of offense; and a wide range of intangible, emotional factors like self-confidence, vulnerability, depression, and anger. While one person might shrug off a racist or religious insult, another might be profoundly affected. I have often left a meeting to hear from a female colleague that she was bothered by a sexist reference or gesture that I scarcely noticed. At other times I discern sexism in places where others don't.

These variations complicate the effort to weigh the harms of speech against the benefits of open discourse. Because our legal system must protect us all equally, it can make limited allowance for the propensity of certain speech to hit particular listeners hard. Courts tend to rely on generalized standards—like whether a "person of ordinary firmness" would feel intimidated by a threat, or whether a "reasonable person" would experience an environment as hostile. These concepts don't always account for the role of race, gender, and experience in rendering speech that might be harmless for most of us but far more toxic to some.

The effective defense of free speech must acknowledge the harms speech can cause and recognize that such harms can vary. Those who ridicule members of minority groups, women, undocumented immigrants, and others targeted by nasty speech as weak or cossetted risk furthering

THE HARMFUL EFFECTS OF SPEECH

- A 2011 study by a Palo Alto University researcher found that microaggressions against LGBTQ individuals of color contribute to higher rates of depression and stress, with results consistent across income and education levels.
- A 2015 study led by a Johns Hopkins University researcher found that microaggressions can lead to depression and thoughts of suicide.
- A 2008 study focused on the effects of microaggressions on black Americans found "a harmful and lasting psychological impact that may endure for days, weeks, months, and even years. Participants reported feelings of anger, frustration, doubt, guilt, or sadness when they experience microaggressions and noted further that the emotional turmoil stayed with them."
- Aggregating dozens of studies, the University of California, San Francisco Medical Center found that "[t]he mental and physical health consequences of perceiving and experiencing discrimination or bias due to some aspect of the self that can be negatively judged appears to be persistent and pervasive."

the unhelpful view that "free speech" as a concept denies these particularized experiences.

Researchers have attempted to isolate the harms associated specifically with speech by studying so-called microaggressions. Psychologists at Columbia University have defined microaggressions as "brief and commonplace daily verbal, behavioral, or environmental indignities, whether intentional or unintentional, that communicate hostile, derogatory, or negative . . . slights and insults." (My own view is that the term "microaggression" is misleading in that it imputes malign intent to passing offenses that, while often callous, are committed out of ignorance or a failure of conscientiousness. While I don't like the term, it has become hard to avoid in discussions of free speech.) Studies of microaggressions offer persuasive evidence that speech and language can measurably hamper mental and physical health.

While some researchers believe that microaggressions as a category is too amorphous to enable conclusive research, they don't deny that these verbal slights can have an impact on mental and even physical health.

With rising awareness and acceptance of transgender rights, the harm of "misgendering" a trans individual—referring to them with a gender with which they do not or no longer identify—has been recognized as hurtful. Misgendering can be entirely unintentional—based on visual cues, ingrained habit, or simple ignorance—or an intentional attempt to deny an individual's chosen identity. Studies show that transgender youth have elevated rates of depression, suicide, self-harm, and eating disorders as compared to peers. When someone identifies as a "him" but is referred to as "her," it can cause stress and embarrassment that compound the challenges of being a transgender youth.

When Harm Is in the Eye of the Beholder

Although speech can cause genuine harm, it is important not to overstate such harms or use them as an excuse to shut down disfavored speech. Most research on harms refers to derisive speech—taunts, slurs, microaggressions, misgendering, and the like. But the language of harm is invoked promiscuously to point to far less proximate effects, such as feelings of unease arising from a campus speaker whom students are not obligated to listen to, or an optional film screening on a controversial topic. I have not come across evidence that supports the claim of lasting harm, as opposed to passing discomfort, from such forms of speech.

Overstating harms can lead to the constriction of the exchange of ideas or art. When a free speech center at Wellesley College invited *The Atlantic*'s Emily Yoffe, who has questioned certain claims about the prevalence of sexual assault on campus, to speak, Becca Pachl, a student, protested in an open letter. Pachl said that by allowing Yoffe on campus, the university was being "negligent in ensuring the well-being of its student survivors." The 2018 talk went ahead despite her objections. In another incident, the University of Michigan initially acceded to requests that it cancel a screening of the film *American Sniper* on grounds that hosting it would make "students feel unsafe and unwelcome." A screening of *Paddington* was planned instead. An administrator expressed "deep regret" for "causing harm to members of our community" before the university came to its senses and reinstated the screening, while offering alternative activities for those opting not to see the movie. Journalist Jesse Singal has argued that simply suggesting to college students that they may be traumatized by speech could trigger such a reaction: "This sort of scaremongering—*Milo is coming and he is shrinking your telomeres!*—could become a self-fulfilling prophecy for some students. . . . And there's no reason to go down this road, because there's no evidence that the mere *presence* of a conservative speaker on campus is harming students in some deep psychological or physiological way."

There is even more reason for skepticism when those claiming harm do so vicariously. When students at Harvey Mudd College planned a "Mudd Goes Madd" party with a mad science theme, they were derided for perpetrating "violence" against those with mental illness. Another student turned the tables, though, accusing the protesters of inflicting harm. She told a neighboring college newspaper that "I am actually bipolar and I am offended that people infantilize the whole issue of mental illness by suggesting we should be protected from anything that could damage our 'fragile' psyches." Psychologists Zachary Rothschild and Lucas Keefer have documented that such professions of outrage-by-proxy can be less an expression of altruism and empathy than "a means of reducing guilt over *one's own* moral failings." They argue not that all moral outrage is self-serving but "simply that outrage can be defensive and can be motivated by underlying feelings of guilt in order to bolster a moral self-concept when people's moral identity is threatened."

Those who believe that the harms of speech must be taken more seriously are most persuasive when they ensure that claimed harms are not speculative, inflated, conflated, or projected onto others. While our goal as a society should be to ensure that all people feel physically safe, whether on campus or on our streets, that objective should not spill over into a guarantee of psychological safety, or freedom from uncomfortable or offensive ideas. Knowing where to draw the line between genuine and exaggerated harms is crucial. Like the harm reduction movement, which focuses on addressing the negative consequences of drug use rather than trying to stop the usage itself, free speech defenders should aim to mitigate the negative effects of certain speech through solutions that do not impinge on expressive rights.

RECOGNIZING THE HARMS SPEECH CAN CAUSE

- Speech can cause genuine and lasting psychological and even physiological harms
- The potential for speech to cause harm can vary depending on the circumstances and the individuals involved
- The harms of speech can be exaggerated or speculative
- The arguments in favor of free speech are strengthened by reckoning with the harms speech can cause
- Overemphasis on the harmful potential of speech can lead to results that are unnecessarily restrictive of speech

12.

Don't Equate Speech with Violence

RECENT CONFRONTATIONS ACROSS THE COUNTRY REFLECT A TENDENCY to answer speech with violence. In 2017 in Montana, Greg Gianforte, a Republican congressman, pled guilty to assault for body-slamming *Guardian* reporter Ben Jacobs after some persistent questioning at a campaign event. In June 2019, conservative journalist Andy Ngo was attacked and beaten at an Antifa counterprotest in Portland, Oregon, where he was taking photographs and video. In October 2019, a driver pointed a gun at protesters outside a Trump rally in Minneapolis.

Today, a surprising number of influential voices seem ready to treat ugly speech as akin to physical violence. Although some forms of speech can be damaging, speech is never the same as physical violence, nor a justifiable provocation for it. As the sociologist Max Weber pointed out a century ago, in a civilized society the state must exercise a monopoly on the use of force. Collapsing the time-honored distinction between speech and action would erode the rule of law, chill speech, upend long-held legal and social arrangements, and invite violence in response to verbal provocation.

Speech and Violence Intersect, but Are Not the Same

Merriam-Webster defines violence as "the use of physical force so as to injure, abuse, damage, or destroy." It's not hard to see why some people alarmed over noxious speech are inclined to equate it with physical harm. The logic is simple, if usually unspoken: We accept that assertiveness is justifiable to prevent and defend against physical violence. By deeming offensive speech a form of violence, the thinking goes, we can underscore its pernicious power and fortify the taboos against it. Calling speech a form of violence lays the foundation to ban and punish it as we do physical assaults.

In her 1993 acceptance speech for the Nobel Prize in literature, novelist Toni Morrison spelled it out: "Oppressive language does more than represent violence," she said; "it is violence." She describes how words have been misused for "menace and subjugation." Taken literally, Morrison's analogy is false. Even the most oppressive language does not involve physical force. But her remark is symbolic—aimed to accentuate the harmful potential of offensive speech, a potency that permissive approaches to expression may seem to deny.

Morrison was right to call on free speech proponents to own up to the psychological, emotional, and social suffering that invidious speech can inflict. In the decades since her entreaty, that damage has become better understood. Even as staunch a traditional free speech defender as the American Civil Liberties Union (ACLU) acknowledges that to deny the harms of speech "flies in the face of lived experience and ignores the costs of free speech." Mass movements have taken hold to counter bullying, stigmatize linguistic offenses against women and people of color, and rid our public lexicon of outmoded, derogatory terms. That denigrating speech seems to be on the rise in society nonetheless is, for the most part, not a result of ignorance about the harms of speech. On the contrary, those who traffic in hateful speech know well the damage it inflicts. When it comes to eradicating lingering pockets of innocent cluelessness about the punch of hurtful speech, education and engagement offer more promise than a confounding accusation that "violence" has been perpetrated through words.

Northeastern University psychology professor Lisa Feldman Barrett has argued that the biological stress induced by menacing speech renders it "literally a form of violence." She notes that "long stretches of simmering stress" caused by speech can trigger sickness, reshape the brain, kill neurons, and even hasten death. She claims that science can provide "empirical guidance for which kinds of controversial speech" provoke these grievous consequences and should thus be prohibited. She gives the example of a classroom debate on eugenics as the sort of edifying intellectual exposure that students' "nervous system evolved to withstand." To Barrett, Charles Murray's ideas are merely "offensive," presenting students with "a scholarly hypothesis to be debated, not thrown like a grenade." On the other hand, she says a speech by "provocateur and hatemonger" Milo Yiannopoulos is "abuse" that should be banned entirely from campuses because it's tantamount to violence. She claims that a clear distinction can be drawn "between permitting a culture of casual brutality" and "entertaining an opinion you strongly oppose." To Barrett, the former is a danger to a civilized society (and to our health); the latter is the lifeblood of democracy.

The problems with Barrett's attempt to demarcate "violent" speech are manifold. First, her dissection of specific speakers and ideas representing subtle shades of offensiveness veers into precisely the sort of viewpoint-specific controls on speech that the First Amendment abhors. Her paradigm illustrates why courts have rejected efforts to parse fine gradations of noxious speech: while Barrett may regard Murray as creditable, the reception he met at Middlebury made plain that others vehemently disagree. While most people (though not all) might concur that Milo Yiannopoulos is obnoxious and unworthy of attention, Barrett offers neither clear criteria nor examples of speech that place him beyond the pale. Her case that the harms of speech intensify with repetition over time flies in the face of her call to ban a one-time, one-day campus engagement for Yiannopoulos. If this type of subjective appraisal of speakers' messages and intent were used to deem certain speakers censor-worthy, it would put immense discretionary power in the hands of institutional leaders and public officials. Perhaps most important, this new definition of violence— which makes the transmission of words into a physical act, interfering with another person's brain—would upend centuries of laws and norms, raising all kinds of questions about banning not just speakers but also protests, demonstrations, books, articles, films, and other forms of communication that have hitherto been routinely categorized as peaceful means of expression but might nonetheless prompt a neurological stress reaction.

Yet Barrett is but one prominent exponent of a perspective that has gained traction. According to a 2017 survey of 800 undergraduates by Yale University's William F. Buckley Jr. Program, 81 percent thought that "words can be a form of violence." Designating speech as a form of violence has won favor as a new tactic to silence disagreeable speech. When former Israeli foreign minister Tzipi Livni spoke at Duke University in the fall of 2019, a student decried her very presence as "an act of violence." The charge of "violence" is thrown around loosely to refer to speech that is merely offensive, and even unintentionally so. Writing in a Concordia University publication, commentator Erika Morris opined that so-called microaggressions are "a very real form of violence." Anni Liu, a contributing writer for *Everyday Feminism* magazine, took it a step further to argue that even inadvertent offenses amount to violence. "Just because a perpetrator of racism is clueless (or in denial) about the impact of their words doesn't mean that their actions were any less violent or that the impact of that violence is changed," she wrote.

Denoting speech as a potential form of violence may, ironically, intensify its harmful impact. The behavioral science field of "mind-set research" holds that the level of stress individuals experience in response to stimuli derives partly from how much anxiety they anticipate ahead of time. By this logic, playing up the possible psychological and biological ramifications of harmful speech can compound its deleterious force. Trinity College student Daniel Nesbit sharpened the point in a 2018 op-ed: "Today's college students are experiencing anxiety and depression at higher rates than ever before. The idea that 'speech is violence' tells students already greatly afflicted with mental health issues that the world is a more violent, hostile, and menacing place than it is in reality."

If Speech Is Treated as Violence, It Will Beget Violence

If speech is violence, then can violence be justified in response? If your words hit me like a punch in the gut, surely I am justified in slugging you back or even, perhaps, smacking you preemptively to protect myself. In the Yale survey, 30 percent of those questioned agreed that physical violence can be permissible to prevent someone from espousing hateful views. In 2014, University of California, Santa Barbara professor Dr. Mireille Miller-Young confronted members of an extremist Christian anti-abortion group who were peacefully protesting on campus using graphic images of aborted fetuses. She ripped their posters and scratched one of the demonstrators until she bled. Miller-Young told police that the gory placards were "triggering" for her and that she acted "in defense of her students and her own safety." She maintained that the display had violated her "personal right to go to work and not be in harm." Miller-Young's argument did not satisfy the court that heard the criminal complaint against her. She pled guilty to three misdemeanor charges. Deeming speech the equivalent of violence may be intended to deter harm, but it can foster violent confrontation by casting it as an inevitable or legitimate response to speech.

The notion that offensive speech may be met with violence lurks beneath a recent trend whereby universities preemptively silence provocative speakers on grounds that their appearance could elicit a volatile reaction that campus leaders and police are powerless to contain. In 2017, Berkeley limited conservative pundit Ann Coulter to speaking before three in the afternoon on grounds that during a later time slot they could not assure her safety. Evergreen State College biology professor Bret Weinstein voiced concerns about a new hiring policy and a proposed "Day of Absence" during which white people were asked to avoid the campus. After ensuing student protests, campus police told him it was unsafe for him to come to campus to teach. He held class in a park instead. In May 2017, the conservative Polish scholar and politician Ryszard Legutko traveled to Middlebury College, in Vermont, to deliver a lecture. Protesters had signaled their intention to assemble peacefully with music, dance, and signs, but once he arrived the college canceled his talk, stating that campus security could not ensure his safety. Political science professor Matthew Dickinson then issued an impromptu invitation to Legutko to visit his class, prompting a lively discussion that went off without a hitch. Those protesting Legutko's presence learned of it only after the fact. While Dickinson and his students demonstrated that discussions about even controversial ideas can proceed peacefully, the university's original decision deprived scores of others from participating in such an exchange. The firm rejection of violence by speakers, protesters, and counterprotesters empowers security officers to do their job in ensuring that controversial expression can go forward and that disputes over speech do not devolve into physical confrontations.

Certain forms of speech tug at the legal bounds of First Amendment, but even then the answer is not to label them as violence. When an Internet troll publishes a target's street address—called doxxing—it may not meet the legal criteria for incitement (since there is no explicit call to arms), yet followers are typically being signaled to harass or endanger someone. Many states are updating their cyberstalking and privacy laws to criminalize such minatory disclosures. One of the more frequent recent invocations of "violence" to describe speech is the deliberate misgendering or dead-naming (referring to someone who has changed their gender and name by the name they used previously) of transgender individuals. Transgender advocates may conflate speech and violence to spotlight a type of harm that is inadequately acknowledged. But unless there is a clear physical threat in the taunt, the cause of transgender rights and the problem of malicious dead-naming are better addressed through the rubrics of harassment and discrimination than by invoking violence.

As a legal matter, violence is subject to harsh punishments, including imprisonment. Blurring the line between speech and physical violence runs the risk that offensive speech could be similarly punished. Nonviolent protest has been the hallmark of some of the world's most venerated and successful political struggles, from Gandhi to Martin Luther King to the Polish and Czech uprisings against communism in the 1980s. When such nonviolent movements meet violent reprisals, their peaceable character confers a profound moral edge, helping to discredit the resort to force. If such protests could be dubbed violent based only on the slogans chanted or speeches given, that advantage would disappear. When it comes to the rights to freedom of association and protest, upholding a strict definition of violence is essential to ensuring the potency of peaceful demonstrations.

Around the world, the conflation of protected free expression and violent action is a prime justification for state-sponsored repression. China treats peaceful dissent and religious expression among the country's minority Uighur, Tibetan, and more recently Hong Kong populations as a form of "terrorism," imposing long jail sentences and other harsh punishments on dissenters. Turkey, Iran, Uzbekistan, Venezuela, Russia, and other authoritarian states deliberately fudge the distinction between peaceful expression and violent crime as a pretext to jail human rights defenders, journalists, and political opponents. If we allow speech and violence to be conflated, such equivalency will play into the hands of governments eager to justify ever-harsher suppression of speech.

UPHOLDING THE DISTINCTION BETWEEN SPEECH AND VIOLENCE

- While the harms of speech should be taken seriously, they don't render words the equivalent of violence
- Calling speech violence is neither necessary nor helpful to the effort to build greater recognition of the harms of speech
- Analogizing speech to violence can compound its harmful effects
- By deeming speech a form of violence we risk legitimizing violent responses to speech
- Treating speech as akin to violence opens the way for official repression of expression, as is done in authoritarian societies

13.

Don't Politicize Free Speech

THE STATUS OF THE FIRST AMENDMENT AT THE FOREFRONT OF THE BILL OF Rights confers a special mystique. But that does not insulate free speech from politics. Free speech values have historically been championed on both the right and the left, and are grounded in distinct ideals and objectives across the political spectrum. Whether your political priority is economic prosperity, individual liberty, social justice, or scientific progress, you have a stake in protecting free speech. Around the world, free speech occupies a place of honor in virtually all major global and regional human rights instruments, cementing its status as a universal value.

But in recent years, as political divisions have deepened, free speech has often been cast as a partisan issue. In particular, many people are coming to regard free speech safeguards as a thumb on the conservative side of the scale. This marks a profound shift, since for the last few centuries, liberals have generally led the fight to uphold free speech—to combat religious and state authority; promote equality and fairness for oppressed groups; and enable personal, sexual, and artistic freedom. But today some prominent self-styled champions of free speech are critics of policies to further equality and inclusion, fueling distrust of the cause among certain advocates of pluralism and diversity. In parallel, some accuse the U.S.

Supreme Court of distorting free speech doctrine to further corporate interests and conservative objectives. In 2018, Justice Elena Kagan validated that critique in a dissent excoriating her conservative colleagues for "weaponizing" speech rights. Furthering the schism, some on the left, concerned about hateful speech and crimes, are skeptical of speech protections that can be cast as inimical to the struggles against racism, xenophobia, and bigotry.

The politicization of free speech represents a dangerous trend. Ideologically, polls show that the U.S. population is moving leftward, as generations that value diversity, equity, and inclusion come of age. If free speech is discounted as a retrograde precept used mainly to provide a safe harbor for hateful ideologies, these protections will be vulnerable as political attitudes evolve. If the only people trying to talk left-leaning youth out of their antipathy toward free speech are right-leaning peers and professors, it is unlikely that they will come around. Reversing the dangerous trend toward politicization of free speech will require both the left and the right to adapt. Right-leaning advocates should take care to defend free speech on an ideologically encompassing basis that includes sticking up for liberal as well as conservative speech. They should also acknowledge and pledge to address the harms of speech and barriers to open discourse including racism, sexism, and xenophobia. Left-wing influentials and organizations must affirm the principle of open expression even for objectionable speech. Political leaders, faculty members, and other voices of authority need to educate young Americans as to how free speech protections are essential to the goals and values that motivate them.

Tilted Bench

When it comes to free speech, hypocrisy abounds. Even its most ardent defenders must admit some propensity to stand up more eagerly for views they believe in than for those they dispute. You're more likely to experience visceral outrage witnessing police arrest a fellow protester than if they target someone for demonstrating against you.

In 2018, political scientists tested whether the tendency to be more protective of speech with which we agree afflicts the Supreme Court jus-tices who are the final arbiters of what speech is legally protected. They studied 2,967 votes cast in 338 freedom of expression cases between 1953 and 2014. The researchers found that liberal justices were more support-ive of free speech claims overall than their conservative counterparts, but that—on both sides—a justice's ideological bent toward the particular speech at issue was more predictive of their vote than their philosophy of free speech rights. The justices, they wrote, "fall prey to in-group bias in freedom of expression cases," meaning that liberal justices are more likely to protect liberal speech and conservative justices to safeguard that which is conservative in content.

In June 2018, *New York Times* Supreme Court reporter Adam Liptak reported on a separate study performed by the same scholars that docu-mented an acceleration of these trends in recent years. Liptak reported that under Chief Justice John Roberts the court had shifted perceptibly right-ward in choosing which free speech cases to hear. While the volume of free speech cases heard by the Roberts court was commensurate with that of prior benches, the court had "trained its sights on speech promoting con-servative values more than any other modern Court." Republican appoin-tees on the Roberts bench were almost three times as likely (67.9 percent of the time) to affirm conservative speech than liberal (just 23.8 percent of the time), a disparity far starker than was documented in prior eras. This study suggests a worrying trend toward more overt politicization in free speech jurisprudence. Justice Kagan has cautioned that the current court's willingness to overturn precedent risks "turning the First Amend-ment into a sword" to achieve preordained political and economic ends. She cautioned that "the First Amendment was meant for better things."

Whose Freedom, Whose Speech

Public opinion polls suggest that political polarization is infecting per-spectives on free speech. Political scientists Joshua Dyck and Francis Talty from the University of Massachusetts at Lowell published a study in 2017 that found wide bipartisan support for free speech alongside great partisan suspicion that the other side doesn't truly hold such ideals. The study found that partisans on both sides were less protective of speech involving ideological positions or personalities they opposed. Republicans surveyed were far more ready to limit the speech of liberal activist Michael Moore than of conservative talk-show host Ann Coulter, and vice versa for Democrats. Both groups viewed their own party as defenders of First Amendment and other constitutional rights but were cynical about the opposing party's commitment to the same freedoms. Several other recent studies confirm sharpening partisan divisions over what speech merits protection. According to a 2017 Cato Institute survey, staunch liberals were most likely to believe that it was morally acceptable to punch a Nazi, whereas Republicans were more inclined to believe that individuals who burn the flag should be stripped of their citizenship (the Supreme Court has held that flag burning is a form of "symbolic speech" protected by the First Amendment).

The divide over campus speech has worsened as conservative politicians have sought to counter what they see as a bias against right-wing opinion, particularly on campus. Because faculty, students, and administrators at universities skew liberal, conservatives on campus may be relatively isolated and find it difficult to create space for their views. In the Cato survey, conservatives were more than twice as likely as staunch liberals to say that "the political climate prevents me from saying things that I believe, because others might find them offensive." Administrators and faculty must work to address the chilling effects of ideological homogeneity on campus to ensure that students and faculty from across the political spectrum can be heard and are willing to listen to one another. Public universities have an educational obligation to see to it that the campus environment does not lead to de facto muting of certain viewpoints.

When governments weigh in, however, they should do so cautiously. Many campuses need to make greater efforts in hiring and classroom management to ensure that conservative viewpoints are welcome. But a recent trend toward government-sponsored executive orders, legislation, political pronouncements, and lawsuits has focused on defending speech with a particular ideological bent. While uproars over campus visits by conservatives like Yiannopoulos have earned high-level condemnations from government officials, including the president, those leaders were silent when, for example, five Kennesaw State University cheerleaders were cut from the squad for kneeling during the national anthem.

The Trump administration has shown no concern that its interventions might be seen as partisan. Former attorney general Jeff Sessions proclaimed that the First Amendment was "not a partisan issue. Constitutional rights are for all Americans—not just those in one party or one faction." But the setting of his address on the topic of campus speech (before a conservative student group), the contempt he expressed for liberals (calling them "a generation of sanctimonious, sensitive, supercilious snowflakes"), and his choice to intervene legally only in speech cases involving conservative expression made his profession of bipartisanship ring hollow. The president continued in a similar vein in March 2019 when he introduced an executive order on campus speech. By announcing the measure at a meeting of the Conservative Political Action Committee and signing it flanked by right-wing activists and students, he made plain whose side he is on. Rather than being greeted as a step to foster open discourse on campus, the executive order met with criticism even from First Amendment advocates who dismissed it as grandstanding and unconstitutionally vague. A growing number of states have introduced their own campus speech bills, often including terms—such as the creation of politically appointed oversight bodies to enforce the law—that risk deepening divides. Rather than such legislative edicts, the better approach is to call on university leaders to examine whether their campuses reflect a breadth of views, and how well those outside the ideological mainstream are able to voice their opinions and pursue their interests. Where problems are identified, measures such as hiring for viewpoint diversity and intensified dialogue between administrators and ideologically heterogeneous student groups are preferable to speech-related regulation by the state.

On the flip side, some liberal politicians have wrongheadedly endorsed bans and punishments for offensive speech. In 2017, former Vermont governor Howard Dean waded into the controversy over Ann Coulter's planned Berkeley visit, saying that the university was within its rights to cancel her event since he could predict it would entail "hate speech," which "is not protected by the First Amendment." Dean's assumptions and legal analysis were flawed, and his call for a public university to pre-emptively shut down speech based on the speaker's past utterances fed perceptions that the left is soft on free speech. In September 2019, California senator and then presidential candidate Kamala Harris wrote to Twitter CEO Jack Dorsey urging that President Trump be blocked for his menacing and harassing tweets. Harris was right that Trump's flouting of the rules would have gotten an ordinary user kicked off. But the suggestion that he be shut down by a platform that is central to our political discourse played into the notion that liberals are quick to silence speech with which they disagree.

A Skeptical Generation

Polls indicate that members of so-called Generation Z, born between 1995 and 2010, are more liberal, more supportive of diversity and inclusion, and more open to government solutions to social problems than their forebears. Some analysts have suggested that these trends pose a long-term danger to the Republican Party. Unless free speech can be restored to its rightful position above politics, such shifts may represent a similar threat to free speech protections. A 2018 study of Smith College compared current student views with those captured in a survey during the 2000–2001 academic year. The researchers were startled to discover a dramatic shift in attitudes during that time, toward wider support for censorship. The study found that the more recent cohort of students placed far lower priority on free expression relative to social justice concerns, and documented a "special skepticism" toward free speech rights among self-described strong liberals. When asked whether "free speech should be granted to everyone regardless of how intolerant they are of other people's opinions," 70 percent of Smith students responded yes in 2000, a figure that dropped to 50 percent by 2017. A 2015 Pew poll similarly found that millennials, born between 1981 and 1997, were far more supportive of government curbs on speech offensive to minorities than were older generations. Forty percent of millennials supported such censorship, compared with just 12 percent of those over age 70, and 24 to 27 percent of those age 35 to 69.

At PEN America we see this trend. In October 2019, there were a spate of incidents involving left-leaning students seeking to shut down speech. At Harvard students protested the *Crimson* student newspaper for contacting Immigration and Customs Enforcement (ICE) for comment on a story about immigration protests; the paper was accused of endangering fellow students by following a basic journalistic practice of offering the subject of a story the chance to comment. Immigration-related protests disrupted campus events at Georgetown University (where the event proceeded once protesters were removed) and the University of Pennsylvania (where the event was canceled when organizers could not contain the disruption). When PEN America spoke out against the exercise of a heckler's veto at Penn, we were accused by some of condoning ICE policies. This spate of incidents revealed a troubling tendency on the left to sweep aside liberal precepts like press freedom and free speech in the name of other values. While concerns over the cruel mistreatment of many immigrants are compelling grounds for protest, potent opposition need not ride roughshod over free speech.

As students graduate, their attitudes toward speech will permeate society at large, influencing how teachers, scholars, courts, and citizens balance values that can stand in tension. If younger Americans come to believe that the First Amendment is a tool of white, male-dominant culture, long-standing protections for speech may give way over time. In the long run, those who have the greatest to lose from a withering of free speech norms are those most vulnerable to government suppression of speech, or to being shouted down by the mob, namely the powerless and voices of dissent. It would be ironic for those whose voices are in greatest danger of being silenced to lead the charge to dismantle the norms and principles intended to guarantee them their say.

Progressives in positions of influence bear a special responsibility to defend the neutral principle of open expression. Liberal talk show host Bill Maher, who once had a show pulled off the air for political remarks he made, and whose planned 2014 commencement address at UC Berkeley was met with calls for cancellation, uses his program to defend the speech rights of leftists, liberals, and conservatives. President Barack Obama, in a 2016 commencement address at Rutgers University, criticized the univer-

sity's decision to acquiesce to student protesters and allow the cancellation
of a planned graduation speech by former secretary of state Condoleezza
Rice. (Rice technically withdrew, but seemingly in deference to the university administration's change of heart.) Obama reminded listeners that
he disagreed with Rice's policy views but continued:

> The notion that this community or the country would be better
> served by not hearing from a former secretary of state, or shutting
> out what she had to say—I believe that's misguided. . . . If you
> disagree with somebody, bring them in and ask them tough ques-
> tions. Hold their feet to the fire. Make them defend their positions.
> If somebody has got a bad or offensive idea, prove it wrong. Engage
> it. Debate it. Stand up for what you believe in. Don't be scared to
> take somebody on. Don't feel like you got to shut your ears off.

HOW TO AVOID POLITICIZING SPEECH

- Beware of the universal tendency to be more protective of the speech rights of those with whom you agree
- Defend the speech rights of those who do not share your ideology
- Be mindful of the skepticism that younger people evince toward free speech and seek ways to overcome it
- Reject politically one-sided government interventions in the name of free speech
- Mobilize progressive influentials to support free speech

14.

Don't Caricature the Arguments For and Against Free Speech

A COLORFUL ROSTER OF NICKNAMES HAS ENLIVENED RECENT FREE SPEECH debates. A Yale student who publicly harangued a professor was dubbed the "shrieking girl." Fox News personality Laura Ingraham labeled two young feminist writers "little journo terrorists." Right-wing analysts dubbed a University of Massachusetts student who vociferously protested conservatives "Trigglypuff." Protagonists in free speech debates are frequently dubbed fascists, chauvinists, or racists or, on the other side, politically correct, social justice warriors, or snowflakes.

While the nicknames may make for vivid prose—and hyperbole and invective are necessary ingredients of satire and polemic—there can sometimes be more caricature in free speech debates than genuine argument. This descent into mutual caricature is counterproductive. Some free speech advocates on the right dismiss those voicing concerns about the harms of speech as coddled. On the other side, those arguing to protect the vulnerable and empower previously excluded groups sometimes deride free speech as a stalking horse for racism and white supremacy. Neither portrayal is broadly accurate, fair, or productive. Moreover, the penchant for hyperbole has fueled a climate of antagonism between free speech proponents and advocates of social and racial justice, unhelpfully pitting these two essential causes—which can more constructively be seen as part of a joint project—against one another. To forge a consensus that involves safeguards for free speech amid a more diverse, inclusive, and equal society, both sides need to listen attentively, stop assuming the worst, and refrain from demonizing the other.

To some extent, the hyperbole, insults, and derisive mimicry in free speech simply mirror our public conversation writ large. On social media, mocking memes travel farther and faster than measured reasoning. That online conversations often take place in algorithmically reinforced echo chambers of the like-minded—what left-wing author and activist Eli Pariser dubbed the "filter bubble"—exacerbates the problem. If what begin as outlandish characterizations go unchallenged, there is no incentive to moderate. Taunts and denigration beget more of the same. The result is a game aimed at virtue-signaling, profile-building, and point-scoring rather than finding common ground, clarifying differences, or revealing truth.

At PEN America we've found that when we can convene representatives of varied sides of these arguments face-to-face—including brash student leaders demanding harsh reprisals for offensive speech and even stubborn First Amendment advocates—we can transcend caricature. Sometimes it's best to begin in private, where people don't have to worry about being quoted out of context. When we organized a series of closed-door roundtable discussions in the aftermath of crises at Middlebury College, the University of California, Berkeley, and the University of Virginia, we found that divisions portrayed in the media between agitated students, embattled faculty, and besieged administrators became somewhat more bridgeable.

Members of the College Republicans at Berkeley shared that their drive to bring Yiannopoulos to campus was motivated partly by a sense of being ostracized within that left-leaning community. Struggling to recruit faculty advisers for their clubs and departmental cosponsors necessary to reserve certain rooms for events, they became determined to assert their rights. Even left-leaning students of color at the meeting acknowledged that being a conservative on campus could be lonely. When a professor at the University of Virginia spoke in personal terms about his multiracial family, left-leaning students in the room were prompted to question their assumption that his support for the rights of white supremacists marchers reflected personal racism. In these private settings people were able to say things that they might have been called out on had they spoken publicly. The result was that new information came to the surface and people on opposing sides could appreciate perspectives they hadn't before.

While the opportunity for such in-depth dialogue is rare, the empathy (and curiosity) that can emerge behind closed doors is sorely needed on op-ed pages, in social media, and in lecture halls. This involves taking a moment to think through what legitimate concerns might lie behind viewpoints with which you disagree and how those interests might be addressed in ways you could accept. Where possible, opposing sides should try to meet face-to-face. Once you've sat across a table from people and heard them out, you are less prone to exaggerate or overreact to their views.

The Snowflake Label

The most prevalent caricature of students who challenge derisive speech is the designation "snowflake." The notion that a rising generation of students evince a self-indulgent intolerance for offense gained traction through the publication of Jonathan Haidt and Greg Lukianoff's 2015 *Atlantic* cover story, "The Coddling of the American Mind," and bestselling 2018 book of the same name. Haidt is a professor of ethical leadership at the NYU Stern School of Business and a founder of Heterodox Academy, an organization devoted to fostering viewpoint diversity in academia, and Lukianoff is president and CEO of the Foundation for Individual Rights in Education. The two have been scathing in their critique of a movement of students aiming to "scrub campuses clean of words, ideas, and subjects that might cause discomfort or give offense." They marshal a raft of troubling examples, including professors backing off the teaching of rape law for fear of triggering students, lists of forbidden "microaggressions" including "America is the land of opportunity" (purportedly offensive because some people don't experience it that way), and comedians afraid to do shows on college campuses because students can no longer take a joke.

Critics characterize student demands to blunt offensive speech as an emotionally driven quest to shield themselves from psychological unease. They note a sharp rise in reported rates of mental illness among young people and link it to a growing willingness to credit subjective feelings of emotional distress that they believe society should challenge rather than validate. Haidt and Lukianoff fault efforts to alert students to course material that could stir memories of abuse on the basis that "according to the most-basic tenets of psychology, the very idea of helping people with anxiety disorders avoid the things they fear is misguided." They note that oversensitivity to microaggressions risks fostering a generation of students prone to blowing up small blips into major catastrophes and dwelling on the negative.

Haidt and Lukianoff astutely analyze a series of trends on campus and pinpoint instances of misguided overreach in efforts to shield students from uncomfortable ideas. But they gave comparatively limited attention reckoning with the underlying preoccupations of many of those who call for speech constraints. Those concerns include pervasive racial stereotyping, harassment, and sexism. Haidt and Lukianoff are right that many of the measures that students have demanded, and universities have entertained—including the publication of lists of microaggressions and requiring so-called trigger warnings on syllabi to put students on alert to material that might offend—are wrongheaded. They are also correct that subjective feelings of hurt or offense should not trump dispassionate judgments of a reasonable observer about whether, for example, words heard as a slur were actually a slur. But Haidt, Lukianoff, and other free speech advocates can be too sweeping in dismissing subjective perspectives. In a diverse society, varied backgrounds and identities shape how events and speech are experienced. For a society to treat all people equally, it must be willing to consider these divergences.

At first, the phrase "all lives matter" sounded like a truism to the white politicians who used it—many of whom were not hostile to the Black Lives Matter campaign. Yet to members of the movement the phrase was heard as a repudiation, undermining their point that society devalues the lives of black Americans in particular. Language that seems utterly harmless to some may be painful to others. That doesn't mean such speech should be punished or banned, but neither should such reactions be dismissed or derided. As a society, we must both sustain objective, universal rules about the permissible bounds of speech (both legally and socially), *and* respect individuals who may justifiably have a reaction that departs from the norm. This is not simply a capitulation to political correctness. A showing of empathy toward individuals who react more acutely to particular speech can mitigate the discomfort they experience and blunt their impulse to call for the speech to be silenced.

When Haidt and Lukianoff turn to the question of how to remedy student grievances without resort to speech-suppressing methods, they emphasize rewiring the students themselves. They urge universities to offer training in cognitive behavioral therapy aimed to get students to reevaluate and reframe their consternation. They argue that students' "perpetual anger" could be overcome by teaching them to recognize their own propensity for "blaming," "catastrophizing," and "overgeneralizing" and teach themselves to interrupt these thought patterns.

In essence, Haidt and Lukianoff maintain that the best solution to young people's concerns with issues of racism, sexism, homophobia, and other forms of bigotry lies in a bootstrap effort to get them to take these phenomena more in stride—to stop being snowflakes. While they call on parents and educational institutions to drive that effort, there is comparatively little about the need for society, or the university, to pry away the calcified detritus of bigotry that continues to leach into our academy and communities. By downplaying that essential complement to the effort to fortify respect for free speech, Haidt and Lukianoff may undercut their ability to be heard by those who might have the most to learn from their thinking. Their work was intended to issue a call to action and has successfully done so, helping to jump-start a variety of efforts to fortify campus speech protections and even catalyze more hands-off forms of parenting. But those who have subsequently echoed and built on Haidt and Lukianoff's thesis have sometimes done so in ways that inflame the debate, rather than advance a constructive point of view.

The Risk of Writing Off a Rising Generation

A 2015 Fox News segment featured an essay by the president of Oklahoma Wesleyan University titled "This Is Not a Day Care, It's a University!" which addressed what he calls the "snowflake rebellion" and involved giving the show's hosts T-shirts printed with College #NotADaycare (the A is a safety pin). The essay itself makes a fair point about overly sensitive students who feel victimized by sermons that cause them to question their own behavior. But instead of treating undergraduates as young adults still developing their faculties, the riff gleefully ridicules them as self-centered wusses. These types of caricatures aim to antagonize rather than to convince. And they sometimes turn their backs on, and try to distract from, legitimate concerns of racism, misogyny, homophobia, and other forms of bigotry.

By now the sobriquets used to belittle left-leaning viewpoints have cleared the campus walls to inflect our wider discourse. Shortly after President Trump's victory in 2016, his top aide Kellyanne Conway dismissed nationwide protests against his victory saying, "We are just treating these adolescents and millennials like precious snowflakes." The writer Bret Easton Ellis decried the "little snowflakes" and "sniveling little weak-ass narcissists" who he believed led the feminist backlash against a piece of his in the *LA Weekly*. The lampooning of political expression as "feelings" run amok is a frequent trope of conservative political commentators, most notably Ben Shapiro, who has used his "Facts Don't Care About Your Feelings" tagline to back his refusal to use gender pronouns that do not correspond with a person's sex at birth and other positions that defy "political correctness."

Whatever satirical power these put-downs once possessed has now dissipated in a volley of name-calling. While the "snowflake" label is most often used to tar left-leaning youth, the same insult was levied after Montana congressional candidate Greg Gianforte physically attacked *Guardian* reporter Ben Jacobs for his hard-hitting questions. Jacobs was dubbed a "snowflake reporter" on Fox News and the Twitterverse took up the chant, with one post reading, "Crying little snowflake got his glasses broken. Boohoo." When conservative *New York Times* columnist Bret

Stephens became outraged at being called a bedbug on Twitter, he was derided as a snowflake, too.

The "snowflake" label lumps together all concerns about offensive expression—legitimate and not—as equivalent emotional claptrap. But individuals who have been physically attacked, confronted with the repeated use of the n-word as a slur, nooses hung in trees, swastikas graffitied on walls, or white supremacist flyers under doors are not being precious when they demand that something be done. They are right to ask insistent questions about how we can shape a discourse in which they don't feel threatened. By dismissing even serious concerns about harmful speech as the simpering of cossetted snowflakes, some free speech proponents can come off as oblivious or even willfully indifferent to bigotry.

Who Is Served by Free Speech?

At PEN America's first symposium on free speech on campus, involving administrators, faculty, and students from around the country, one comment stood out. A black female student leader from the University of Missouri was asked if she would favor rescinding a campus invitation for a speaker known for racially offensive views, and whether doing so would violate the First Amendment. She replied, "The First Amendment wasn't written for me." I found her answer jarring. She was a smart, high-achieving young woman. She had helped mount protests that led to the resignation of her university's president and provost, enjoying free speech protections that shielded her from official reprisal. I didn't understand why she would feel so alienated from a precept that, for me, had always been at the foundation of democracy.

Over time, though, listening to her and others, I grasped that "the First Amendment wasn't written for me" meant at least two things. First, she meant that her forebears, as African Americans, would not have been considered citizens when the Constitution was penned. Second, in the high-profile campus cases that make news, the First Amendment is invoked mostly to protect speech that is offensive to a particular group—a right-leaning speaker who opposes affirmative action, the use of the n-word, or a message like "build a wall." At the University of Missouri, the First Amendment had been invoked in the case of two students found to have placed cotton balls in front of the black cultural center in a display intended to insult black students by evoking slavery, and another instance involving the spray-painting of a racial slur on a sculpture. Though both incidents raised cognizable First Amendment questions, when it seems as though the amendment comes up mainly to safeguard speech that you find abhorrent, you might wonder if it was written for you. Her comment and perspective underscored the risks of politicization of free speech: namely that a rising generation becomes alienated from this core precept and indifferent toward its protection.

Free Speech as a Stalking Horse

Caricatures of free speech are not unique to the right. The frustration over stubborn manifestations of racial and other forms of inequality in American society have led some to deride free speech as an instrument of the powerful. The writer P. E. Moskowitz, in *The Case Against Free Speech,* goes so far as to argue that "free speech has never really existed because freedom and liberty have never really existed for the vast majority of Americans." Having witnessed the white supremacist march and violence in Charlottesville in 2017, Moskowitz argues that free speech has only been selectively honored in the past and does not deserve deference going forward. Rather than looking at the politicization and manipulations of free speech as scourges in need of redress, Moskowitz judges them grounds to dismiss the very principle of open expression as inherently corrupted and empty, a coat of thick paint that unhelpfully obscures the rot beneath. Of note, Moskowitz's account does not address what life is like in China, Russia, Iran, or anywhere else where free speech lacks all protection. A comparison with those societies helps reveal that, blemishes notwithstanding, free speech precepts are fundamental to protecting individuals from the wrath of the state, fostering open debate, and enabling social and political change.

One lodestar for left-leaning free speech skeptics is the late German

American theorist Herbert Marcuse, who argued in his 1965 essay "Repressive Tolerance" that creating a broadly tolerant society demands intolerance of certain ideas, including right-wing ideologies. Marcuse argued that rights of speech and assembly should be suspended as necessary to protect against dangerous ideas. His arguments echo today in calls that new categories of speech and opinion be delimited as beyond the pale, and that free speech considerations be subordinated to other values. The arguments Marcuse made more than fifty years ago are now enjoying a comeback.

Historian and writer Jelani Cobb set out a different case in a November 2015 essay in *The New Yorker* titled "Race and the Free Speech Diversion." For Cobb, free speech was a tool less of repression than of distraction—in the service of maintaining the status quo on racial politics. He argued persuasively that campus controversies that are ostensibly over speech actually have more to do with racism and marginalization that reaches a breaking point. He writes, "That these issues have now been subsumed in a debate over political correctness and free speech on campus—important but largely separate subjects—is proof of the self-serving deflection to which we should be accustomed at this point." He judges the debate over campus speech as a diversion from essential conversations about race, saying "This is victim-blaming with a software update."

Cobb is right that much coverage and debate over campus speech stresses threats to free speech while ignoring underlying tensions concerning race. A 2018 article by Linfield College English professor Rashmi Dutt-Ballerstadt went still further, arguing that free speech was a weapon to beat back the struggle for racial and ethnic equality. She cited several instances of left-leaning speech being punished, including a professor suspended for blaming white men for carrying out acts of violence, calls to expel a professor who had demanded a probe of white supremacist incidents, and a college investigation of student protests against a far-right speaker. She concluded that college campuses are "the frontline of the right wing's battle against diversity and multiculturalism." She accused conservatives of "using outright hate speech as 'free speech'" and called out groups by name that she said purported to champion viewpoint diversity but instead had a "sole agenda" "to legitimize ideologically racist and culturally conservative indoctrination." She decried calls for civility as a "smoke screen to silence speech that wants to dismantle racism, white supremacy and fascism," arguing that "any critique or outrage over discriminatory and vile rhetoric marks one as being 'uncivil.'"

In the fall of 2017, shortly after the deadly white supremacist rally in Charlottesville, the executive director of the Virginia ACLU branch was invited to speak at the College of William and Mary. The event sparked controversy because of the ACLU's role in representing the white nationalists who sponsored the "Unite the Right" demonstration. Boisterous protesters shouted, "Your free speech hides beneath white sheets" and "Liberalism is white supremacy," preventing the ACLU official from speaking. As Harvard Law School professor Jeannie Suk Gersen put it, such expressions reflect "the notion that invocations of 'free speech' most often enable domination, oppression, and hate. For some, the idea that free speech can be weaponized to harm the vulnerable not only justifies shutting down speech they hate but also makes free speech itself deeply suspect." After Charlottesville and the criticism of the organization that it spawned, the ACLU quickly announced it would be more selective in supporting the demonstration rights of those wielding weapons, and later introduced a nuanced, case-by-case approach to defending civil liberties in instances that raise conflicts with the organization's commitment to racial or other forms of justice.

In all of this, there lies some risk that free speech becomes the baby cast out in the effort to rid ourselves of the foul bathwater of bigotry. Critics of free speech frequently decry the straw man of "free speech absolutism" painting staunch First Amendment champions as heedless toward concerns of equality or even justice. But that too is a caricature. Even ardent First Amendment defenders acknowledge that some speech is unprotected, and for good reason. They may also be every bit as passionate about racial justice as they are about free speech. Free speech concerns should neither be allowed to distract from questions of racial equality nor take a deferential backseat to them. The challenge of realizing a society dedicated to both is to articulate how they interact and can reinforce one another. Free speech was an enabler of the catalytic student protests Cobb describes; without it Missouri students could have been punished for efforts to oust administrators or for causing campus-wide disruption. Free speech protects Professor Dutt-Ballerstadt from reprisals for questioning the motives of her university leaders.

While free speech can be invoked cynically, it is not the wellspring of bigotry or racism. Those evils derive from history, belief systems, socialization, power structures, fear, and other sources. While free speech principles sometimes safeguard bigots from certain forms of reprisal, to blame "free speech" for social and racial inequality, or suggest that curtailing free speech will somehow redress these ills, is a red herring. On the contrary, free speech is essential to enable the bracing and confrontational protests, demands, and debates that have historically been the engine of equality.

WHY AND HOW TO AVOID CARICATURING FREE SPEECH DEBATES

- Caricatures used by both defenders of free speech and those who question its primacy tend to inflame debates and obscure understanding
- Free speech defenders can be too quick to dismiss legitimate concerns regarding the harms of speech, particularly for less powerful communities
- Free speech skeptics can be too ready to cast concerns about free speech as disingenuous or a veiled effort to entrench inequality
- Where possible, engage in face-to-face dialogue with those on the opposing side of free speech debates
- Remember that no matter which side of the debate you're on, the objective should not be to ridicule or scorn, but rather to persuade those who don't already agree with you

15.

Prevent Free Speech from Reinforcing Inequality

DISPARITIES OF WEALTH, POWER, BACKGROUND, RACE, AND GENDER IN-
fluence who gets to speak when, where, and to whom. In a country
predicated on ideals of equality, we must recognize how advantage and
disadvantage affect who can command attention and shape discourse.
Free speech defenders must look beyond the most obvious constraints
on speech—state censorship, corporate controls, and online outrage—to
consider what it would take to create a marketplace for speech in which
everyone is an equal participant. All markets are subject to flaws and fail-
ures; it should not come as a surprise that interventions are necessary to
make the market for speech open to all comers.

In his seminal 2019 book, *How to Be an Antiracist,* Ibram Kendi seeks
to show how racism pervades every facet of American society. Free speech
is no exception. Many of the most formidable barriers to expressing yourself don't come in the form of laws punishing speech or bans on certain
content on YouTube or Facebook. Rather, there are educational, cultural,
historic, and other forces that dictate who enjoys important outlets for
speech—publishing contracts, newsroom jobs, public speaking slots,

plum jobs, and opportunities to make art or films. There are myriad forms of mentorship, recognition, and acclaim with the power to raise visibility and propel expressive careers. Access to these abetments is shaped by the forces of inclusion and exclusion that pervade society at large, including racism, sexism, and other forms of discrimination and inequity. Kendi argues that it is not enough, or even possible, to be a nonracist. He argues that individuals and institutions must be explicitly antiracist, meaning that they are working assiduously to dismantle, reverse, and reinvent the forces of racism that pervade society. To be a true advocate of open expression similarly demands insisting on—and working for—the eradication of constraints, biases, and inequities that make speech freer for some than others.

Discourse is not fully open as long as some groups face heightened obstacles in speaking out. The Holmesian ideas of a "marketplace" is premised on the notion that unconstrained give-and-take is necessary to surface the most compelling ideas and enduring truths. The corollary is that exclusion and underrepresentation in such debates impoverish the deliberation and compromise the result. Also, when free speech is seen as benefiting only the powerful, it becomes discredited as a tool of privilege. Amid the energetic drives now under way to eradicate racism, sexism, homophobia, antireligious bias, and prejudices, the drive to defend and revitalize free speech will benefit from being seen as compatible, and where possible aligned, with these causes.

Formal Versus Substantive Equality

Equality means different things to different people. Some critics have faulted First Amendment jurisprudence for excessive focus on formal equality and denial of the ways in which speech can compound disadvantage.

University of Michigan Law professor Catharine A. MacKinnon argues that judicial interpretations of the First Amendment have moved gradually in a corrupting direction, such that "once a defense of the powerless, the First Amendment over the last hundred years has mainly

FORMAL EQUALITY

The belief that, to achieve fairness, people must
be treated the same way at all times, regardless
of individual background or circumstance.

SUBSTANTIVE EQUALITY

The belief that because individuals' situations can differ vastly,
in order to achieve equal opportunities or results, it may be
necessary to adjust for those differences and, in some cases, treat
people distinctly in order to foster greater equality as an outcome.

become a weapon of the powerful." She decries that a one-time shelter for radicals, artists, and activists is now used to protect Nazis, Klansmen, racists, and misogynists. She identifies a few fleeting moments when courts seemed inclined to recognize how adjudicating speech could either enhance or set back the cause of equality, but reports that—for the most part—jurists have sidelined such considerations.

MacKinnon cites the Supreme Court decision of *Beauharnais v. Illinois* (1952), which upheld the conviction of a man for distributing blatantly racist pamphlets. The prosecution was based on a state statute that prohibited portrayals of "depravity, criminality, unchastity, or lack of virtue" that "expose the citizens of any race, color, creed or religion to contempt, derision, or obloquy." The court recognized that the statute was passed in an effort to quell rising racial tensions among a fast-diversifying population in the state. While not opining on whether such a statute would effectively ease racial tension, the majority concluded that the legislature had the authority to give it a try. The Supreme Court upheld Illinois's extension of the reach of libel beyond individuals to groups. The court acknowledged the harm that "group libel" could inflict, recognizing "that a man's job and his educational opportunities and the dignity accorded him may depend as much on the reputation of the racial and religious group to which he willy-nilly belongs, as on his own merits."

There is a logic here, but also some peril. It is worth noting that this was the same Supreme Court that upheld the convictions of Communist Party leaders in *Dennis v. United States,* finding that by subscribing to a philosophy that supported the overthrow of the U.S. government, the men were not protected by the First Amendment. The weaker interpretation of the First Amendment that protected minorities from racist pamphlets also allowed for the conviction of political dissidents. (The *Dennis* decision was narrowed and in effect overturned just a few years later.)

Two dissenters in *Beauharnais,* Justices Hugo Black and William O. Douglas, argued that the racist pamphleteer was being impermissibly punished based on viewpoint. They maintained that by affirming the Illinois statute the high court would give state legislatures the authority to restrict speech based on virtually any legislative objective at all. Black and Douglas also rejected the concept of group libel. Their reasoning was later adopted by the Supreme Court in *New York Times v. Sullivan* (1964) and *RAV v. City of St. Paul* (1992). In MacKinnon's analysis, the court's turn away from *Beauharnais*—and implicit repudiation of the notion that the First Amendment can make space for government efforts to achieve substantive equality—has opened the door toward unjustifiable protections for noxious and abusive speech that only reinforces inequity.

Critics have faulted a series of more recent Supreme Court First Amendment decisions for further buttressing an unequal status quo. The court's decision in *Citizens United* (2009) struck down limitations on corporate campaign expenditures. The court maintained the long-established holding that campaign spending was a form of speech—and went further to find that Congress's effort to foster a more level playing field for candidates irrespective of money violated the free speech rights of corporations. Other recent decisions have relied on the First Amendment to curtail the power of unions and limit states' ability to inform women of their abortion rights.

MacKinnon's notion of a First Amendment aimed to advance substantive equality would allow prohibitions on a broader range of hateful speech, including advocacy of racial supremacy, that are today protected by law. While the current court is unlikely to adopt these arguments, her work reminds us that such interpretations are not foreclosed entirely and have some precedent. Other legal theorists, including Columbia's Timothy Wu, are entertaining other ideas to update First Amendment jurisprudence to better address online hate. University of Virginia historian James Loeffler has argued that group libel should make a legal comeback. Courts are perpetually balancing the strictures of the First Amendment against other legitimate government objectives that may impinge on free speech. While this task should be approached cautiously, with a recognition that more constraints on speech generally cause more harm than good, there is scope for debate and innovation in how the First Amendment is interpreted to meet the demands of an evolving society.

Lift Every Voice

While the First Amendment demarcates the permissible range of government *constraints* on free expression, free speech defenders also need to consider the *enablers* of open discourse. Cultural theorists and ethicists have examined inequities inherent in expression and how to rectify them. Ethicist Miranda Fricker, in her 2007 work *Epistemic Injustice,* introduced the concept of "testimonial injustices," or ingrained prejudices that "give a deflated level of credibility to a speaker's word" based on who they are. Members of minority groups, Fricker writes, are saddled with testimonial injustices that make audiences take their words less seriously. When a woman addresses a heavily male professional group, listeners' prejudices inflect how she is heard. Female political candidates are more prone to be evaluated based on their dress, hairstyles, vocal register, and propensity to smile. Fricker's work built on earlier contributions, including by African American scholar Anna Julia Cooper, who wrote in 1892 about the suppression of black women's ideas, as well as Sojourner Truth, who similarly commented on black women's struggles to establish themselves as full participants in society. Fricker calls for "testimonial justice," an active attempt by listeners to correct for testimonial injustice in order to advance substantive equality.

A 2003 study published by the National Bureau of Labor Relations aimed to prove that minority contributions are discounted, by studying the impact of individuals' names on their employment prospects. In "Are Emily and Greg More Employable than Lakisha and Jamal? A Field Experiment on Labor Market Discrimination," researchers responded to job ads with fictitious résumés that had "either a very African American sounding name or a very White sounding name." The white-sounding names received 50 percent more callbacks for interviews regardless of occupation, industry, or whether the employer cited an emphasis on equal opportunity. A 2017 Northwestern aggregate study found that hiring discrimination against black people in particular was undiminished fifteen years later. Discrimination in hiring may not precisely mirror discrimination in getting one's ideas heard, but similar prejudices undoubtedly operate.

Achieving a truly open marketplace for ideas requires steps to rectify such unfairness. On an individual level, the person sitting at the Thanksgiving table can pivot the conversation so that an excluded younger member of the family, elderly relative, or a visitor can join in. When a group comes together to make a choice, for example on what time of day PTA meetings should be scheduled, those who are concerned with ensuring full participation and substantive equality should consider who is missing from the table or email chain and involve them before plans are finalized.

New tools and approaches have been piloted to advance substantive equality of participation and speech. "Progressive stacking" is a technique used by classroom teachers and group facilitators who prioritize calling on members of minority groups first, before permitting others to take the floor. Teachers may call on students from excluded groups before recognizing white students who have raised their hands in an effort to ensure that traditional power dynamics do not drive the conversation. The tactic generated controversy in 2017 when University of Pennsylvania teaching assistant Stephanie McKellop tweeted: "I will always call on my black women students first. . . . Other POC [people of color] get second-tier priority. [White women] come next. And, if I have to, white men." The rigid and brazenly exclusionary (and possibly illegal due to its explicit basis in race) approach adopted by McKellop triggered concerns that progressive stacking could amount to reverse racism, virtually excluding white students from classroom participation. Commentators also noted that hard and fast rules of priority could misfire, for example excluding individuals who for reason of disability, nationality, or other less visible characteristics might themselves be vulnerable to testimonial exclusion. This has prompted new proposals aimed to achieve more egalitarian participation without strict hierarchies or overt exclusion, for example by requiring all students to take part in class discussions or calling on those who have not yet spoken before anyone gets a second chance to take the floor.

One concept taking hold of late involves "centering" and "decentering" groups and experiences based on historic proximity to power. The notion is that white voices, ideas, and institutions have long occupied center stage in American society, and that it is important to now center people of color and their narratives as a way to upend traditional hierarchies that impair equality. "Decentering whiteness" avoids assuming that white people will dominate, or that whiteness is the norm. For example, white families raising children can decenter whiteness by introducing books, shows, museums, and events that feature diverse characters and cultures, by inviting diverse friends home, and by pointing out racism so that kids know it when they see it. Talking about or studying "whiteness" can be a move toward decentering it by treating white-dominated culture as one among many, rather than a standard from which the other subcultures depart. Ultimately achieving greater narrative justice will require a shift away from viewing white culture as a baseline and instead treating a range of experiences and backgrounds on a more equal footing.

Various initiatives, movements, and mantras aim to widen the range of voices heard. The impetus generally begins with someone calling out a pattern of exclusion and rallying others to challenge it. Attention to "manels" (all-male panels) became more visible and widespread in early 2015 after the launch of a Tumblr website and Twitter hashtag #manel. This movement has prompted event sponsors in academia, business, and civil society to rectify gender disparities in conferences and symposia. In June 2019, National Institutes of Health director Francis S. Collins published an open letter titled "Time to End the Manel Tradition," pledging not to participate in speaking engagements unless scientists from a range of backgrounds and identities were included. More than two thousand people have signed "The Pledge," which think tank leader Owen Barder published on his website. It reads, "At a public conference I won't serve on a panel of two people or more unless there is at least one woman on the panel, not including the Chair." The Pledge website includes a list of frequently asked questions, including "What happens if a woman drops out and we end up with a men-only panel?" The answered offered is "there are many brilliant women—please find someone else to take her place."

In 2015, activist April Reign reacted to the 2015 Oscar ceremony with a tweet that read "#OscarsSoWhite they asked to touch my hair." Reign's hashtag went viral, accompanied by reports that all twenty acting nominees were white, while the black director and lead actor in *Selma* (Ava DuVernay and David Oyelowo) had been snubbed. California congressman Tony Cárdenas wrote an open letter to the Academy of Motion Picture Arts and Sciences (AMPAS) calling it "unfortunate" that the nominees "fail[ed] to fully reflect our nation." The following year, yet again, all twenty acting nominees and four out of five directing nominees were white. Reign tweeted, "It's actually worse than last year." Actor Jada Pinkett Smith and director Spike Lee both pledged to boycott the show and actors Lupita Nyong'o and Reese Witherspoon joined the campaign.

With the heat rising, AMPAS announced several policy changes. They recognized that their balloting practices favored an aging, heavily white population of longtime members. Under revised rules, new Academy members would retain voting rights for just ten years, ensuring turnover in who gets a say in the honors. AMPAS also announced three new governance positions and an aggressive recruitment drive to double the number of women and people of color in the Academy by 2020. The effects were felt swiftly. A 2018 study found that in the next class of incoming members 46 percent were women and 41 percent people of color, in contrast with a voting membership that was previously 92 percent white and 75 percent male. In 2018, Reign published a story in *Vanity Fair* acknowledging the progress. She attended the 2019 Oscars for the first time in four years. But the debate isn't over. In 2019, controversy swirled anew over the award of Best Picture to *Green Book,* a story of racial reconciliation that some black critics derided as centering whiteness both on and off-screen.

There hasn't yet been a viral hashtag to jump-start the diversification of newsrooms, where progress has lagged egregiously. In 2017, the Asian American Journalists' Association released a report titled "Missed Deadline: The Delayed Promise of Newsroom Diversity," which cited a pledge that the American Society of News Editors (ASNE) made back in 1978 to ensure that the percentage of people of color in newsrooms would reflect the general population by 2000. In 2017, the ASNE set a new goal for 2025 to hit that pledge, giving itself an extra twenty-five years. The study found that "minorities now make up 17 percent of the workforce among newsrooms . . . far less diverse than the nation's population, which is 39 percent minority." The absence of diverse perspectives in newsrooms can lead to neglect or mishandling of certain stories, failure to account

LITERARY ORGANIZATIONS DEDICATED TO EXPANDING OPPORTUNITIES FOR EXPRESSION

Cave Canem: dedicated to fostering African American poets and poetry

Kundiman: dedicated to fostering Asian American creative writing

Vida: Women in Literary Arts: tracks the number of women reviewing books and published in literary journals

Lambda Literary: nurtures and advocates for LGBTQ writers

Asian-American Writers Workshop: supports writers and curates events

for diverse perspectives in coverage, and gaffes including the use of stereo-types and outdated language. External pressure may be necessary to spur progress. In a 2018 *Columbia Journalism Review* article, journalist Farai Chideya suggested investigations into news organizations' settlements of discrimination claims involving race, ethnicity, age, and sexual orienta-tion as a way to uncover bias and embarrass media organizations into addressing it.

In the literary community of which PEN America is a part, the imper-ative to better reflect American society has prompted legacy organizations to evolve and given rise to new and influential players. Organizations like PEN America have worked to foster diversity and inclusion in our staff and board but also in literary awards judges, public program participants, fellowship recipients, among many others. Of course, representation alone does not equity make. As the composition of an organization changes, there is hard work to be done to ensure that the full breadth of voices and perspectives present have commensurate influence on norms and decision-making and are fully empowered across our full breadth of activities.

Breaking decades of tradition in terms of which voices are most likely to be heard and celebrated takes deliberate effort, often prompted by a measure of shaming and campaigning to force leaders to take equity more seriously. As these debates become more visible, the hope is that they are prompting more industries and subcultures to look hard at who is in-cluded and who is left out, taking steps to advance inclusion before the hashtag goes viral.

WHY AND HOW TO PREVENT FREE SPEECH FROM REINFORCING INEQUALITY

- Recognize the ways in which inequities impair the exercise of free speech rights
- Appreciate that an open landscape for speech depends on the ability of all to freely and fully participate

- Acknowledge that achieving true freedom of speech requires dismantling barriers that impair the expression of particular groups
- Seek to interpret and apply free speech principles in ways that address, rather than reinforce, inequality
- Take steps to amplify and enable less-heard voices, including by supporting organizations that do so

PART IV

PRINCIPLES TO FOLLOW IN CONSIDERING SPEECH-RELATED POLICIES

16.

Know the Legal Limits of Free Speech

FREEDOM OF SPEECH IS NOT ABSOLUTE. ALTHOUGH THE FIRST AMEND-ment provides that the government "shall make no law abridging the freedom of speech," that doesn't actually mean everything we say is legally protected. In considering whether our current system of stringent safeguards for free speech does enough to shield against harm, it is essential to understand the boundaries of what speech is and is not protected. When a noxious image is displayed or intimidating words are uttered, it may be that an exception to the First Amendment applies, allowing authorities such as police or public university administrators to take legal or disciplinary action. In its 1942 decision in *Chaplinsky v. New Hampshire*, the Supreme Court spelled out a partial list of categories of speech beyond the First Amendment's protective umbrella, including obscenity, defamation, and—in Chaplinsky's own case—"fighting words" that "inflict injury or tend to incite an immediate breach of the peace." Later court decisions have added categories to this list, among them fraud, incitement, speech integral to criminal conduct, and "true threats." This list of exceptions has been relatively stable over the years. Courts have both progressively narrowed their scope and hesitated to add new categories, while not ruling out the possibility that additional exceptions will someday be recognized.

Incitement

The First Amendment does not protect express advocacy of immediate illegal action where the action is likely to occur and the potential harm serious. The legal test for unprotected incitement (defined as spurring or urging someone to action, including violence) comes from the 1969 case of *Brandenburg v. Ohio.* In *Brandenburg,* the Supreme Court held that the state of Ohio could forbid advocacy "directed to inciting or producing imminent lawless action" and "likely to incite or produce such action." In practice, this is a strict, highly speech-protective test. Most speech that might *seem* to be inciting (much less merely provocative) does not qualify. The case concerned Clarence Brandenburg, a Ku Klux Klan member who had urged violence against the federal government in the abstract, but stopped short of goading his followers to engage in imminent lawlessness. The court found the Ohio statute under which he was prosecuted overbroad and his conviction was overturned. The court held that for incitement to fall outside the First Amendment's protection, it must meet a three-part test.

BRANDENBURG TEST FOR INCITEMENT

1. must *advocate* lawbreaking
2. advocacy must be of *imminent* lawbreaking, and
3. must be *likely* to cause such lawbreaking to occur

To be clear, *advocacy* of violence alone, without the elements of *imminence* and *likelihood,* falls short of the definition of incitement and is thus protected. *Brandenburg's* test expanded the scope of First Amendment protection beyond prior iterations, which dated back to the era of World War I. In its initial confrontations with this issue, including the 1919 case of *Schenck v. United States,* the court, following the lead of most lower courts at the time, allowed restrictions on speech that had a "tendency" to bring about a harm that the government had a right to prevent. In effect, the court held that critics of the war or the draft could be punished because such speech might encourage men to refuse induction into the military, harming the U.S. war effort.

But shifts in thinking were already under way and burst into public view later that year in a landmark dissent written by Justice Olive Wendell Holmes in *Abrams v. United States*. After thoughtful reflection, reportedly including consultations with friends and fellow judges, reading European philosophers, and attentiveness to aggressive Justice Department prosecutions of peaceable political dissenters, Justice Holmes made the case for far more sweeping protections for political speech. He opined that five Russian Jewish émigrés who had been prosecuted for antiwar pamphleteering under the 1918 Sedition Act were wrongly convicted. He found that their propaganda efforts did not constitute a "clear and present danger." Holmes argued that the only basis for suppressing speech was an "emergency that makes it immediately dangerous to leave the correction of evil counsels to time." Holmes's reasoning, the foundation for modern First Amendment jurisprudence, was as follows:

> [M]en have realized that time has upset many fighting faiths, they may come to believe even more than they believe the very foundations of their own conduct that the ultimate good desired is better reached by free trade in ideas—that the best test of truth is the power of the thought to get itself accepted in the competition of the market, and that truth is the only ground upon which their wishes safely can be carried out. That, at any rate, is the theory of our Constitution . . . we should be eternally vigilant against attempts to check the expression of opinions that we loathe.

While revolutionary at the time, Holmes's shift toward more muscular, viewpoint-neutral protections for speech became an anchor of American jurisprudence and is among the elements that distinguish the United States' approach to free speech protections as the world's most robust.

The definition of incitement to *imminent violence* that falls beyond the scope of First Amendment protection has come into new focus in our era of smash-mouth politics. In September 2018, a Cincinnati-based federal appeals court ruled that protesters attacked at a 2016 Trump campaign rally could not sue the president for incitement. The president had urged the crowd to remove the demonstrators, saying: "Get 'em out. Get 'em out of here. . . . Get 'em the hell out. . . . Don't hurt 'em." The protesters were then pushed and shoved. Relying heavily on the "don't hurt 'em" admonition as evidence that Trump did not intend for violence to occur, the court found that he "did not specifically advocate imminent lawless action."

Courts have found that illegal incitement doesn't take place when the speaker calls for lawless activity to take place at a future time, or when the call to violence is couched or contingent on an intervening development. The use of emotive and fiery rhetoric, even if it clearly could stoke angry feelings and actions, is also protected if it stops short of directly calling for immediate violence. As disturbing as it is to witness a leader goading followers into frothing hatred that may later cross over into violence, it does not meet the Supreme Court's test for incitement. Indeed, much of what people may intuitively view as stoking violence falls short of that legal definition.

It is also important to appreciate the distinction between incitement and provocation. While the term "incitement" is sometimes used to refer to speech that may elicit a hostile or even violent *reaction* from those who *oppose* the message, this is not incitement. Incitement involves *urging* people to carry out a violent act, not saying something that might prompt a violent response. In practice, the definition of incitement is so narrow that convictions are very rare.

Fighting Words

The "fighting words" exception to the First Amendment was established by the Supreme Court's 1942 decision in *Chaplinsky v. New Hampshire*. The case involved the prosecution of a Jehovah's Witness proselytizer for sharp words shouted at a town marshal. The doctrine of "fighting words" can apply to speech that provokes rather than incites. Some commentators

have argued that the armed demonstrations carried out by white supremacists in Charlottesville in 2017 might have been shut down under the
"fighting words" exception to the First Amendment. But while rising political temperatures may render the concept newly relevant, the Supreme
Court has not sustained a conviction on the basis of the "fighting words"
doctrine since it was first propounded in 1942. Because of this, some
have suggested fighting words no longer constitutes exception to the First
Amendment at all.

FIGHTING WORDS

More than rough or offensive talk—"a quite
unambiguous invitation to a brawl."

In the 1971 case of *Gooding v. Wilson,* an antiwar protester was convicted of a misdemeanor for saying, during a scuffle with police, "White
son of a bitch, I'll kill you" and "You son of a bitch, I'll choke you to
death." He was prosecuted under a Georgia statute that prohibited "op-
probrious words or abusive language, tending to cause a breach of the
peace." The court overturned his conviction, finding that a prohibition
on "fighting words" could punish only words directed to a particular individual and having a tendency to directly provoke acts of violence by
that person. In a case involving similar facts, Justice Powell suggested in
a concurrence that the fact that vulgar words were addressed to a police-
man was relevant. A well-trained police officer, in Powell's view, could be
expected to show greater restraint than the average citizen. The court has
also said that the "fighting words" doctrine doesn't apply to flag burning,
which, it held, does not constitute "a direct personal insult or an invitation
to exchange fisticuffs."

Expletives also are not considered fighting words. In *Cohen v. California* (1971), a case involving a defendant who wore a jacket with the
words "Fuck the Draft" in a courthouse, the court held that "fighting
words" must directly insult individuals, not ideas or policies. The court

found that the government had no business policing coarseness in public discourse: "Surely," Justice John Marshall Harlan wrote, "the State has no right to cleanse public debate to the point where it is grammatically palatable to the most squeamish among us."

In evaluating whether the disturbance created by speech places it outside the realm of First Amendment protection, courts look to the interplay between speaker and listeners. Where speech elicits a combative response, the Supreme Court has been reluctant to recognize an exception to the First Amendment rights of the original speaker, even if a melee ensues. The justices want to avoid ratifying a "heckler's veto," in which an individual can react to speech fiercely and thereby achieve the desired result of getting the government to silence the speaker in order to preserve public safety. In the 1949 case of *Terminiello v. Chicago,* the court overturned the conviction of a vitriolic priest for "breach of the peace" based on a fiery oration denouncing Jews, Franklin and Eleanor Roosevelt, and others. The speech had prompted a riotous protest outside the auditorium, but the court found that to hold Terminiello responsible and punish his speech would violate the First Amendment. Justice William O. Douglas wrote that free speech "may indeed best serve its high purpose when it induces a condition of unrest, creates dissatisfaction with conditions as they are, or even stirs people to anger."

The First Amendment exception for fighting words has been narrowed in another important sense: the government cannot consider viewpoint in deciding whether the doctrine is satisfied. This was the court's holding in *R.A.V. v. City of St. Paul* (1992), a case involving the prosecution of a white minor for burning a cross in a black family's yard. A municipal ordinance prohibited the placement of symbols that could provoke anger or alarm on the basis of race, color, gender, religion, or creed. The Supreme Court reversed the defendant's conviction on the grounds that the regulation unfairly discriminated among viewpoints: it singled out racist (as well as sexist, antireligious, etc.) fighting words and punished them on the basis of the message they conveyed. To put it another way, the court said that even a generally *unprotected* category of speech like fighting words cannot be policed in a way that privileges certain viewpoints over others. The bottom line is that the fighting words doctrine has been construed so narrowly as to have virtually disappeared as an exception to the First Amendment.

True Threats and Intimidation

"True threats" are also outside the realm of First Amendment protection. Unlike "fighting words," while the boundaries continue to be debated, there exists a significant line of cases in which prosecutions of such threats have withstood constitutional scrutiny.

Had the cross-burning case of *R.A.V. v. City of St. Paul* been heard after 2003, the court might have ruled differently. That's because in 2003, in *Virginia v. Black,* the court upheld the core prohibition of an anti-cross-burning law, finding that First Amendment did not guarantee the right to burn crosses *with the purpose of intimidation.* The defendant in the case had burned the cross after attending a Ku Klux Klan rally on a property whose owner had given permission for the display. The court found that "[w]hile cross burning does not inevitably convey a message of intimidation, often the cross burner intends that the recipients of the message fear for their lives. And when a cross burning is used to intimidate, few if any messages are more powerful." The First Amendment offered no protection to "true threats," defined as "statements where the speaker means to communicate a serious expression of an intent to commit an act of unlawful violence to a particular individual or group of individuals." Several states have laws prohibiting the display of nooses on similar grounds, that they meet the test of a "true threat."

Whether speech qualifies as a "true threat" depends on a range of factors, including surrounding circumstances that might render such a threat more credible; whether the target of the threat took it seriously; and whether similar threats had translated into action. In 2002, a divided Ninth Circuit Court of Appeals ruled against the publishers of an anti-abortion website featuring mock-ups of individual doctors in "Wanted" posters, crossing out the names of those physicians who had been murdered. Medical personnel had taken to wearing bulletproof vests and adopting other security precautions. The court concluded that the website expressed an unprotected "true threat" and could be constitutionally subject to civil damages. "While advocating violence is protected," the court said, "threatening a person with violence is not."

But many other prosecutions of threatening language have not passed constitutional muster. The 1969 Supreme Court case of *Watts v. United States* involved an eighteen-year-old who spoke during a rally near the Washington Monument. After noting that he had received his draft classification, he said, "I am not going. If they ever make me carry a rifle the first man I want to get in my sights is L.B.J." Watts was prosecuted and convicted under a law that prohibited making threats against the president of the United States. The Supreme Court reversed his conviction, describing Watts's utterance as a form of "political hyperbole" and noting that the crowd had laughed at it. It fell short of a "true threat."

Harassment

Harassment in the workplace, at school, or on the campus of a public institution constitutes another exception to the First Amendment where the government can restrict speech without violating the constitution. But the boundary lines in terms of what constitutes unlawful harassment tend to be fact-specific, sometimes resulting in tensions between the First Amendment and the equal protection clause of the Fourteenth Amendment, which prohibits the state from denying individuals equal treatment under the law.

In a 1986 decision in *Meritor Savings Bank v. Vinson,* the Supreme Court held that sexual harassment—including the creation of a hostile work environment—is a form of unlawful discrimination under the 1964 Civil Rights Act. The court held that for sexual harassment to be actionable it must be sufficiently "severe or pervasive to alter the conditions of the [victim's] employment and create an abusive working environment." Evidence of a hostile environment can include language, pictures, or behavior. The Supreme Court has held that when pictures or comments contribute to the creation of a hostile work environment, they do not constitute protected expression and can be barred or punished.

Other cases have examined the interplay of First Amendment protections and the anti-bullying and harassment obligations of schools. In *Davis v. Monroe County Board of Education* in 1999, the Supreme Court determined that to be held liable for a civil rights claim of harassment, the school must have *actual knowledge* of harassment to which it is *deliberately indifferent*, and that the harassment must meet a three-part test of being so "*severe, pervasive, and objectively offensive*, that it effectively bars the victim's access to an educational opportunity or benefit." Some of the thorniest current issues relating to harassment are not fully addressed by legal precedents or other policy directives. Most people would probably agree that for a student to be periodically exposed to racial slurs, stereotyping, or sexual innuendo on campus could interfere with their right to an equal education. Yet it is not clear whether harassment at that level, particularly if perpetrated in passing by many individuals rather than a single person, would meet the Supreme Court's test of severity and pervasiveness. In the online era, where there have been relatively few test cases to date, conduct that an individual could unquestionably experience as harassing—being targeted by a barrage of nasty social media posts, let's say—may not involve any behavior that would meet a legal definition of harassment sufficient to allow the government to step in. This is particularly so if the messages were posted by many different people, none of whom did more than a tweet or two.

Obscenity

Obscene speech falls outside the protection of the First Amendment, although the court has struggled to define its parameters. An early English law formulation, from the *Hicklin* case, defined obscenity as material tending to corrupt people who were vulnerable to immoral influences. It was on this basis that prosecutors challenged literary works including D. H. Lawrence's *Lady Chatterley's Lover* and Theodore Dreiser's *An American Tragedy*. The *Hicklin* test, with its reference to susceptible consumers, fell out of favor as it was recognized to "permit censorship of serious works of art and literature based on the effects of its most sensuous or erotic passages on the most squeamish or sensitive readers." While this seems quaint in light of present-day mores in the United States, PEN America still assists writers elsewhere in the world who are prosecuted under similarly outdated standards.

In 1957, in *Roth v. United States,* the Supreme Court faced the question of whether obscenity falls within the constitutional protections for speech and the press. Justice Brennan answered with a resounding "no": "implicit in the history of the First Amendment," he wrote, "is the rejection of obscenity as utterly without redeeming social importance." Rather than settle the law of obscenity, *Roth* gave rise to a raft of Supreme Court cases, including the famous statement from Justice Potter Stewart regarding hard-core pornography, in which he admitted that it was hard to define but concluded, "I know it when I see it."

But for the most part, obscenity law is shaped by the test the court set forth in *Miller v. California* (1973):

THE MILLER TEST

1. whether the average person, applying contemporary community standards, would find that the work taken as a whole appeals to the prurient interest

2. whether the work depicts or describes, in a patently offensive way, sexual conduct specifically defined by state law

3. whether the work, taken as a whole, lacks serious literary, artistic, political, or scientific value

In 1990, a Cincinnati jury ruled that an exhibition of photos by the artist Robert Mapplethorpe, including depictions of men in sadomasochistic poses and of children with exposed genitalia, was not obscene, because they had artistic value. The museum's director had testified that she saw in those depictions examples of "striking . . . light and composition." Similarly, the rap group 2 Live Crew's album *As Nasty As They Wanna*

Be, which included songs with titles like "Me So Horny" and "The Fuck Shop," escaped conviction on appeal, owing to expert testimony that the work had artistic merit.

Despite the broad dictionary definition of obscenity, the court has been clear that its meaning for First Amendment purposes is confined to depictions of sex. In *Brown v. Entertainment Merchants Assn* (2011), the court rejected the state of California's argument that it could prohibit the sale of violent video games to minors on a theory that they were akin to obscenity. The court was not persuaded by this "attempt to shoehorn speech about violence into obscenity." While child pornography is categorically unlawful because of the acts of exploitation involved, today many forms of pornographic content can flourish online because private possession of pornographic material, unless it involves minors, does not violate federal law.

Defamation

Defamation refers to injury to a person's reputation based on a false statement of fact. It includes both libel (written statements) and slander (spoken statements).

Defamation law has come into the news in recent years in light of calls by President Donald Trump to loosen the law and make it easier to win a defamation claim against a media outlet. In early 2019, Supreme Court justice Clarence Thomas chimed in to support the president in a concurring opinion in a case involving a libel claim against comedian and convicted rapist Bill Cosby. Thomas opined that the court's precedents on defamation were "policy-driven decisions masquerading as constitutional law" and argued that states were well equipped to strike the right balance between free speech and reputational protection. But a majority of justices continue to back more strict limits on libel claims.

The landmark case that confined the scope of illegal defamation was *New York Times Co. v. Sullivan* (1964). The paper had run a full-page paid ad soliciting donations to support civil rights groups in the South. The ad included a handful of inaccuracies—for example, it misstated the number of times Dr. Martin Luther King Jr. had been arrested and the reason a group of students had been expelled in Alabama. L. B. Sullivan, a Montgomery police commissioner, sued, arguing that the inaccuracies damaged his reputation. A state court jury awarded him $500,000.

The U.S. Supreme Court reversed the judgment, citing First Amendment protections. Public debate, the court said, "may well include vehement, caustic, and sometimes unpleasantly sharp attacks on government and public officials." The court set out new limits on libel actions brought by public officials (later expanded to include "public figures"): to prevail, a public official had to prove that the false statement was published with "actual malice"—either knowledge that the statement was false or reckless disregard of its truthfulness. The newspaper's mere failure not to check the ad's statements against the paper's own reporting (which would have contradicted the ad's claims) did not satisfy the "actual malice" standard. Rather it requires that at the time of publication, the defendant must have actually lied, or borne in mind, and then disregarded, significant doubts about the veracity of the published statements.

In short, you have no First Amendment right to intentionally publish false statements damaging to the reputation of another person. If the person is a public figure, though, the First Amendment protects your ability to make inadvertent false statements about them—but if you know those statements are false, or have serious doubts but publish anyway, you may be liable for defamation.

Time, Place, and Manner Restrictions

No matter how benign your message, you don't have the right to blare through a loudspeaker in the middle of the night or to hold a protest on the White House lawn. The government may—and does—impose reasonable restrictions on the time, place, and manner of speech. The permissible parameters of such restrictions were set out in the 1984 case of *Clark v. Community for Creative Non-Violence*. The court held that these types of restrictions are valid as long as they:

1. apply universally without regard to the content of particular speech;
2. are "narrowly tailored" to serve a significant governmental interest; and
3. leave open ample alternative channels for communication of the information.

In *Clark,* a National Park Service regulation that banned camping in certain parks was held not to violate the First Amendment when applied to activists seeking to sleep in a symbolic tent city to demonstrate the plight of the homeless. The regulation was neutral as to viewpoint—it would have applied regardless of the aims of the protest. When it came to the question of whether the regulation was "narrowly tailored," the court found that the demonstrators had ample alternative ways to spotlight the plight of the homeless, including by standing vigil overnight, since only camping was banned.

To qualify as a constitutionally permissible time, place, and manner regulation, the rule in question must not "burden substantially more speech than necessary" to achieve the government's aims. Under this test, a state law creating a "buffer zone" on public sidewalks outside abortion clinics failed the "narrow tailoring" requirement, because the court found that the state could protect the rights of clinic visitors without such buffers, including through stronger enforcement of existing laws barring protesters from interfering with someone obtaining reproductive health services.

Reasonable time, place, and manner restrictions can take the form of a permit requirement for public assemblies. Such requirements were once rare but now many jurisdictions have a default rule requiring permits for just about any gathering of a certain size. Some object that the mere fact of having to obtain a permit unnecessarily impairs First Amendment assembly rights but such restrictions are mostly upheld as constitutional as long as they are viewpoint neutral. In recent years, sixteen states have enacted or considered new legislation allowing more stringent curbs on protests. These are likely to be tested constitutionally.

The legal definitions of just about all categories of exception to the First Amendment are all intentionally narrow, safeguarding a good deal of speech that might intuitively seem unworthy of protection. But if the exceptions were too wide, that would undercut the governing premise of our open society that most forms of speech are permissible. More encompassing of vague standards would force speakers to be cautious for fear of crossing an unseen red line.

KNOWING THE LEGAL LIMITS OF SPEECH

- Courts have delineated a series of categories of speech that sit beyond the protection of the First Amendment and thus can be banned and punished
- Certain types of hateful speech meet the definitions of incitement to imminent violence, true threats, and harassment, enabling government to restrict them
- Other categories of speech that can be constrained include defamation and obscenity
- Governments can impose reasonable "time, place, and manner" restrictions to govern where and when potentially disruptive speech may occur
- Courts have generally interpreted these exceptions narrowly, so as to protect the maximum amount of speech

17.

Beware Expanded Government Controls on Speech

THE IDEA OF THE FIRST AMENDMENT IS THAT FREEDOM AND DEMOCRACY demand strict controls on the government's authority to suppress speech. While the exceptions to the First Amendment may seem surprisingly narrow, we should be wary of efforts to expand them. In Hong Kong, policemen with brickbats can come after peaceful protesters, but in the United States, law enforcement must allow people to have their say, as long as their expression does not transgress that narrow set of First Amendment red lines. Having mounted a rebellion against British rule, the Constitution's Framers recognized the importance of newspapers, pamphlets, and public speeches in articulating a cause and rallying the public. If they had all been silenced or locked up for challenging the crown, the revolution might have been stillborn. The First Amendment was drafted to reflect a fourfold progression from the most individual forms of expression, including freedom of thought to outward manifestations, such as assembly and advocacy, that can catalyze political and social change.

The founders of the United States were passionate about these rights. George Washington warned that if "the freedom of speech may be taken

FORMS OF EXPRESSION PROTECTED
BY THE FIRST AMENDMENT

FREEDOM OF THOUGHT → addressed as freedom of "religion"

FREEDOM TO COMMUNICATE YOUR THOUGHTS →
addressed as "freedom of speech, or of the press"

FREEDOM TO MOBILIZE AND JOIN WITH OTHERS →
addressed as freedom "peaceably to assemble"

FREEDOM TO PRESENT YOUR CASE TO THE AUTHORITIES →
addressed as freedom "to petition the government for
the redress of grievances"

away, and dumb and silent we may be led, like sheep, to the slaughter."
Thomas Jefferson famously wrote, "Were it left to me to decide whether
we should have a government without newspapers, or newspapers without
a government, I should not hesitate a moment to prefer the latter." Despite these clarion statements, until the early twentieth century, the courts
permitted laws and policies that suppressed speech on the basis of viewpoint. This allowed the federal and state governments to target abolition-
ists, suffragists, labor organizers, antiwar protesters, religious minorities,
and other dissenters. If the government had reason to believe that any of
these rabble-rousers posed a challenge to law and order or other government interests, officials were empowered to shut their speech down, First
Amendment notwithstanding.

It was not until Holmes's 1919 dissent in *Abrams v. United States* that
our modern notion of strict constraints on viewpoint-based government
interference with speech took hold. That controversial speech was challenging or hostile to official policy was no longer enough to shut it down.
The courts slipped somewhat during the McCarthy era, succumbing to
the witch-hunt mentality of the time and holding for a brief period (in

decisions that were later overturned) that, for example, teachers could be fired for being subversive. But in 1969, *Brandenburg* established the current standard that speech can only be banned if it is both intended and likely to produce "imminent lawless action." That legal boundary line strictly limits the government's power to regulate advocacy of ideas. The narrow discretion that government here in the United States has to police political speech renders ours the most protective regime for free expression anywhere in the world. The First Amendment has influenced international legal forums including the United Nations' Human Rights Committee as well as national courts in jurisdictions throughout the world.

Does the First Amendment Need a Rethink?

In recent years, some people have begun to ask whether the First Amendment should be narrowed. Some scholars have explicitly called for the U.S. government to introduce new laws that would restrict particular types of speech—for example, white supremacist vitriol. Others have called into question the breadth of the First Amendment, arguing that certain kinds of speech—racial slurs, for example—should not be constitutionally protected, although they do not typically specify how they would be carved out or what strictures should apply.

In March 2019, Facebook founder and CEO Mark Zuckerberg wrote an op-ed in the *Washington Post* calling for a "more active role for government and regulators" in protecting society from Internet-related harms. He suggested that new regulations could require that Internet companies remove harmful content appearing on their platforms (and that the law define "harmful content"). He also called for the government to set standards for how to determine whether an online user's posting or publication should be considered a political ad.

Zuckerberg's op-ed didn't mention the First Amendment. He wrote as the representative of a private company that already regulates speech on its platform. He seemed to be partly motivated by a desire for consistency across platforms ("[W]hen people use dozens of different sharing devices . . . we need a more standardized approach"), and partly by a desire to relinquish responsibility for formulating complex, contested, and highly influential content regulation standards. ("I've come to believe that we shouldn't make so many important decisions about speech on our own," he wrote.) While Zuckerberg may not think of himself as advocating a redrawing of the rules in terms of how far government can go in regulating speech, his proposals raise the question of whether more intrusive government regulations of online speech would be constitutional or desirable.

Others have called for stricter government regulation of hate speech. In the name of fighting anti-Israel and anti-Semitic sentiment on campus, there have been repeated efforts at the state level, including in New York, to introduce laws that would bar funding to student organizations that promote "hate speech" or advocate boycotts of U.S. allies. Proponents of enhanced strictures posit that hate speech causes real harms that government should do more to prevent. Richard Delgado and Jean Stefancic, professors at the University of Alabama School of Law, in 2018 reissued their 1997 book *Must We Defend Nazis? Why the First Amendment Should Not Protect Hate Speech and White Supremacy.* The new version argues that hate speech can directly affect the health and academic performance of minorities and thus should be curtailed. They also question the argument that sweeping free speech safeguards have helped advance other civil rights, pointing out that the First Amendment coexisted with slavery and did not prevent the suppression of abolitionist speech. They argue that since the First Amendment was once interpreted to permit far more intrusive regulation of speech, new restrictions are not out of the question.

Many of those who question whether the breadth of First Amendment protections is excessive are imprecise about precisely what new restrictions they would favor. They often simply point out that other industrialized democracies regulate hateful expression without sliding down a slippery slope toward authoritarianism, maintaining that the United States should follow their model without fear. In 2017, in the *Los Angeles Times,* Northwestern sociologist Laura Beth Nielsen called for American courts and legislatures to "allow the restriction of hate speech as do all of the other economically advanced democracies in the world." But Nielsen did not explain which specific European, Canadian, or other constraints she would favor—and there is significant divergence among different countries' models.

It is fair for these critics to raise the questions they do. The radical transformation of our discourse in the digital age demands thoughtful consideration of how to balance the benefits and harms of untrammeled speech. We should not assume that rules developed decades ago are necessarily optimal for the future; we need to continually interrogate them in the context of new technologies and controversies. Demographic, political, and social change all demand an open-minded approach toward how norms and strictures must evolve. But that debate should be informed by a full grasp of the logic behind our current set of rules, and a hardheaded appraisal of whether we'd actually be better off doing things differently.

This open-mindedness should also be informed by an appreciation of why our nation has historically favored broad speech protections. We should not assume that other countries have struck a better balance, as a quick look beyond U.S. borders shows. PEN America advocates daily on behalf of writers, journalists, and scholars around the world who face harsh punishments for the crime of expressing their opinions. According to the Committee to Protect Journalists, in 2018 some 251 journalists were jailed for their work. In the same period, 88 scholars were imprisoned and 60 prosecuted for the crime of expressing themselves. Their ordeals are a living reminder that empowering governments to go further than the U.S. Constitution allows in controlling speech has serious pitfalls. Increasingly, at PEN America we find ourselves having to come to the defense of writers who hail from countries that claim to be democracies— including India, Turkey, and Poland—yet nonetheless face devastating risks for voicing controversial views.

As we contemplate calls for greater government regulation of speech in the States it is worth reminding ourselves of what exists at the other end of the spectrum, in China. Although China's constitution mentions the freedoms of speech, press, and assembly, the country guarantees these freedoms in name only.

In 2018, PEN America published "Forbidden Feeds," a report documenting the breathtaking scope of online repression in China. The report enumerated eighty known cases of individual Chinese citizens threatened,

SUPPRESSION OF SPEECH IN CHINA

- Chinese courts lack independent review powers, leaving the government free to breach these rights without interference.
- All Chinese media and publishing organizations are controlled by the government.
- Foreign entities wishing to reach a Chinese audience can do so only with permission from the government, meaning that Google, Facebook, and countless other international platforms are unavailable.
- The government issues daily coverage directives to media outlets and Internet platforms, spelling out banned topics and directing how major national events should be covered.
- Journalists who defy orders are jailed, often held incommunicado, their alleged crimes, sentences, and whereabouts unknown.
- The government maintains a massive system of surveillance of online speech, and private online messages have been cited in court decisions as evidence supporting punishment for prohibited political or religious expression.

detained, interrogated, fined, and even imprisoned for online posts. The posts themselves, which touch on the Tiananmen Square protests of 1989, land rights, corruption, and other topics, implicate governmental vulnerabilities that are so widely understood that very few Chinese dare raise them. Many essential topics of public concern are precisely the subjects that the Chinese government has declared off-limits.

Laser-focused on preventing the rise of an Arab Spring–like protest movement, China is unyielding on speech that might galvanize a domestic audience. This can mean a virtual blackout of information about events like public-health scares and the sinking of a cruise ship. Western companies operating in China must play by the rules. As the thirtieth anniversary of the Tiananmen Square massacre approached, the government demanded that a data firm partly owned by Reuters remove articles relating to the massacre from its news feeds. The firm complied. In just the last year Chinese repression has stepped up dramatically with a million or more ethnic Uighurs forced into prison-like reeducation camps.

The Chinese are working to instill their notion of "cyber-sovereignty" through the United Nations and other international forums, seeking to legitimize the idea that states should have unbridled authority to control the Internet at home, without regard to international protections for free speech. If they succeed, the Internet as we know it could splinter into thousands of distinct global pieces, losing its power to unite and mobilize across borders. China is just one example of dozens of countries around the world that lack protections for freedom of speech. PEN America works in places like Saudi Arabia (which had *Washington Post* columnist Jamal Khashoggi butchered in its Istanbul consulate because the crown prince did not appreciate his writings), Myanmar (where two reporters were jailed for exposing a massacre that the country's military later confessed to have committed), Russia (where dissident journalists, artists, and writers face harassment and imprisonment if they antagonize the Kremlin), and elsewhere. In dozens of countries, if the government comes to believe that disfavored political opinions are spreading, it simply shuts down the Internet entirely, sometimes for days or weeks. While we recognize that our own U.S. approach to free expression is imperfect, a global perspective reminds us of Winston Churchill's famous saying on democracy—that it is "the worst form of government except all those other forms that have been tried."

Speech Regulation in Democracies

There is a wide distance between the harsh repressiveness in China and constitutionally enshrined free speech in the United States. As critics of U.S. permissiveness toward speech like to point out, virtually every other democracy in the world—including the United Kingdom, Canada, Norway, and elsewhere—allows greater government restraints on speech than does our First Amendment. These countries generally hold themselves to international law as codified in the International Covenant on Civil and Political Rights (ICCPR), adopted in 1966.

INTERNATIONAL COVENANT ON CIVIL AND POLITICAL RIGHTS (ICCPR)

ARTICLE 19

"Everyone has the right to freedom of opinion and expression; the right includes freedom to hold opinions without interference and to seek, receive and impart information and ideas through any media regardless of frontiers." Article 19 permits legal restrictions on speech as "necessary for respect of the rights or reputations of others, for the protection of national security, public order, or public health or morals."

ARTICLE 20

Prohibits "propaganda for war" and says, "Any advocacy of national, racial or religious hatred that constitutes incitement to discrimination, hostility or violence shall be prohibited by law."

As interpreted by the UN's Human Rights Committee, to pass muster under Article 19 speech bans must:

1. be provided by law (excluding laws that are too vague);
2. be necessary (which means they must be the least intrusive means to achieve the desired ends);
3. achieve an enumerated legitimate public interest.

The language of Article 19 is far-reaching and prescient, insofar as it encompasses "all media regardless of frontiers," a phrase that has become the predicate for insisting that international free speech protections are as robust on-line as off. The concerns raging now in the United States over hateful speech and bigotry are not unlike those that informed the treaty, which was drafted in 1954, in the aftermath of the Holocaust. The United States signed that treaty but entered a "reservation" to Article 20, meaning that it committed to implementing Article 20 only insofar as it is consistent with the First Amendment. This departure encapsulates one key difference between the American approach to hateful speech and that of much of the rest of the free world—the United States bans only incitement to "imminent violence" and not incitement to discrimination, hostility, or even violence in general.

There's a strong case to be made that the U.S. system is superior. The constitutions of many European countries, including Austria, Germany, Hungary, Italy, and Poland, guarantee freedom of expression but permit considerable restrictions. The United Kingdom lacks a written constitution but has a Human Rights Act that seeks to balance freedom of expression and equality. Provisions aimed to curtail forms of hateful speech exist in a wide range of European national laws and regulations. These include certain criminal law provisions, administrative restrictions that can sanction and fine errant speech, and civil law remedies that allow hate speech victims to seek compensation through the courts. One of the most evident problems in the European approach is that the application of anti-hate laws is discretionary, which can mean that they are used selectively to target speech that is unpopular or considered unfriendly by the government. The results are frequent charges of double standards, politicization, and the abuse of the law to suppress unwelcome viewpoints. In France, the former head of ACT UP, the HIV/AIDS activism group, was fined in 2016 for using the word "homophobic." In 2019, the head of the French #metoo movement (known by the hashtag #balanceton-porc or #exposeyourpig) was found guilty of defamation for publicizing comments that her harasser did not deny making. In another instance, activists were fined for wearing T-shirts advocating a boycott of Israel. Moreover, speech-suppressive laws may succeed in banning words and phrases, but not sentiments. In Germany, prohibitions on Nazi nomenclature have led to the emergence of a subversive lexicon of terms (such as

88, named after "H," the eighth letter of the alphabet, to allude to "Heil Hitler") meant to evoke bigotry to those in the know.

A variety of European restrictions on speech, including genocide denial laws, blasphemy laws, laws that protect royalty from criticism, and criminal defamation laws, lead to contentious results that call into question adherence to Article 19. During the debate over banning the defamation of religion (recounted in the Author's Note), when the U.S. delegation argued that such a prohibition would violate international free speech safeguards, diplomats from the Islamic Conference countered that many European countries ban Holocaust denial. They argued that there was a double standard in prohibiting speech offensive and potentially harmful to Jews while objectionable speech related to Muslims was permitted. While the two examples are far from identical, the discrepancy nonetheless fed into their sense of vulnerability and victimization, since they didn't believe the law was being applied fairly.

As the U.S. delegation, our credibility in these discussions was enhanced by being able to say that Holocaust denial laws would be every bit as unconstitutional in the United States as would prohibitions on depicting Muhammad. The minute we begin delineating new categories of hateful speech that are beyond First Amendment protection, we will open the door to charges of unfairness and double standards. On the flip side, if we were to vow to fully protect all groups that feel victimized by denigrating speech, the quantum of prohibited expression could be boundless.

Journalist Glenn Greenwald has cataloged cases that he believes represent politically motivated efforts by democratic governments to target and punish left-wing activists. Greenwald points to a trend of using such laws to punish critiques of Israel, a sensitive subject given Europe's history of anti-Semitism and a recent spike in anti-Semitic sentiment and activity. Greenwald cites the conviction, upheld by France's highest court, of twelve pro-Palestinian activists who wore shirts advocating a boycott of Israel, on the grounds that they violated a ban on provoking discrimination or hatred based on national origin or religion. Nadine Strossen has collected similar cases, such as the 2014 arrest of a British political candidate for quoting a passage from a book by Winston Churchill criticizing the treatment of women in Islam. As Strossen writes, hate speech laws in these countries "uniformly vest enforcing officials with enormous discretionary power, and consistently have been enforced to suppress unpopular views and speakers, including political dissent and minority speakers."

Others have critiqued the vague standards that European hate-speech restrictions often employ. Danish human rights lawyer Jacob Mchangama has critiqued the "hopelessly arbitrary standard" used by the European Court of Human Rights that purports to distinguish between expression intended to inflict "gratuitous offence" and is thus unlawful, and expression on a "question of indisputable public interest." He points out that these categories can easily be one and the same. Mchangama points to the troubling example, also cited by Strossen, of an atheist campaigner in the United Kingdom receiving a six-month prison term—for "religiously aggravated intentional harassment, alarm or distress"—for placing satirical drawings of Jesus, the pope, and Muhammad in a prayer room at the Liverpool airport.

Another worry is that such laws, by suppressing speech, lead to malign views being spread surreptitiously through coded language and underground Web platforms. Such surreptitious dissemination of noxious ideas is arguably more dangerous because it spreads mainly to those who are susceptible to it and is shielded from rebuttal or counterspeech. Pushing noxious speech into encrypted channels makes it more difficult for law enforcement to track the spread of extremist ideologies. When bigoted sentiments are out in the open, you can trace who is expressing them, dispute them, and protect against attempts to act on them. Outlawing hateful speech can also deepen social fault lines. German American political theorist Yascha Mounk has written about how, growing up Jewish in Germany, he witnessed the chilling effect of prohibitions on Holocaust denial firsthand: "Worried that one careless formulation might tar them with the brush of anti-Semitism, many people were visibly nervous even to talk to me and other German Jews." At the same time, Mounk writes, the very same speech restrictions emboldened the far right by giving them a basis for claiming to be victims of censorship.

Flemming Rose, the former foreign affairs editor of *Jyllands-Posten*—

the Danish newspaper that published a controversial set of cartoons of the prophet Muhammad in 2005—has made a related point about the inefficacy of hate-speech laws. Researching his book *The Tyranny of Silence,* Rose learned that the Weimar Republic had hate-speech laws that were enforced rather robustly. He notes that Nazi leaders like Joseph Goebbels and Julius Streicher were prosecuted for anti-Semitic speech, with Streicher twice sent to prison. But the prosecutions did not deter Nazi anti-Semitism: to the contrary, according to Rose, "the many court cases served as effective public-relations machinery, affording Streicher the kind of attention he would never have found in a climate of a free and open debate." Rose's point is not that anti-Semitic speech was benign; he believes that Nazi propaganda fomented anti-Jewish hatred. His contention, rather, is that strict laws against hate speech did not prevent the Nazis' rise: "This type of legislation proved ineffectual on the one occasion when there was a real argument for it." The sort of boost that Nazi propagandists enjoyed by crying persecution when their hateful sentiments were punished is a version of the same sort of moral victory that is claimed today when a provocateur is silenced and accuses his critics of censorious cowardice. Because they only bottle up rather than eliminate hateful sentiments, laws banning noxious speech have a way of intensifying rather than alleviating underlying hatreds.

That government regulation of speech can go badly wrong does not mean we should foreclose discussion of how the law might need to evolve. The less absolutist free speech regimes in place in Europe have allowed some important trials in the regulation of hateful speech online. For example, in June 2017, Germany implemented something called the Network Enforcement Law, which requires social media companies to remove content that violates the country's laws against hate speech and defamation. The law depends heavily on the tech platforms for enforcement, pressing them into service as content regulators charged with implementing government mandates. The law imposes stringent deadlines (twenty-four hours for the removal of "manifestly unlawful" content) and stiff penalties (up to €50 million or $56 million) for violations. Critics worry that as companies step into the role of regulating the legal perimeters of speech, they may err on the side of removing all potentially offensive speech to avoid risk. Others object that the enforcement of the law against far-right politicians, such as leaders of Germany's right wing Alternative fur Deutschland (AfD) party, has allowed these polarizing figures to cast themselves as martyrs.

Some early evidence suggests that drawing the proper lines will be tricky. Under the law, both Germany's Jewish weekly newspaper and an individual Social Democratic officeholder had their Twitter accounts blocked in May 2019 because of tweets critical of AfD, which Twitter said contained misleading election-related information. The newspaper's tweet linked to a quote from the Israeli ambassador to Germany criticizing the propensity of some AfD lawmakers to cast doubt on the Holocaust. The politician's tweet questioned why a photo of an AfD politician with wine bottles labeled with a picture of Adolf Hitler (an image that is illegal in Germany) had not disqualified her from seeking office. While the accounts were restored quickly, they demonstrated that laws designed to prevent hate speech can hurt those who see themselves as fighting it.

About eighteen months into the application of the Network Enforcement Law, it appears to have prompted significantly more muscular enforcement of the Internet platforms' own community standards, resulting in the removal of substantial amounts of content. While it's too soon to judge the law's effects, the prospect of Americans from every political and ideological stripe filing reports to complain about one another's speech with the specter of hefty fines under a similar law here (somehow assuming away the First Amendment) is cautionary at best.

Similar concerns have been voiced regarding the "Christchurch Call," an agreement drafted after the terrorist attack on mosques in Christchurch, New Zealand, that killed fifty-one Muslim worshippers in March 2019. The nonbinding pact among seventeen governments (mostly European but also Japan, India, and others, as well as, of course, New Zealand) and eight leading Internet platforms, including Google, Facebook, and Amazon, invited social media companies to pledge to do more to eradicate violent and extremist content from their platforms. The Trump administration declined to sign on, a decision one commentator defended because of the agreement's "deliberate, strategic vagueness" about what would be regarded as legitimate free expression under its terms.

Regulations of so-called fake news have also prompted free speech concerns, as in the case of Singapore's anti-misinformation law, which grants the government sweeping powers to suppress and censor unfavorable coverage. The country's Protection from Online Falsehoods and Manipulation Act criminalizes the spread of "false statements of fact" that compromise security, "public tranquility," public safety, or foreign relations. The law imposes harsh sanctions of up to $37,000 or five years in prison for simply sharing false information and $740,000 and ten years in prison for tech platforms that fail to remove such content. Advocates decry the law as yet another tool in the government's hands to suppress anything that challenges state-mandated narratives.

In keeping with Flemming Rose's argument that hate-speech laws did nothing to keep the Nazis at bay in Weimar, there is no sign that Europe's or other nations' tougher approach to hateful rhetoric is tamping down noxious sentiments or acts of bigotry. In the year since the adoption of Germany's Network Enforcement Law in late 2017, anti-Semitic crime and crimes targeting foreigners spiked by nearly 20 percent, a rate of increase slightly above the 17 percent year-on-year jump most recently recorded in the United States. Anti-Semitic attacks are also trending sharply upward in France, the United Kingdom, and Canada. To insist that tough measures be adopted to tamp down hateful speech without any evidence that such regulations mitigate hateful sentiment or actions runs the risk of further politicizing free speech and playing into the hands of those who rally followers by claiming that their speech rights are being trammeled.

Most critics of these measures agree that the potential harms of speech on the Internet—the dissemination of hateful views, the spread of misinformation—are all too real. What concerns them are the risks that have historically accompanied government restrictions on speech: overenforcement, arbitrary enforcement, selective enforcement to protect those currently in power, and the misplaced faith that banning hateful ideas is a substitute for the hard work of addressing them at their roots.

In contrast, some narrowly drawn forms of viewpoint-neutral government content regulation might well pass constitutional muster. The Honest Ads Act, sponsored by Senators Mark Warner, Amy Klobuchar,

and Lindsey Graham, would impose disclosure and reporting requirements for online political campaign ads; the provisions closely resemble
those that have long applied in the offline world for television commer-
cials, print ads, and billboards. The purpose of the act would be to inform
Americans about who is paying for the ads they view online, which would
help defend against the kind of foreign election interference that occurred
during the 2016 U.S. presidential election. Critics of the act fear that
it would impair political trench warfare that depends on the ability to
obscure the movers and motives behind messages. A blanket refusal to entertain digital-content-regulation proposals—or even the mere extension
of offline obligations to the digital realm—is spurious. First Amendment
jurisprudence has always evolved, taking account of new threats to speech
and new harms that may derive from expression.

Perhaps the best argument against progressives seeking new restrictions on speech is a simple reminder of who, as of this writing, would
have the power to enforce them. Were it not for the First Amendment,
it's easy to imagine that President Trump's attacks on journalists and media outlets would become politically motivated prosecutions, or that his
loathing of political antagonists would land those critics in jail. Proponents of greater government curbs on speech seem to envisage a Congress
and Justice Department that would share their own outlook on the harms
of hateful speech and the need to shelter its victims. But experience suggests that, in practice, governments empowered with the ability to restrict
speech use that power not to protect the vulnerable but to preserve their
own prerogatives.

WHY WE SHOULD BE LEERY OF EXPANDING GOVERNMENT CONTROLS ON SPEECH

- Historically and across the globe, government controls on speech have been used to consolidate state control
- In democracies that go further than the United States in terms of restricting speech, the rules can be used in ways that reinforce power structures
- Historical examples suggest that government restrictions on hateful speech are not successful in curbing the spread of hate-based ideologies
- Government repression of speech can backfire, pushing hateful speech underground, where it may be more difficult to expose and counter
- Broadened government regulations on speech will unavoidably involve viewpoint-based distinctions that will privilege certain opinions and ideologies

18.

Beware Expanded Corporate Controls on Speech

NUDITY, BREASTFEEDING, ANTI-VACCINATION CLAIMS, REVENGE PORN, terrorist recruitment, bigotry, gambling, graphic photos of violence—each of these categories, and several dozen more, are designated no-go areas on particular social media platforms. Some of the most pitched free speech debates of the digital age center on the degree to which online platforms should remove or hide offensive or harmful speech, and bar persistent purveyors from the platforms. With Google, Facebook (and their respective sub-properties including YouTube, Instagram, SnapChat, and more), as well as Twitter holding dominion over vast swaths of public discourse, these arenas have become prime vehicles for messages, photos, and videos that bully, harass, stoke hatred, extol violence, and advocate criminality. The global reach and viral potency that make the Internet so compelling as a communication tool have weaponized speech in ways that were unimaginable during the age of the pamphlet or printed political magazine. Technological advances—including the rise of so-called deep-fake videos that aim to defame and mislead and are almost impossible to definitively discredit—hold the potential to further thwart trust in our discourse. Figuring out how to strike a balance that sustains what is best about a free and open Internet while mitigating its manifest harms has bedeviled Silicon Valley executives, government regulators, scholars, and civil libertarians alike.

The early days of the Internet were greeted as the dawn of a new and jubilant era for free speech. Visions of empowered global networks, isolated communities newly connected to information, and outpourings of creative expression inspired tech entrepreneurs and rights activists. I was part of an Obama administration team that paved the way for the first ever United Nations resolution on Internet freedom, codifying that principles of unfettered exchange of information and ideas should apply equally online. We wanted governments to adopt a hands-off approach, allowing the Internet to govern itself free from surveillance, interference, and censorship.

Utopian visions of a pure, self-regulating Internet gave way long ago to a harsher reality. Rampant online harassment and trolling have driven some social media users, writers, and journalists offline, fearing their mental well-being and physical safety. Victims of crimes and tragedies are taunted with conspiracy theories and accusations of self-dealing. Cyberbullying contributes to rising teenage suicide. The glorification of violence influences perpetrators of assaults and killings. Dangerous quackery, including anti-vaccination pseudoscience, has fueled public health crises. Targeted misinformation has skewed election outcomes, pulling the rug out from under democracy. These damaging digital side effects are now recognized as not just bugs in the system, but entrenched features of it. There is growing evidence that online platforms may structurally favor some of the most nefarious forms of content. Their algorithms are designed to select for content that users find most compelling, and it turns out users gravitate toward more incendiary and extreme messages.

Cascading evidence that digital media has intensified the harms of speech has strengthened calls for social media companies to more aggressively moderate content on their platforms. (Content "moderation" refers to controls by a private Internet platform, as distinct from content "regulation" by government. Corporate "moderation" efforts include those undertaken based on corporate policy as well as those directed at removing content prohibited by law, such as child pornography or copyright infringement.) Internet companies are not subject to the First Amendment and, as a legal matter, can suppress content at will with few restrictions. Many critics have urged the platforms to exercise this discretion far more sweepingly, to expand and enforce strict usage rules aimed to rid the forums of vituperation, propaganda, and advocacy of violence.

The failure of platforms to more aggressively moderate content is explained in significant part by the almost complete immunity from liability that they enjoy for content posted by others on their platforms as a result of Section 230 of the 1996 Communications Decency Act (more on that in the next chapter). But companies face rising public pressure to go well beyond what the law requires in terms of policing content on their platforms.

But there are clear risks to empowering private, profit-driven companies to exert untrammeled control over the huge proportion of our public discourse under their purview. There is no precedent for allowing—or asking—a small group of private corporations to dictate what opinions can be expressed, images shown, ideologies expounded, political views advanced, scientific theories disseminated, and campaigns mounted on platforms that are so pervasive in daily life. Many of the fears we associate with government controls over speech—that dissent will be suppressed, that the open exchange of ideas will shrivel or skew, and that power over speech will be abused to benefit those that wield it—are as applicable to conglomerates as they are to a national government. While a tech company doesn't have the authority to arrest and prosecute you, its ability to delete your posts and shut down your accounts is a potent form of social control, and not subject to the appeals and other constraints of our legal system. Fears that Silicon Valley giants are consolidating domination over our public debate have helped fuel a drive to regulate or break up these companies, and limit the size of the markets for information, communication, and commerce that are under each one's control.

While some demand that Internet platforms be more assiduous in governing content, others decry such moves as a new and invidious form of corporate censorship. Navigating between these competing pressures, tech platforms announce new policies almost daily. Lawmakers, Internet moguls, algorithmic engineers, legal scholars, free speech advocates, and journalists grope to understand how each new tweak tilts the balance between mitigating the harms of online speech and keeping online platforms free and open.

Ordinary citizens rarely follow the intricacies of these debates, which involve complex legal rules, technical capabilities, and political and moral questions. It is hard to fault the average Facebook or Twitter user for not having a clear opinion on knotty questions that confound renowned free speech and digital experts. But informed citizens should understand enough about these deliberations to have an opinion on whether our political leaders and the platforms we depend on are upholding their responsibilities. The right solutions to the dilemmas posed by digital content will both limit the discretionary power that companies wield over speech and hold them accountable for addressing serious harms to which they contribute. The devil lies in the details.

Internet Companies' Free Speech Obligations

We often say that platforms like Facebook have become the new "public square." But lower courts have rejected attempts to treat Internet companies as if they resemble the village greens of old. Courts almost never apply First Amendment obligations to private entities. One exception, which the Supreme Court recognized in 1946 in *Marsh v. Alabama,* applied the First Amendment to limit the latitude of the Gulf Shipbuilding Corporation, owner of a company town where it performed governmental functions like overseeing safety and sanitation. The court held that the company could not prevent a Jehovah's Witness from proselytizing on a sidewalk, though it was technically private property. Justice Hugo Black wrote, "The more an owner, for his advantage, opens up his property for use by the public in general, the more do his rights become circumscribed by the statutory and constitutional rights of those who use it." But the exception requires that the business owner "be actually doing a job normally done by the government."

The Supreme Court recently made clear that social media does bear some connection to the First Amendment. In a 2017 ruling the court unanimously held that a state law prohibiting registered sex offenders from accessing certain social media sites violated plaintiffs' free speech rights. In his opinion, Justice Anthony Kennedy raised the question of whether Internet platforms perform a "quasi-municipal function." Kennedy noted that the Internet now constitutes a primary source of information, including practical necessities like job ads, and one purpose of the First Amendment is to guarantee everyone "access to places where they can speak and listen."

If Internet platforms like Twitter, Facebook, or Google indeed constitute our modern public square, performing a quasi-governmental function, they could prohibit only content that meets the legal definitions for harassment, true threats, incitement to imminent violence, or other specific categories that courts have placed beyond First Amendment protection. The sites would have to allow users to post most hateful material—as if they were publishing their own newspapers or speaking on a street-corner soapbox. Under such a regime, platforms could no longer set their own rules and would have to allow many forms of content—such as racist and sexist vitriol—that they have long banned. Given the widely held view that social media platforms need to do more rather than less about

SAMPLING OF NEW MEASURES IN CONTENT MODERATION IN SUMMER 2019

- A wholesale ban on white supremacist content on YouTube
- A new alert system on Twitter that informs readers when politicians violate the platform's guidelines
- A new Facebook initiative to suppress misleading health-related content
- Introduction in the U.S. Congress of the Ending Support for Internet Censorship Act, which would allow companies to be held liable for favoring one political ideology over another

harmful forms of content, the notion that they should be subject to First Amendment constraints is not popular.

All Fun and Games Until Someone Gets Hurt

New York Times tech journalist Kara Swisher has led calls for Silicon Valley to clamp down on harmful content, hammering companies for what she sees as negligence and worse. She has lambasted Twitter for not joining other platforms in banishing radio talk show host and right-wing conspiracy-monger Alex Jones from its platform in 2018, badgering Twitter until it did so. More recently she called for the platform to ban President Donald Trump for "dangerously weaponizing" the medium. In 2019, after Facebook users widely shared a doctored video that made House Speaker Nancy Pelosi look like she was slurring her words, Swisher blamed the company for "abrogating its responsibility as the key distributor of news on the planet." The headline of a column she wrote in the summer of 2019 addressed Internet CEOs: "If You've Built a Chaos Factory, You Can't Dodge Responsibility for the Chaos."

Swisher's list of allies is growing. A profusion of organizations, initiatives, and proposals now seek to press Internet companies to excise and suppress more content. When you hear about gunmen radicalized online, families of shooting victims who are menaced on social media by opponents of gun control, or the spread of propaganda that distorts election outcomes, the sense that platforms must somehow stanch the harm is understandable. Pious pronouncements by tech company CEOs about free expression and their platform's role in propelling social goods can come off as self-serving in the face of hard evidence of harms from online speech. But you do not need to be a fan of Facebook, Google, or Twitter to recognize that there are perils in asking them to regulate content more aggressively. As we debate what should be banned online, it is worth keeping in mind a series of risks associated with commissioning the world's most powerful companies to exercise vast and unprecedented controls over speech. Some of these risks can—and must—be mitigated through more assiduous effort and investment by the companies. Others are less tractable, and offer enduring cautions about moving down the road toward more aggressive corporate moderation of online speech.

TEN REASONS TO BE LEERY OF INTENSIFIED CORPORATE CONTENT CONTROLS

1. Volume and variety of content at stake make fair, logical, and consistent moderation virtually impossible;
2. By relying on user flagging, the methods platforms use to moderate content are subject to manipulation;
3. Those doing the moderation often lack adequate training and expertise;
4. The tech platforms are notoriously and determinedly nontransparent;
5. The basis for content moderation decisions is often opaque to users; platforms do not offer ready channels for explanation or appeal;
6. Company decisions on where to draw the line on content can be arbitrary, leading to illogical and sometimes indefensible results;
7. Content moderation systems are vulnerable to both the perception and reality of politicization;
8. Greater content controls may tend to favor the powerful at the expense of the disenfranchised;
9. Companies are ultimately motivated by profit above the public interest or the principle of free expression;
10. Automated moderation systems are imperfect and may make errors hard to detect.

Boiling the Online Ocean

To assess proposals to more tightly control digital content, it helps to get a sense of scale and process. The volumes of content being distributed online are staggering, as is the potential for abuse.

A VAST DIGITAL PUBLIC SQUARE

- 300 hours of video uploaded to YouTube every minute
- 5 billion videos viewed on YouTube each day
- 500 million tweets per day
- 20 percent of the election-related tweets posted in the lead-up to the 2018 midterm ballot were by bots
- 88 million Facebook profiles, out of 2.5 billion global users, are fake

Trying to sort through this morass is like driving up to a mountainous landfill and setting about to pick out piece by piece various categories of recyclable materials that don't belong. The volumes of content involved raise a question of whether any moderation scheme can avoid egregious lapses and pitfalls. That said, the propensity of the companies to cite their own vastness as an excuse for unfulfilled promises and harmful results is galling. These colossal user bases help generate gargantuan profits that should be plowed into improving how content moderation works.

The rules governing online content moderation are set by the platforms themselves, with limited outside input. Facebook has its "Community Standards," YouTube its "Community Guidelines," and Twitter its "Rules." The standards set out what the platforms permit and forbid when it comes to nudity, violence, hateful speech, and other contentious content.

The scale and nature of this method of content moderation by platforms poses a host of risks. Most content inquiries and takedowns are prompted by "flagging"—reports from users who alert the platforms to content they believe problematic. Governments, political movements, or anyone with an axe to grind can systematically flag disfavored content, as long as they can point to a violation of the platform's guidelines. Those determined to hijack the process for their own ends, sometimes called "snitches," can set in motion overly punitive enforcement of the rules, thwarting messages that they don't want spread. It can be hard for less sophisticated or well-heeled users to fight back. UN Special Rapporteur on Freedom of Expression David Kaye recounts how in war-torn Syria, pro-government forces would manipulate Facebook and YouTube into taking down informational posts from antigovernment or rebel groups or individuals, thwarting their ability to mobilize. While companies have made some efforts to root out politically motivated flaggers, propagandists are becoming savvier about snitching surreptitiously. As long as "flagging" remains the prime means by which troublesome content is brought to the attention of the platforms, this manipulation will persist.

Once content is flagged for evaluation, the problems can be compounded. No set of written rules can implement themselves. The social media sites rely on tens of thousands of low-wage "content moderators," usually employed by outside contractors, who pore endlessly over content that has been flagged as violating the rules, either rendering judgment on its permissibility or, in rare cases, referring the decision to a supervisor. Content moderation contractors at Facebook and elsewhere have described depressing work conditions, including rampant pot smoking on the job, inadequate breaks, panic attacks, employees embracing fringe views after prolonged exposure, and salaries that are a small fraction of that of the average Facebook worker. University of California, Los Angeles professor Sarah T. Roberts has written about the widespread post-traumatic stress disorder experienced by content moderators who are forced to review reams of explicit, violent, and otherwise disturbing material, and the limited resources and support the companies offer them. A February 2019 investigative report by technology website The Verge detailed "near-daily changes and clarifications" to the site's content rules, moderators who misconstrued posts due to a lack of cultural or political context, and "frequent disagreements among moderators about whether the rules should apply in individual cases." In February 2019, Brian

Amerige, a former Facebook employee, wrote that the moderators lack the education and experience to make subtle judgments and must rule on each case within a matter of seconds. There's no excuse for this. Facebook and other tech companies pride themselves as top-drawer places to work, with great salaries and even better perks. Given the importance and difficulty of content moderation, the companies should bring this function in-house and substantially upgrade the qualifications required and working conditions offered.

These concerns are compounded by a lack of transparency in how content is being parsed and adjudicated. Facebook has made some efforts to render its content moderation policies more transparent through reports and the release of statistics about the amount of offending content it takes down. But these disclosures are sharply bounded. Contractors who perform frontline content moderation have told journalists that they are subject to strict nondisclosure contracts.

Moreover, published standards represent only a small portion of the guidelines that dictate content removal decisions. Facebook's tools also include "more granular" internal directives, a document called "Known Questions" that addresses "thorny questions of moderation," and on-the-fly judgments hashed out among individual moderators. In 2018, a Facebook employee leaked more than 1,400 pages of previously undisclosed global content moderation instructions spread over assorted PowerPoint slides and spreadsheets. Even when the company commits to opening itself up to scrutiny by outside experts, the follow-through can fall short. In the fall of 2019, the *New York Times* reported Facebook was delaying the release of data to academic researchers studying how to prevent election-related disinformation because the company couldn't figure out how to strip out personally identifying information. Company officials cited privacy, technical constraints, and a fear of sharing trade secrets with outsiders as grounds for stonewalling the project. This persistent lack of transparency about moderation should be rectifiable through more public and regulatory pressure, but has been intractable to date.

Despite reams of rules, users struggle to find out why content has been removed or to appeal the companies' decisions. Facebook's own "Help" community includes plaintive pleas from frustrated users who haven't been told why their posts disappeared and feel powerless to do anything about it. A small example: a couple of months ago I tried to alert a private Facebook group page for alumni from my law school class to let people know that one of our classmates was running for office. The post was rejected by Facebook, without explanation. I am guessing it fell afoul of some restriction on political ads or content. I appealed the decision but never heard back. That one simple personal experience illustrates several troubling facets of the content review process: it is opaque; it's often impossible to know why something was removed or how to adjust it so it passes muster; and appeals often land in a black hole. I hear frequently from people who believe they have been wronged for reasons they don't fully understand—accounts disabled, posts rejected, or content made inaccessible. Those frustrations over systems that seem mercurial and unaccountable can fuel a sense of discouragement with participation in public discourse. A meeting of artistic freedom groups with Facebook and Instagram in the fall of 2019 surfaced a host of concerns, including the imposition of culturally specific standards to censor art and photos globally, shadow-banning practices whereby content is present but removed from searches and hashtags so it's available only to those who know to seek it out (and thus presumably won't be offended by it), and dead-end appeals. The absence of accessible, efficient, and clear appeals channels is among the most glaring gaps in the platform's approach to content moderation and one that they should be forced to remedy.

Alongside challenges of administration, the underlying policies that the social media companies apply are themselves labyrinthine and, at times, illogical. For example, Facebook bans speech targeting people on the basis of protected characteristics, but does not prohibit speech that targets discrete subsets of those groups. This has meant that while hate speech targeting "females" was prohibited, that targeting women athletes or "female drivers" was not. The official policy protected "white men" from hate speech (since both race and gender are listed among Facebook's protected characteristics) but not "black children" (since age is not a protected trait). This glaring inconsistency was reportedly behind the seemingly disparate results in a pair of widely publicized cases: a post by U.S. representative Clay Higgins calling for the murder of radicalized Muslims was allowed to stay online, while a post by a poet and Black Lives Matter activist saying "All white people are racist" was removed. These and other examples reveal the seemingly arbitrary and at times unwarranted results that content moderation schemes yield. In fairness, though, trying to promulgate rules that cover every potential form of self-expression known to mankind is an overwhelming task, even for a tech behemoth. If content moderation became more aggressive, it seems almost inevitable that such anomalies and inconsistencies would multiply.

Politics Stops at the Platform's Edge

Online platforms have come under persistent criticism for allowing political leanings to color content decisions. Conservatives frequently complain that the liberal bent of Silicon Valley tilts the companies' approach to patrolling content. In May 2019, the White House tweeted out a survey asking users to report bias that they had encountered on social media. Stating that "too many Americans have seen their accounts suspended, banned, or fraudulently reported for unclear 'violations' of user policies," the effort struck Democratic lawmakers as a shot across the bow to deter platforms from removing inflammatory content by the president's supporters. Although some scholarly studies suggest that the claims of bias are baseless, several former company insiders have confessed, anecdotally, that they have seen employees' values, worldviews, and political attitudes color discretionary decisions. After all, tech company engineers and information architects are only human; ordinary employees cannot be expected to assume the impartial professional ethos of a courtroom judge. Fighting back against perceived bias may create its own distortions. In October 2019, it was revealed that Facebook CEO Mark Zuckerberg had mounted a charm offensive involving wooing conservative politicians and pundits at one of his Palo Alto homes. At a moment when companies are fearful of antitrust scrutiny and other forms of federal regulation, it's hard to imagine that their decisions could be fully insulated from an effort to appease overseers. All companies must manage political risk and many court regulators. But the intense pressures on social media outlets to do so ought to make us wary of asking them to exercise unfettered control over online content, lest they do so in ways that are politically tainted.

There are also reasons to worry that when corporations apply a heavier hand in moderating content, it can have a disproportionate impact on less powerful speakers. ProPublica found in 2017 that Facebook routinely removed black activists' strongly worded posts about racism and the killings of African Americans at the hands of police. Some activists opened up backup accounts so they could continue organizing after their primary pages were suspended. The ability to get such decisions reversed often depends on the speaker's public profile and ability to draw press attention. That means that while those with large followings and media access may be able to sound alarm bells over unfair treatment by the platforms, those without such influence are often powerless.

The platforms' treatment of white supremacist speech relative to Islamic extremist speech has also been faulted as inconsistent, or worse. A 2016 study comparing white nationalist and Islamic State Twitter activity found that while Islamic State accounts were subjected to frequent disabling and removal, white nationalist accounts were allowed to post with little disruption. The tech companies have said that one cause of the differential treatment is that it's "easier to identify content related to known terrorist organizations." For instance, in the wake of the Christchurch attack in March 2019, YouTube's press account tweeted an explanation of why they could readily take down copyright-violating or Islamic terrorist accounts, but could not swiftly remove Christchurch video. In the cases of copyright violations or Islamic terrorism, YouTube explained, the site had a library of "reference files" either provided by publishers or deriving from the "common footage and imagery" that Islamic terrorists use, enabling the offending content to be identified and removed en masse. The same was not true for a breaking-news event like the Christchurch shooting, although YouTube also said it was "continually working to improve our detection systems." But some, like Drexel law professor Hannah Bloch-Wehba, claim that the sites are comparatively less rigorous in their enforcement of white nationalist content because of a mix of less pressure from regulators and the threat of "political blowback from the right." While pressure to rectify this imbalance is forcing progress, the problem is illustrative of the ways in which online content moderation is subject to all kinds of bias, intended or not.

Principle and Profit

The profit motive dictates that media companies act in their own self-interest. To attract and sustain users, engagement, ad dollars, and transaction revenues, the platforms favor gripping content including surprising, shocking, up-to-the minute posts with the potential to go viral. While vitriol and bigotry may drive some users offline, plenty of others come to the Internet to indulge in conspiracy theories, spew prejudice, or just to enjoy a good fight. If platforms make their sites too tame, users may tune out. A major 2018 study conducted by the Massachusetts Institute of Technology found that on Twitter, falsehoods consistently travel farther and wider than truthful posts, undercutting the incentive for traffic-hungry content czars to crack down on misleading information.

There is no question that market considerations influence content decisions. *Vanity Fair* reported that in 2013, Facebook reversed course on posts containing rape jokes that it initially said were permitted satire because they stopped short of stoking harm. The company rewrote its policies after several clients started pulling ads from the platform. All the platforms engage in "geo-blocking" (that is, blocking access to particular content within specific countries) to maintain access to global markets, even when the content that they are required to block is expression that should be protected under international law. For example, Google agreed to block videos mocking the king of Thailand in order to comply with that country's laws against insulting the monarch. For companies that want to operate globally, there is no choice but to comply with local law in each country. But this often means that platforms' professed commitment to free speech is traded away to stay on the good side of repressive governments and maintain access to markets. While the companies often argue that affording international users even partial access to their platforms can be a boon for information flows in repressive settings, the willingness of these highly influential global behemoths to cooperate with authoritarians in curbing speech gives some implicit legitimacy to these suppressive tactics.

Platforms are addressing some of these criticisms by gradually automating content moderation, honing algorithms and artificial intelligence to be able to screen impermissible content without human intervention. "Hashing" is a technique by which prohibited content is tagged for removal the minute it appears online—a way to thwart the whack-a-troll system whereby malign actors stymie flagging-based moderation schemes by simply reposting offending content over and over again via different accounts. Nine major Internet platforms now share a database to "hash" terrorist content and simultaneously expunge it from their outlets. If they are making sound decisions, such collaboration sounds like a good idea. But with borderline cases such as antigovernment rebels in Syria or Crimea, we probably don't want dissident messages instantly and permanently deleted from virtually the entire Internet. Such collective action places enormous power in the hands of a united Big Tech. If Twitter's terrorist may be Facebook's freedom fighter, the prospect of universal, automated identification and deletion of content starts to look Orwellian.

Machines simply can't always be trusted to make nuanced and consequential distinctions. In one instance, YouTube removed a video channel tied to California State University San Bernardino's Center for the Study of Hate and Extremism—a channel that was educating users about bigotry, not promoting it. Center director Brian Levin commented, "Artificial intelligence has not been honed to the level where it can distinguish between content that is promoting the most odious bigotry, and that which is reporting and analyzing it." In another instance, YouTube pulled a series of videos involving fighting dinosaur robots on the grounds that they depicted "deliberate infliction of animal suffering or the forcing of animals to fight." Automated content moderation also has difficulty accounting for regional and cultural differences and the speed with which language and usage evolve. These limitations are compounded by the utter lack of transparency that results when content-specific decisions are rendered with no human being even involved.

One of the more promising innovations in online content moderation is rising emphasis on viewpoint-neutral tracking of so-called coordinated inauthentic behavior. This approach focuses on detecting problematic posts not based on the content itself, but rather on the patterns of dissemination. Algorithms are trained to pick up on content that moves across the network in ways that suggest the involvement of bots or foreign actors that are operating deceptively. For example, Facebook can now disable campaigns that are made to look as if they are coming from one place (rural Texas, for example) when they originate elsewhere (Moscow). This approach has the benefit of avoiding putting the companies in the position of adjudicating the content itself.

Internet Platforms' Duty of Care

This book is not the place for an in-depth discussion of the rules that should govern the many specific forms of content that spark controversy online. But those debates should be informed by an understanding of the distinct roles that Internet platforms play, and the duties that should attach in each.

When platforms are serving as an *algorithmic conduit* for information posted by others, they should be permissive in allowing as broad an array of content as possible to be shared, largely avoiding judgments of taste or truthfulness. That a Google search can turn up an endless breadth of unvetted content makes the platform uniquely useful. It should be possible to hunt down the arguments against vaccinations or climate change, just as you could have once looked up similar information in a library. In terms of the breadth of available content, this slice of platforms' role resembles that of a wireless provider that does not evaluate the truthfulness or lawfulness of information transmitted via the network.

When platforms serve as *curators of content* through news feeds, favorites, elevated search-engine results, or recommended answers to questions, their role is closer to that of a publisher judging whether information can be trusted or is worth knowing. When a platform places its imprimatur on content, it should be confident that it can stand by it. In Google News (as opposed to Google Search), the company says that it excludes sites that impersonate others, conceal their ownership, or systematically "mislead users." The company is right to apply higher standards on this subplatform.

In their capacity as *commercial and advertising platforms,* when clients buy access to consumers, platforms' responsibilities are greatest. Here platforms profit from the opportunity to expose their users to messages and offers from parties with whom the companies hold a business relationship. They have an obligation to verify their clients' identities, what they are selling, and that their claims are accurate. The Federal Trade Commission enforces rules regarding truth in advertising that apply on- and offline. In the fall of 2019, controversy erupted over whether Facebook was right to allow deceptive political ads on its platform. CEO Mark Zuckerberg argued that to forbid them would amount to censorship. It is true that political candidate ads that are broadcast in the United States cannot be censored at all (unless they are sexually explicit). But Facebook is not subject to this rule, and the logic behind it does not apply. The very nature of a broadcast ad means that it goes to a wide audience, allowing for false information to be exposed and rebutted. Online ads can be targeted to reach only those audiences who will be most receptive to them, and many never learn that they are deceitful. The democracy-distorting power of micro-targeted deceptive messages was evident in the 2016 U.S. presidential election and the 2016 campaign for Brexit in the United Kingdom. While the line between political hyperbole and abject falsehood may blur, companies make thousands of similar hard calls on content daily. While a political campaign may be free to lie on its free Facebook account, when it enters a transactional relationship with Facebook, a higher duty of care attaches. Refusing to run deceptive ads is not censorship. Facebook, like any business, has a right to choose its customers as long as the criteria it uses do not violate discrimination law. It and other platforms should make clear that they will not transact with advertisers, be they political or commercial, that traffic in false claims.

Of course, there are gray areas between these categories, and each platform governs content differently. The all-powerful algorithms that dictate what content users see involve a level of intermediation that falls between traditional editorial oversight and nothing at all. To the extent that the quest for eyeballs algorithmically elevates hateful, incendiary, or misleading content so that it reaches audiences beyond what it otherwise would, the platforms have a responsibility to prevent what amounts to active—if automated—promotion of harm.

Corporations' Right to Say—or Not to Say—It

If the U.S. government were to follow the lead of countries like Germany or Singapore in requiring social media companies to remove content that harmed individual reputations or fomented unrest, would the First Amendment offer these companies any protection? In short, the answer is yes. A series of Supreme Court decisions have upheld the free speech rights of corporations as comparable to those of individual citizens. In 1976, in *Virginia Pharmacy Board v. Virginia Consumer Council,* the Supreme Court recognized First Amendment protections for "commercial speech." Two years later the court held that governments could not dictate to corporate "persons," any more than they could to individuals, the permissible subjects on which they could speak (the court held that corporate campaign spending could not be legally confined to advocacy on matters directly affecting the company). The current Supreme Court's approach to corporate speech rights was summed up by Justice Samuel Alito in his majority opinion in *Burwell v. Hobby Lobby,* a case involving the First Amendment right not of speech but of free religious exercise: "A corporation is simply a form of organization used by human beings to achieve desired ends. . . . When rights, whether constitutional or statutory, are extended to corporations, the purpose is to protect the rights of these people."

A decision by the Supreme Court to recognize the platforms as performing something akin to a government function—the maintenance of a public square—would involve a dramatic departure from recent jurisprudence affirming and expanding corporations' own speech rights. Whether and when the U.S. Congress may take action to regulate the tech platforms, what such rules will entail and how they will square with the First Amendment, remains a huge open question.

The struggle to find a suitable method of online content moderation is one of the most important free speech challenges of our time. A small handful of giant companies have more or less complete control of what has become one of our central marketplaces of ideas. We do not wish them to overregulate, but if they imposed no restraints at all, the discourse would become so flooded with misinformation and venom that reasoned debate would be subsumed. While no content moderation scheme will ever be perfect, the powerful implications of these rules and processes for our public discourse demand that the companies move more affirmatively and aggressively to remediate the most flagrant flaws.

REASONS TO BE WARY OF INCREASED CORPORATE CONTROLS ON CONTENT

- Given the vast swath of public discourse they control, asking the platforms to more tightly regulate speech would afford them even more power
- Tech companies are motivated by profit and their interests won't necessarily align with the public good or the protection of free speech
- Current systems for content moderation reveal significant flaws
- Tech companies are notoriously nontransparent, making it hard to hold them accountable for how they arbitrate content
- Many of the risks we associate with government controls on content apply equally to the tech companies

19.

Hold Tech Platforms Accountable for Their Influence on Public Discourse

REGULATING DIGITAL CONTENT IS A MESSY BUSINESS. BUT MOST PEOPLE agree that the answer cannot simply be to allow anything and everything to be posted online. Justice Louis Brandeis's idea that the answer to offensive speech is simply more speech is being tested in a world where tens of thousands of online users can reply to a single tweet. When it comes to harassment, trolling, and doxxing, "more speech" is not an unalloyed good. Our wariness of more aggressive policing of speech by platforms should not mean we throw up our hands and accept that even the most egregious harms of online discourse are ones we must live with.

The expansion of corporate influence over public discourse, via online platforms, is staggering. A democracy relies on checks and balances to constrain power, but few such mechanisms exist for these giants. Their leaders can act as president, legislature, judge, and jury, with the public unaware of what has been decided and why. The government alone cannot figure out how to rein in these content titans. Watching congressional hearings on the subject can be cringe-inducing, as legislators stumble over technical terms and reveal a lack of familiarity with even the basics of social media. As described later in this chapter, the creation of a Public Content Defender system modeled on similar structures in other public and private realms is one important way to rectify the imbalance of power between the tech companies and the consumers they serve. All of us—scholars, advocacy groups, journalists, and citizens—have a role to play in holding the Internet giants accountable. If we opt out of these conversations because they are too technical or because we despair of having any influence, we cede our voice to those with the strongest self-interest in the outcome or the most extreme views.

HOW TO BE A RESPONSIBLE ONLINE CITIZEN

- Follow major news on platforms' products, operations, and terms of service.
- Express yourself publicly and within your circle of influence on issues that matter to you.
- Ask questions about how the platforms work and what they are doing.
- Voice outrage when user trust and expectations are breached.
- If you see something on a platform that seems unlawful, or inconsistent with the company's standards, report it.
- Don't share dubious content.
- Vote with your clicks—reject platforms that betray their responsibilities to society.

Giants Walk the Earth

The sheer size and reach of the tech companies is one reason why no civic-minded citizen should look away. Seventy-two percent of American adults use some form of social media and sixty-eight percent rely on social media as their prime source for news. Among young adults, the proportions are even higher. Opting out of online discourse is not a realistic option for those whose social and professional lives depend on the digital realm.

Even more jaw-dropping than these statistics are those detailing online platforms' revenues, profits, and rates of growth.

SOCIAL MEDIA REVENUES (2018)

- Alphabet Inc. (Google): $137 billion
- Facebook: $56 billion
- Twitter: $3 billion

The nine top publicly traded traditional news media companies (including News Corporation, the *New York Times,* Tribune, and others as ranked by Investopedia) had a combined market capitalization of just $23 billion, about 3 percent of Alphabet's. These companies exert control over our speech—and our lives—and we have a duty to pay attention to what they're up to and insist that they wield their vast power responsibly.

Platform, Police Thyself

The track record of these companies in addressing matters of public concern is generally poor. In 2016, tech reporter Charlie Warzel detailed a decade of evasions and inaction by Twitter's leadership in response to the spiraling problem of online trolling. Despite numerous exposés and policy updates, trolls and hate groups still flourish on the site. "We suck at dealing with abuse and trolls on the platform," conceded Twitter's former CEO, "and we've sucked at it for years." PEN America has documented the pervasiveness of trolling on Twitter and other forums, particularly targeting women and people of color who attract hostility from racists, misogynists, white supremacists, and ideological antagonists. While part of the excuse for inaction may lie in a justifiable reluctance to police speech,

that doesn't explain why the platform has failed to implement technical measures—such as modifying Twitter's "lists" function, which can
be used to enable wholesale harassment of entire categories of users. This
track record of passivity in the face of harms wrought by the platforms
goes well beyond trolling. Whistle-blowers at Facebook and Google have
disclosed litanies of malfeasance and ineptitude involving grand-scale
violations of user privacy, intrusive surveillance, defiance of government
orders to protect user data, and security breaches. Privacy infringements
can undercut free expression by making users fear that their opinions and
searches may come back to haunt them. Despite its immense power and
sweeping social implications, the Internet ranks among the least regulated
industries in the entire U.S. economy. The idea that Internet platforms
can simply be trusted to do what's best for the public on their own initiative is fantasy.

Yet because the First Amendment would bar government from making or enforcing content-specific rules for most of the categories of online
expression, we have little choice but to depend on responsible, voluntary
content moderation by the platforms. The bottom line is that we need
companies to step up and do far more to prevent and redress the harms of
online content, but they must do so in ways that maximize protection for
free expression and address head-on the flaws and gaps manifest in current content moderation schemes.

While this will be a multipronged, multiyear effort there are five principal areas that warrant focus:

1. increased transparency;
2. meaningful accountability for malfeasance and negligence;
3. respect for international human rights law and norms;
4. adequate redress for individuals who are harmed, including
   through the unwarranted suppression of their speech;
5. credible and empowered external oversight.

One of the biggest obstacles to taming the negative impact of Big
Tech on our discourse is that so much of their decision making occurs in
secret. Without more transparency about what speech is being suppressed,

why, and with what consequence, it's impossible to judge the companies' behavior. The companies may view this opacity as an advantage, in that it throttles public debate, impedes research, and defeats accountability. Some methods of content moderation compound the problem. Increasingly, instead of removing entirely content that skirts platform rules, the companies *demote* problematic posts, limiting how often they are seen but without excising them entirely. While perhaps preferable to out-and-out deletion, this system creates a shadowy realm of quasi-censorship that is almost invisible to users. Websites may observe sharp reductions in traffic due to tweaks by Google, Facebook, or other referring sites, but usually cannot find out why their content was downgraded nor what they can do about it. Most ordinary users have no way to know whether a tweet or post failed to get traction because it was simply unexciting or because— unbeknownst to them—it was demoted and never saw the light of day. Shadow banning is the practice of suppressing social media users so that, without their being notified, their posts and comments cannot be seen by others.

Demotions and shadow bans tend to be based on unpublished rules rather than official guidelines. Companies sometimes argue that such obfuscation is necessary so that malevolent actors will not game content detection. But users have a right to know what boundaries are being policed. If boundaries are invisible and content that veers close to them is surreptitiously suppressed, the playing field for expression becomes substantially narrowed. Moreover, sophisticated propagandists and political operatives have managed to manipulate the platforms thoroughly as is, calling into question whether all the secrecy is actually protecting anything.

The Santa Clara Principles, developed by open-expression advocates in 2018, offer one blueprint to expand disclosures and enable greater public accountability. They call on companies to reveal how many posts are removed, provide notice and an explanation to anyone whose content is taken down or account is suspended, and to create an accessible appeals process. If adopted, these principles would substantially improve platform transparency. Transparency, in turn, would facilitate expert and public debate on the limits of permissible online content, ensuring that Silicon

Valley is not deciding in a vacuum. Opening the process to wider scrutiny and participation would also address concerns of politicization and bias toward the powerful in content moderation.

Additional recommendations come from UN Special Rapporteur on Freedom of Expression David Kaye, who argues that the companies should issue public statements with rationales accompanying all changes to their content policies. Such disclosure would allow users and experts to not just monitor the implementation of content rules, but help shape them. Kaye also recommends that companies' decisions on content be assembled into a cumulative jurisprudence of online content moderation that would be open for analysis. This would include specifying whether content was removed at the request of a government or pursuant to a company's own rules, and why. A bank of evolving, publicly available written decisions on content would help foster reasoned evaluation, facilitate research, and allow the public to meaningfully weigh in. Kaye's proposal could be expanded to reveal the methods used to detect and adjudicate the impermissible content, allowing for greater scrutiny of the benefits of reliance on human versus automated moderation.

BENEFITS OF MORE TRANSPARENT CONTENT MODERATION

- Greater user input and public debate
- Increased predictability in how rules are implemented
- Errors of judgment could be more easily identified and rectified
- Researchers and analysts could play a larger role in interpreting online content trends and help recognize and address problems

Perhaps the most far-reaching, elusive facet of content moderation occurs passively through algorithmic amplification of content that elicits the most user engagement. Many analysts have argued that the fundamental driver of Internet platforms—user activity that can support advertising and transaction revenues—inherently privileges the most dangerous and divisive types of content, particularly on social media. They point out that white supremacist, misogynist, and politically polarizing content has surged in the digital era because of the way algorithms are calibrated to serve us the content we are most likely to view and share. The platforms themselves don't actively promote specific content but instead allow the algorithms to work their will, prioritizing content only by click- and shareworthiness and paying no attention to whether the expression is lofty or lecherous. While platforms suppress particular types of content (muting or muffling it to counteract amplification, in effect), it is not clear that they have done enough to address the algorithmic propensity to prioritize content that hits sensitive societal nerves. This most thorny and important aspect of content moderation needs to be opened up to far greater scrutiny and debate over the values that inform how algorithms prioritize. Platforms must allow researchers to probe how content moves and escalates across populations, how it correlates with offline actions, and how well countermeasures, including downgrading, fact checking, and algorithmic adjustments, work to counteract it.

Mandated transparency is one area where government regulation of online content may be a positive step and would not entail viewpoint-specific intrusions on content in violation of the First Amendment. Past practice suggests that the only way to get companies to provide meaningful transparency may be to require it by law.

Meaningful Accountability for Malfeasance and Negligence

Since the passage of the Communications Decency Act in 1996, Internet companies have enjoyed immunity from liability for content posted by users. A newspaper or a magazine that publishes defamatory or libelous material can be sued but Google, Facebook, or Twitter cannot. Section 230 of the act provides that websites can't be held legally accountable for content that others create on their platform. While violations of criminal and intellectual property laws can be pursued, those whose privacy or reputation is damaged have no remedy against the hosting platform. The legislators who established the immunity were concerned about a trend in court decisions whereby platforms were more likely to be treated by courts like publishers for liability purposes if they had made editorial or filtering decisions regarding the content they hosted as opposed to just offering users a free-for-all to post anything they chose. Such rulings created the "perverse upshot" that a website "faced a much higher risk of liability if it failed to eliminate all defamatory material than if it simply didn't try to control or edit the content of third parties at all." By immunizing websites from liability even when they exercised editorial judgment, Section 230 allowed these sites to host all kinds of content without worrying about whether it violated the law. Section 230 imagines online platforms to be like cell phone providers, not newspapers. We don't hold a wireless company responsible for the content of messages transmitted on its service, even if they are used to plot a criminal conspiracy. But a publisher who printed and distributed a call to imminent violence could be held accountable. With a few narrow carve-outs for copyright law, federal criminal law, child pornography, and sex trafficking, Section 230 dictates that platforms be treated as though they have no control over the content they host.

Free speech groups have supported Section 230 as a safeguard for unfettered online speech. If every Facebook post or tweet had to undergo libel vetting, the Internet as we know it would not exist. On the other hand, this protection now allows oceans of illegal, immoral, and dangerous content to wash ashore. One of the foremost hurdles to getting online platforms to take more seriously their obligation to mitigate harms is the absence of threatened legal liability. To counter this, several analysts have begun to call for reform of Section 230.

While advocates are right to insist on extreme caution in any tinkering with the legal foundation of the Internet, creating an online content moderation system that better fosters open discourse may require some reexamination of Section 230 to increase the incentive of online platforms to come to grips with some of the harms their services enable. One simple suggestion would be to retract the immunity for content that is paid for by either the platform or the user. This would reflect the idea that companies should assume different levels of responsibility depending on whether they are simply algorithmic hosts to content versus business partners of the content purveyor. This could help address the risks posed by, for example, democracy-distorting political ads and paid campaigns, while protecting the vast bulk of online content from any new form of intervention.

Legal experts Danielle Citron and Benjamin Wittes have argued that courts have applied Section 230 immunity far more broadly than lawmakers intended, particularly insofar as it shelters even platforms that knowingly provide venues for unlawful activity. Citron and Wittes argue that companies that implement reasonable monitoring mechanisms to address lawless activity should be held blameless if those efforts fall short, but that those that foster or invite unlawful online activity, or make no effort to prevent it, should be stripped of immunity. Fordham University law professor Olivier Sylvain has made a similar argument, focusing particularly on the ways that Section 230 has allowed the development of an online sphere that reinforces the vulnerability of women, children, and racial minorities. He cites examples including gossip sites that allow the anonymous posting of images of underage girls, social media sites that allow men to lure teenagers into situations of sexual assault, online commercial platforms that enable exclusions of minorities and older people from seeing certain job or housing ads, and online harassment that disproportionately targets women and people of color.

New approaches may be necessary to clarify the terms of Section 230 immunity and put more focus on whether companies have exercised appropriate care in the various roles they play. Any reforms must be carefully crafted to avoid a perverse incentive for companies to err on the side of content removal for fear of lawsuits and fines. But by introducing some risk of liability, a change in how Section 230 is implemented could incentivize companies to beef up content moderation, investing in better-qualified personnel, and elaborating the rationales for decisions.

Allegiance to International Human Rights Law

Another proposal that would bring needed rigor to online content moderation would be a commitment by companies to comply with international human rights law. This would involve two elements: conforming companies' own content moderation rules to international human rights precepts and utilizing human rights rules to push back against national content regulations that are overly restrictive. While companies are not themselves subject to the international human rights laws applicable to nation-states, the UN has ratified guiding principles that urge companies to avoid interference with those rights. Conforming content moderation practices to international human rights precepts would require following the formula set out in Article 19 of the ICCPR, which mandates that content can be restricted only (1) when pursuant to an articulated and sufficiently specific law (or, in the case of a private company, a standard or rule); (2) when the constraint is the least intrusive means of achieving the goal in question, and (3) when that goal serves the public interest. Such an approach would tighten up content moderation practices by putting the burden on companies to publicly articulate all the content moderation rules they follow. It would also require them to rigorously pursue solutions that minimize the impairment of speech (for example, better blocking tools to defend users against trolling or harassment, as opposed to banning such content). A more formal effort to evaluate and articulate whether content moderation rules serve the public interest (as opposed to, for example, advertiser demands) would also be a step in the right direction.

When it comes to fending off censorious national content regimes, a simple proclamation by companies that they intend to abide by international human rights law will not wish away contrary governmental regulations. A social media company that cited international law in declining to take down satirical posts deemed to be hateful speech in Germany would still face stiff fines. Such an undertaking would, however, give companies a concrete, principled basis on which to resist government overreach, including the repression of dissent and censorship of disfavored views. Companies may also gradually recognize that they have more leverage than they realize to withstand government demands that contravene international human rights standards. Given the platforms' popularity, political leaders are reluctant to trigger the uproar that results from shutting them down.

The idea that international human rights law provides a useful global reference point to guide content moderation is slowly taking hold. In 2018, Twitter CEO Jack Dorsey said that the company's values needed to be rooted in human rights law. A year later, Facebook announced that in weighing the public interest value of content against the risk that it could cause harm, the company would hereafter "look to international human rights standards."

Redress for Harms, Including Infringements on Speech

To better guarantee that an evolving Internet continues to respect freedom of speech, Internet companies and civil society organizations should come together to establish a robust global system for content defense. Given growing momentum to remove harmful content from online platforms, the flaws in both human and algorithmic methods of evaluating content, and the many novel questions that arise, such a function is necessary to ensure that, as companies take responsibility for cleaning up their platforms, expressive rights remain intact.

With a reliable, universally accessible, and publicly accountable system to ensure that erroneous content removals could be quickly reversed, the prospect of companies becoming more aggressive with policing their platforms would be less worrisome. We would have a fail-safe to address the inevitable false positives quickly enough so that the impairment to free speech resulting from content moderation would be minimized (though, admittedly, not eliminated).

Such a system would bear some resemblance to a series of different mechanisms that are familiar and perform somewhat analogous functions in other realms. Think of the services we contact when our credit card is unexpectedly declined at a point of sale. Alert to fraud, credit card companies have become quick to disable charges that trigger a flag, either because they occur in an unexpected geography or due to the suspicious nature or patterns of expenditures. Inevitably, a good deal of these declines are unwarranted—we use our credit cards when traveling and, every so often, we splurge. When this happens, though, it takes only a phone call to a toll-free number—and some inevitable and agonizing wait time—to get the matter resolved.

A similar type of service should operate for content. If an account is disabled or an individual post is flagged for deletion or demotion, the account holder should be notified immediately. Available via a customer service line should be a Public Content Defender, empowered to examine straightforward cases and, where appropriate, overrule disablings, take-downs, or demotions of content in collaboration with the platform in question so that your service can be restored "while you wait." Every report should be logged and given a tracking number (think FedEx or UPS) so that you can look online and understand exactly what has been done on your case and where it stands.

The service should have available experts on staff to deal with more complex cases or those that raise novel issues including changes in community standards or terms of service that impinge on expressive rights. For such cases, the Public Content Defenders should be equipped to deploy high-level advocates able to marshal research, expert testimony, and novel theories in defense of content, as would a public defender representing a client in a court of appeals.

The cost of the Public Content Defender Service should be borne by online platforms, perhaps in proportion to the number of claims filed in relation to their services. They should commit up front to the creation of a significant pool of funds from which settlements and compensatory payments can be made to individuals whose expressive rights are violated. The Content Defender Service would need to be resourced to enable straightforward determinations to be made and communicated in Internet time.

While the initial focus of the service would relate to claims of content unfairly removed or suppressed, it might eventually also address claims of individuals who believe that certain content (for example, nude pictures or a defamatory message) should be removed for violating companies' terms of service or local law. It could augment current "flagging" systems by offering expert assistance to mount more complex claims and by ensuring that such claims can be tracked. But the main initial purpose of such a service would be to mitigate the risk that more assertive content moderation strategies—demanded to curtail harmful speech in particular categories—avoid encroaching on legitimate content. By empowering users with expert assistance to challenge contestable determinations, such a service would balance out considerations of mitigating harm with the importance of preserving freedom of expression. By operating independently and transparently, the service would also provide a check on the unfettered power and discretion of the companies.

Online platforms are unique in that the level of service they offer today to consumers is virtually nil. If companies are committed to owning up to their responsibilities as venues for public discourse, they need a massive build-out of user service arms that rectify this lack of accessibility. Though they may not pay to use the service in the same way as customers in a retail store, users have immense value to platforms, making it worthwhile to keep them satisfied and respect their rights. The creation of an independent Content Defender Service and corresponding user service departments would go a long way toward helping allay concerns that the platforms governing so much of our discourse care little about our rights and needs.

Content Review Boards

In November 2018, Mark Zuckerberg announced that Facebook was examining the creation of an independent expert body to hear users' appeals of content removal decisions. The idea for a so-called Supreme Court of Facebook—the company prefers the term "oversight board"—originated with Harvard law professor Noah Feldman, who initially pitched the concept to Facebook chief operating officer Sheryl Sandberg and then helped develop the idea. The oversight board's purpose would be to "uphold the principle of giving people a voice while also recognizing the reality of keeping people safe," and its decisions would be "transparent and binding." In September 2019, the company set out a charter for the board providing that it would be composed of up to forty members, representing diverse nationalities and areas of expertise. The board is to have authority to request information from Facebook to facilitate its deliberations, to interpret Facebook's policies, and to instruct Facebook to allow or remove content, including by reversing the company's decisions. To enhance Facebook's public accountability, the board will need a series of powers and protections.

If the proposed board is prevented from wading into content-related matters that are of grave concern to users on the basis of corporate security, privacy, or technical constraints, it will quickly earn a reputation as feckless. If the board works only after the fact and is unable to weigh in on pressing issues in real time, it may be seen as irrelevant. Overall, though, the effort to engage diverse expertise to inform and mediate content moderation decisions is welcome.

Another proposal is for industry-wide rather than company-specific self-regulation. Just as in some countries media companies have established press councils to promote journalistic ethics and receive complaints over unfair coverage, so the tech companies could create "social media councils" for the same purpose. To the extent such proposals formalize input, consultation, and influence for qualified experts in shaping content moderation decisions, they represent a step in the right direction.

One of the biggest changes being discussed is the breakup of the tech giants, either through antitrust enforcement action (some of which is under way) or legislation. The implications of the forced breakup of Google and Facebook into smaller entities might lead to a wider array of distinct sets of content standards online. There may be merit in having a greater breadth of platforms deciding where to draw the lines on content, offering consumers more choice among the content rules they opt to live within. But ultimately, if the companies are to balance mitigating the worst harms of online content and unduly impairing free expression, it will be because users, citizens, and civil society groups pushed them to do so.

HOW TO HOLD TECH COMPANIES ACCOUNTABLE FOR THEIR INFLUENCE ON PUBLIC DISCOURSE

- Demand greater transparency in terms of content moderation policies and their implementation
- Consider reforms to platforms immunity from liability for content
- Press platforms to adhere to international human rights laws
- Push for the establishment of a Public Content Defender
- Support greater oversight for content moderation

20.

Know the Case for Free Speech

BECAUSE AMERICANS OFTEN THINK OF FREE SPEECH AS SYNONYMOUS with the First Amendment, discussions of why it matters can center on the Constitution and Bill of Rights—effectively an argument that "free speech matters because the Founders said so." But when James Madison drafted the Bill of Rights, he wasn't inventing new rights but rather codifying liberties that were thought to be inherent in individuals, and that this new American society and government should be bound to respect. While modern defenders of free speech don't need to be experts on philosophy, it is worth reviewing why leading scholars, thinkers, and leaders have hewed to free speech as a bedrock of open and democratic societies, and to inventory the ways in which free speech benefits our lives both individually and collectively. Free speech is not without its risks, demands, and sometimes harmful side effects. That makes it all the more important to keep sight of—and be able to explain—the reasons why we protect and treasure it.

A survey of the reasons for defending free speech also reminds us that keeping speech free means more than getting government out of the way. The concerns that underlie our commitment to free speech are at stake when speech is silenced in everyday life or suppressed on social media, when certain voices are excluded from the debate, or when the weight of self-censorship suffocates controversial but important ideas. If we remind ourselves why we are protecting free speech in the first place, those rationales compel us to go further than simply enforcing the First Amendment's prohibition on government interference to consider the myriad ways in which free speech must be defended and supported in daily life.

American notions of free speech have their roots in the ancient Athenian concepts of *isegoria* and *parrhesia,* both roughly translated today as "freedom of speech," but carrying distinct meanings. *Isegoria* referred to the universal right to speak out in public settings and try to persuade fellow citizens to a point of view. *Parrhesia* was less about who was speaking than what they were free to say. It covered speech outside the political assembly, including in the theater, and encompassed a right to provoke and offend. The concept made space for the biting satirical plays of Aristophanes, but did not protect Socrates from being poisoned to death for challenging the sanctity of the gods and purportedly corrupting Athenian youth. *Parrhesia* was a less stable privilege, which could be revoked at will by mercurial rulers or thugs, as when fellow citizens would "shout down or even drag speakers they disliked" off a speaker's platform (an ancient version of "no platforming").

Although it did not specifically protect free speech or expression, the Magna Carta is considered a landmark in the history of the freedom of speech in that it established the idea of individual liberty and the notion that everyone, including the king, was subject to the law. In his 1644 "Areopagitica," John Milton argued against prepublication censorship of books on the grounds that readers ought to be free to confront and reject bad ideas on their own. British philosopher John Locke's 1689 "Letter Concerning Toleration" focused on freedom of religion but established the principle that a functioning society need not mandate a common set of beliefs and that toleration for heterodox opinions could ameliorate rather than foster conflict. Nearly seventy-five years later French philosopher Voltaire published his 1763 "Treatise on Tolerance," arguing for religious pluralism and against fanaticism.

Here in the United States, the 1735 trial of newspaper printer John Peter Zenger, in which Zenger's defense against an accusation of seditious libel by a New York governor was based on the truth of the facts published, became a landmark in establishing public appreciation for the value of a free press. The Bill of Rights in the U.S. Constitution adopted affirmative protections for freedom of speech and the press from government intrusion. After World War I, these provisions were reinterpreted to form the speech-protective regime that governs today. Freedom of speech is a broadly recognized liberty in Western democracies, and the UN Universal Declaration of Human Rights, adopted in 1948, enshrines rights to freedom of thought, conscience, religion, opinion, expression, peaceful assembly, and association.

Though the conceptual and legal underpinnings of free speech relate mostly to curtailing the power of government relative to individual rights, the early Athenian notions of free speech are more encompassing, elaborating that individuals have an affirmative right to participate in public life and to express dissent. The case in favor of free speech goes above and beyond the rationale for limiting government encroachments on expression. It also implies affirmative steps to make sure all individuals and groups have the means and opportunity to be heard. If free speech matters, we need to ask not only whether the government is respecting it, but whether individuals feel able to exercise it in daily life. The nature of the societal advantages of free speech help explain why it is not enough to define free speech simply as the right to be shielded from government interference. To unleash both the individual and the collective benefits of free speech requires the creation of an enabling environment for a broad array of speech and a public discourse open to all.

Free Speech as a Route to Truth

A principal rationale for protecting free speech is to promote the discovery of truth. In "Areopagitica," Milton wrote, "Though all the winds of doctrine were let loose to play upon the earth, so Truth be in the field, we do injuriously, by licensing and prohibiting, to misdoubt her strength. Let her and Falsehood grapple; who ever knew Truth put to the worse in a free and open encounter?" Justice Oliver Wendell Holmes famously elaborated this justification in his dissent in *Abrams v. United States* in 1919, where he introduced the metaphor of a "marketplace of ideas": "[T]he best test of truth," Holmes wrote, "is the power of the thought to get itself accepted in the competition of the market."

Holmes's premise is that a free exchange of ideas, hotly debated, is the most efficient and reliable way to sort through what is wise and foolish, true and false. Barriers to open exchange such as government censorship or the punishment of dissent would obstruct the natural propensity of good ideas to win out, as well as stifling the spirit of open inquiry, which produces new and original thoughts. John Stuart Mill embraced the truth-promotion rationale for free speech in *On Liberty,* decrying censorship for the twin evils of suppressing new and valid ideas and impairing society's ability to refine its discernment of truth by witnessing the encounter of veracity and falsehood.

University of Virginia law professor Frederick Schauer has further developed the truth-finding theory with an account of how the competition of ideas can promote the discovery of truth, even when the public may not be consistently capable of separating truth from falsehood. Schauer theorizes that the role of the public at large is to provide an endless bounty of ideas and concepts that are then filtered by people with specialized knowledge and expertise that enables them to detect the truth in specific areas. "Although the public may not be the body to identify most effectively sound policies and true statements," Schauer writes, "its size and diversity make it the ideal body to *offer* the multitude of ideas that are the fuel of the engine for advancing knowledge."

Freedom of Speech Is Essential to Self-Government

Another major reason to keep speech free is that it is essential to self-government. In a democracy, where government is "of, by, and for the people," free debate is necessary to ensure both that the public can consider all arguments and that the popular will is ultimately reflected in the choice of leaders. James Madison, who authored the First Amendment, made this case in arguing against the Sedition Act, which the governing Federalist Party passed in 1798 during a conflict with France. Madison argued that the act, which criminalized "false, scandalous and malicious" criticism of the government, violated the First Amendment's function of "binding the hands of the federal government from touching the channel which alone can give efficacy to its responsibility to its constituents."

Jurists returned to this rationale often over time. In his concurrence in the 1919 case of *Whitney v. California,* Justice Louis Brandeis opined that "the greatest menace to freedom is an inert people; that public discussion is a political duty, and that this should be a fundamental principle of the American government." University of Chicago legal scholar Harry Kalven crisply summarized the "essential to self-government" rationale in his comment on the 1964 *New York Times v. Sullivan* case, where he stated that "defamation of the government is an impossible notion for a democracy. . . . Political freedom ends when government can use its powers and its courts to silence its critics."

Philosopher Alexander Meiklejohn, one of the great free-speech theorists of the early twentieth century, was a prime proponent of the self-governance rationale for free speech, emphasizing that free speech rights mattered as much if not more to the democratic polity as a whole as they did to the individual rights holder. Analogizing to a town meeting, Meiklejohn argued that the First Amendment did not mandate "unregulated talkativeness" but rather could be interpreted to allow for controls that would ensure orderly and open discussion, as long as no speaker could be denied a hearing "because we disagree with what he intends to say." Meiklejohn's ideas have been relied on to argue in favor of constraints on corporate campaign donations as distorting an open and fair marketplace for political deliberation.

At first blush, it might seem as if protecting free speech to guarantee its role as a requisite for democracy and a check on government power might require simply warding off intrusions by government on the individual liberty to speak out. But today's political discourse reveals a variety of factors outside government itself that affect the vitality of our political deliberations, from political disinformation to the underrepresentation of certain racial groups in newsrooms. For free speech to serve its purpose in enabling self-government, its defenders must look at the full range of factors that allow for and impede that objective.

Freedom of Speech Promotes Tolerance and Reduces Violence

Another principle animating the protection of expression is that robust free speech promotes civic character, helping to nurture citizens who are more tolerant, more willing to engage opposing viewpoints, and less prone to lash out with violence and fear. Columbia Law School professor Vincent Blasi describes this rationale as rooted in the "ideal of civic courage," and an "engaged, confident, innovative citizenship." This premise is one of several tenets in Justice Brandeis's concurrence in *Whitney*, which Blasi credits with establishing "the conviction that the essential character of a political community is both revealed and defined by how it responds to the challenge of threatening ideas." As Brandeis wrote in *Whitney*:

> Fear of serious injury cannot alone justify suppression of free speech and assembly. Men feared witches and burnt women. It is the function of speech to free men from the bondage of irrational fears.

This motivation for the defense of free speech values the distinctive character that exposure to open discourse inculcates in the citizenry, a mind-set that deals with disfavored viewpoints not with panic, but rather by engaging them in vigorous, reasoned debate.

The "civic courage" rationale resonates powerfully today, particularly in relation to debates over speech on college campuses. In a diverse society, you will inevitably confront some ideas you do not like, and the more equipped you are to handle and respond to them, the better.

Free Speech as Essential to Personal Autonomy

A fourth rationale for free speech—and more broadly, free expression—is its role in the development and manifestation of personal autonomy. The notion here is that the freedom to speak is intertwined with the freedom to be yourself, make your own decisions, and live as you choose. This also encompasses freedom of conscience and belief—the liberty to think and value what you choose. This rationale is linked to the freedom of individuals to reflect their sexual preferences and gender identity, a set of expressive rights that are inextricably interwoven with individuals' ability to live as they wish and be who they are within society. In societies where being gay is punishable by law, the most fundamental freedom to express oneself is denied. Supreme Court justice Anthony Kennedy embraced a capacious concept of constitutionally protected liberty that included personal dignity and self-fulfillment. Kennedy cited George Orwell's *1984* in his opinion in *United States v. Alvarez* (2012) in which the court overturned on First Amendment grounds a criminal conviction for an individual who had lied about having been awarded the Congressional Medal of Honor. Kennedy referred to *1984* in saying, "Our constitutional tradition stands against the idea that we need Oceania's Ministry of Truth." He warned of granting government "a broad censorial power" whose potential exercise casts "a chill the First Amendment cannot permit if free speech, thought, and discourse are to remain a foundation of our freedom."

Free Speech as a Catalyst for Progress

Free speech has also been recognized as a catalyst for a range of social goods. One of the most canonical arguments for freedom of speech appears in Galileo's 1615 "Letter to the Grand Duchess Christina of Tuscany," in which he defends the doctrines of Copernicus against religious and political censure. Galileo argues that God would not have endowed humankind with the powers of reason and judgment had he not intended for scientists to use them in an unbounded quest for knowledge.

Legal scholars have also recognized the importance of free speech as a prerequisite for scientific progress. In 1979, Northwestern's James R. Ferguson argued against proposed state and federal legislation that aimed to control areas of scientific inquiry out of concerns for public security, safety, and morality. Ferguson argued that the history of scientific thought and human progress has rewarded societies that allowed knowledge to be disseminated even if "it conflicted with central assumptions of received tradition," as in the epistemic shifts effected by Copernicus, Galileo, and Darwin.

Economists have long argued that freedom of speech and related protections stimulate innovation and economic prosperity. Harvard's Amartya Sen has argued that human rights, including protections for free speech, help boost economic development, income, and growth. He points out that lack of respect for freedom of expression can foster political volatility, clouding the investment environment and lowering returns. Economics researcher Adam Millsap has written about the role of innovation and entrepreneurship in driving economic growth for developed economies, positing that the free exchange of ideas and opportunity to meet and debate with others is what spurs fresh thinking and creative breakthroughs.

Some analysts have pointed out that China's dramatic and sustained economic expansion in recent decades runs counter to this theory. While many Western critics predicted that Chinese expansion would be impaired by its tight restrictions on individual freedom, the statistics and trend lines have not born that out. Sen argues that China's authoritarian ascent is attributable to wise decisions on the part of Beijing's leadership to prioritize addressing hunger and illiteracy, thereby sustaining the support of its population. He cautions that leaders who are not held accountable by a free populace empowered to speak its mind are subject to an "inescapable fragility" in that when they take policies in a destructive direction—such as during China's Great Famine in 1959–62—their closed and brittle political system is unable to surface the problems and correct course. As of this writing mass protests over the fate of democracy in Hong Kong are exposing those vulnerabilities, forcing a protracted stand-off between a restive freedom-loving population and a ruling government whose authority and effectiveness are grounded in repression.

Free speech is also a catalyst for artistic expression and creativity. Many now-classic works of art, literature, and film faced censorship or social opprobrium in their own time but earn our admiration today precisely because they shattered the existing boundaries of what was deemed proper or acceptable. Accordingly, courts have long recognized that, alongside political speech, artistic expression merits a degree of special deference when it comes to the exceptions to First Amendment protection such as obscenity. Legal scholar Edward J. Eberle has explicated the distinctive character of artistic expression as a vehicle for exploring ideas that may be out of reach in more traditional discourse. He writes that art "addresses aspects of human life that are difficult to reach or, even, ordinarily beyond comprehension; and constitutes a domain of freedom beyond the normal rules of society . . . art speech furthers the pursuit of truth, constitutes self-realization, checks entrenched power, and acts as a safety valve to diffuse tension." At a time of tensions over offensive speech, art offers a vehicle to explore provocative or contrarian ideas that can be high-risk when voiced within mainstream discourse.

Foundation for All Other Freedoms

Free speech is the foundation for all other rights. If we did not enjoy the freedom to write, speak, publish, assemble, and protest, the great movements for reproductive freedom, racial justice, environmental accountability, immigrants' rights, and other essential causes would be hamstrung. Every major manifestation of social progress—passage of civil rights laws, women's suffrage, environmental protection, gay marriage, and countless other examples—was driven forward by the exercise of protected speech: people who voiced ideas that were novel and debatable and used their powers of persuasion to win gradual support. This notion that freedom of speech is a foundational right, a fount out of which all other freedoms flow, is codified in Supreme Court case law in the words of Justice

Benjamin Cardozo, who refers to it in *Palko v. Connecticut* (1937) as "that freedom [of which] one may say that it is the matrix, the indispensable condition, of nearly every other form of freedom."

For progressives who may be confounded by the power of free speech to protect the expression of retrograde attitudes, it is worth remembering that, historically speaking, free speech precepts have been invoked most often and most powerfully to shield dissenters and change makers from the heavy hand of government.

A long litany of famous Supreme Court cases have involved left-leaning speech. The 1943 case *West Virginia State Board of Education v. Barnette* rejected the government's claim that it could compel students to recite the Pledge of Allegiance against their conscience. The court also protected the rights of antiwar expression and similar political statements in *Tinker v. Des Moines Independent School District,* which protected high school students' rights to wear black armbands or execute other forms of protest of the Vietnam War. First Amendment jurisprudence also involved social justice issues on the question of the individuals' right to privacy, as in the 1965 case of *Griswold v. Connecticut,* the successful culmination of years of challenges to the 1879 statute that had made birth control illegal. In *Texas v. Johnson* in 1989, the court made explicit that burning a United States flag in protest against the government (in that instance outside the Republican National Convention) was a protected form of free speech and could not be prohibited. Time and again the United States' robust free speech protections have been invoked to safeguard liberal activists and movements from efforts at suppression.

The distinct rationales for free speech are interlacing. It is individual autonomy that allows for the free thought that can expose falsehoods and uncover truths. The instantiation of civic courage is what makes possible the kinds of open political deliberations that democracy requires. Different rationales for free speech may have greater or lesser resonance depending on whether you are a scientist, a member of a fringe political party, an artist, a scholar, or a journalist. We don't all have to be in complete agreement about *why* free speech must be defended as long as these and other arguments, in totality, convince us that it *must* be defended.

WHY WE DEFEND FREE SPEECH IN THE FIRST PLACE

- Free speech enables society to uncover truth
- Free speech promotes tolerance and lessens violence
- Free speech is essential to individual autonomy, identity, and self-actualization
- Protections for free speech foster economic prosperity, scientific progress, and creative achievement
- Safeguards for free speech have been essential to virtually every form of social progress attained by democracies

ACKNOWLEDGMENTS

I COULD NOT HAVE COMPLETED THIS PROJECT WITHOUT THE HELP AND SUP-
port of coworkers, family, and friends. I am grateful to my colleagues
at PEN America for helping to navigate and illuminate the rocky landscape of free speech at a time of rising threats. Summer Lopez, Tom Me-
lia, Nora Benavidez, James Tager, Stephen Fee, Polina Kovaleva, Karin
Karlekar, and Viktorya Vilk have helped me time and again to puzzle
through difficult questions. Katie Zanecchia, Rebecca Werner, Praise
Apampa, Michelle Franke, Stephen Fee, Chip Rolley, Shawnna Jannah,
Madison Gonzalez, Clarisse Rosaz Shariyf, Deborah Wilson, Julie Tre-
bault, and many others have been unfailingly supportive and enthusiastic through the contortions required to get this book done. Jonathan
Friedman provided invaluable comments on the manuscript, drawing
from his excellent work leading our campus speech program since 2018.
PEN America COO Dru Menaker filled in for me during a month of
book leave and is a heroic and treasured intellectual and professional
partner. If the expertise, dedication, and passion of the PEN America
staff is any indication, free speech has a bright future. I am also grateful
to former colleagues, including PEN America alumni, partners in the
human rights field, and coworkers at the U.S. State Department and
elsewhere who have been valued collaborators on the issues addressed in
this book.

Deepest thanks go to the PEN America Board of Trustees, Executive
Committee, and especially President Jennifer Egan, for their unflagging
support for this project, including reading through the manuscript. Mi-

chael Pietsch has been a very patient, thoughtful adviser on all things book publishing.

My work on this book was enabled by exceptional assistance with research. Rumur Dowling is brilliant, diligent, meticulous, and indefatigable. Despite meeting only once in person, we worked together seamlessly and his contributions to this book were boundless. Paul Barker provided superb, highly detailed, well-informed, and imaginative assistance with the legal chapters of the book.

I am extremely grateful to Floyd Abrams, Geoffrey Stone, Nadine Strossen, Evelyn Aswad, and Adeline Lee for providing expert, detailed, and thoughtful comments on the manuscript. I am also grateful to Eileen Donahoe, David Kaye, Dan Mogulof, John Witt, and Nicholas Christakis for their careful review of sections of the narrative. David Grann, Kyra Darnton, Joel Simon, and Dan Gerstein were unfailingly helpful with guidance and suggestions for research, writing, and presenting my ideas. Thanks to Michael Massing, James Traub, Dahlia Lithwick, and Matt Connelly for their insights. Some of the ideas of this book grew out of pieces published in the *Washington Post*, the *New York Times*, and Foreign Policy. I am grateful to editors, including Fred Hiatt, Adam Kushner, Clay Risen, Sasha Polakow-Suransky, Cameron Abadi, and their teams.

My agents, Larry Weissman and Sascha Alper, provided encouragement, incisive observations, and unflagging support throughout this project. During our first meeting my editor Alessandra Bastagli casually offered up a suggested structure for the book that turned it from a formless morass of examples and arguments into a coherent concept that I could actually imagine writing. She has been kind, generous, forgiving, and deeply committed throughout the process, driving things forward with determination and good cheer. The entire team at HarperCollins/ Dey Street, including Rosy Tahan, Tatiana Dubin, Heidi Richter, Kendra Newton, and Julie Paulauski, has brought energy and creativity to making the book all it could be.

Finally, thanks go to my family. We are very fortunate to have a wonderful, close extended family, including in-laws Bob and Maida Greenberg; Jonathan Greenberg; Megan Blumenreich; Hank Greenberg; Maggie Greenberg; Judith Greenberg; Ira Joseph; Claire Joseph; and Sasha Joseph as well as my sister, Ilana Nossel; Jordan Kolar; Noam, Ori, and Edan Kolar; and my brother, Deon Nossel. My mother, Renee Nossel, is the anchor of our family whose love and support have undergirded me my entire life. Working away in the evenings in his study at home, my late father, Hymie Nossel, provided a role model of exceptional professional discipline combined with infectious zeal for his work, which has guided me always and which I thought of often during the trying moments of writing and editing.

Finally, greatest thanks go to Leo and Liza Greenberg and David Greenberg. David has been a clear-eyed, insightful thought partner throughout my work in the field of free expression and has provided endless rounds of editing and polishing, making nearly every page and paragraph better. Our family's dinner-table talks, car and subway conversations, world travels, debate preparations, historical explorations, and never-ending dialogues on everything contributed to this book more than any other source. You are my life's greatest inspiration, comfort, and love.

NOTES

Chapter 1: Be Conscientious with Language

14 *special effects:* Jessica Wright, "Teen Blasted Out of Rod Laver after 'Timebomb' Tweet," *Sydney Morning Herald,* July 8, 2013.

15 *powerless to correct:* Jay Caspian Kang, "The Campaign to 'Cancel' Colbert," *The New Yorker,* March 30, 2014.

15 *"that's the game":* Jacque Reid, "So Funny It Hurts? Comedians Who Go Too Far," The Root, June 25, 2011.

16 *"the word 'primitive'":* "Readers Respond: Which Racial Terms Make You Cringe?" *New York Times,* April 2, 2017.

19 *anointed to replace:* Steven Pinker, "The Game of the Name," *New York Times,* April 5, 1994.

19 *to help erase:* Heather Kirn Lanier, "The R-Word," *The Sun,* May 2015.

19 *punch of the n-word:* Ibid.

19 *"Spread the Word to End the Word":* Todd Youngblood, "It's Time to Stop Saying the R-Word, and Everyone Needs to Play a Part," Huffington Post, May 4, 2015.

19 *many federal documents:* Luke Cyphers, "Meet the Little Girl Who Wiped Out Government Use of the R-Word," ESPN, July 20, 2015.

20 *the word "queer":* Michael M. Ego, "'Chink in the Armor': Is it a Racist Cliché?" AP News, October 27, 2018.

21 *Oriental medicine programs:* Jayne Tsuchiyama, "The Term 'Oriental' Is Outdated, but Is It Racist?" *Los Angeles Times,* June 1, 2016.

22 *"the thought that we hate":* Robert Barnes, "Supreme Court: Rejecting Trademarks That 'Disparage' Others Violates the First Amendment," *Washington Post,* June 19, 2017.

22 *"an unknown person, uncomfortable?":* Walter Mosley, "Why I Quit the Writers' Room," *New York Times,* September 6, 2019.

23 *"honor the pronoun choice":* Terry Gross, "Random House Copy Chief: Stand Tall, Wordsmiths! (But Choose Your Battles)," Public Radio Tulsa, February 5, 2019.

24 **winning wider recognition:** Suyin Haynes, "'Special Forces Change Language.' Merriam-Webster Adds Gender-Neutral Pronouns to Dictionary," *Time,* September 17, 2019.

Chapter 2: Fulfill a Duty of Care When Speaking

28 **culpability is heightened:** Keith N. Hylton, *Tort Law: A Modern Perspective* (Cambridge: Cambridge University Press, 2016), 102–21.

29 **duty of care applies:** Hylton, "Duty in Tort Law," *Fordham Law Review* 75, no. 3 (2006): 1501–28.

29 **among other categories:** Ibid.; Reynolds C. Setiz, "Legal Responsibility Under Tort Law of School Personnel and School Districts as Regards Negligent Conduct Toward Pupils," *Hastings Law Journal* 15, no. 4 (1964): 495–519; Vincent R. Johnson et al., "The Tort Duty of Parents to Protect Minor Children," *Villanova Law Review* 51, no. 2 (2006): 311–36.

30 **ouster as president:** Lois Romano, "Harvard President Resigns After Battling with Faculty," *SFGate,* February 22, 2006.

30 **women in the field:** Sarah Whitten et al., "Papa John's Founder John Schnatter Resigns as Chairman After Apologizing for N-Word Comment, Shares Surge," CNBC, July 12, 2018; Lara O'Reilly, "Saatchi & Saatchi Chairman Kevin Roberts Has Resigned Following His Controversial Gender Diversity Comments," Business Insider, August 3, 2016.

31 **dressing up as a character:** Tom Kludt, "Megyn Kelly Apologizes for Defending Blackface Halloween Costumes," CNN, October 25, 2018.

31 **axe her program:** John Koblin, "After Racist Tweet, Roseanne Barr's Show Is Cancelled by ABC," *New York Times,* May 29, 2018; Geoff Edgers, "Roseanne Barr Just Can't Shut Up," *Washington Post*, March 21, 2019.

32 **"a call to destroy anything or anyone":** Oliver Darcy, "CNN Severs Ties with Liberal Pundit Mark Lamont Hill After His Controversial Remarks on Israel," CNN, November 30, 2018.

32 **"assault on a people":** Alyssa Biederman, "What Does 'From the River to the Sea' Mean?" *Temple News,* December 4, 2018.

32 **"I am deeply sorry":** Marc Lamont Hill, "I'm Sorry My Word Choices Caused Harm," *Philadelphia Inquirer,* December 1, 2018.

33 **learning environment at Yale:** Christine Hauser, "A Yale Dean Lost Her Job After Calling People 'White Trash' in Yelp Reviews," *New York Times,* June 21, 2017.

33 **treat white students fairly:** Susan Svyluga, "After a Professor Wrote about Hating White People, Rutgers Considers the Limits of Free Speech," *Washington Post,* August 22, 2018.

34 **have legal representation:** Isaac Chotiner, "A Harvard Law School Professor Defends His Decision to Represent Harvey Weinstein," *The New Yorker,* March 7, 2019.

34 **the vocal students:** Shera S. Avi-Yonah, "'With Us or Against Us': Current, Former Winthrop Affiliates Say Faculty Deans Created a Toxic Environment Stretching Back Years," *Harvard Crimson,* May 10, 2019.

35 **culminated in Spellman's resignation:** Zaid Jilani, "Are College Students Really Against Free Speech?" Greater Good, October 12, 2018.

37 **"same identity group":** Kat Rosenfield, "What Is #OwnVoices Doing to Our Books?" Refinery29, April 9, 2019.

37 **one commentator taunted:** Ibid.

37 **stripped of its honorific star:** Alexandra Alter, "In an Era of Online Outrage, Do Sensitivity Readers Result in Better Books, or Censorship?" *New York Times,* December 24, 2017.

38 **"their way into bookstores":** Dhonielle Clayton, "Let's Talk About Sensitivity Readers," *Publishers Weekly,* January 12, 2018.

39 **"Imagine it, create it":** Toni Morrison, "Write, Erase, Do It Over," *NEA Arts Magazine,* no. 4 (2014).

Chapter 3: Find Ways to Express Difficult Ideas

43 **collapsed into violent trauma:** Saturday Night Live, "Dinner Conversation," filmed January 2018, YouTube.

44 **question of reparations:** Ta-Nehisi Coates, "The Case for Reparations," *The Atlantic,* June 2014.

44 **discussion on touchy topics:** Paul Bloom, *Against Empathy: The Case for Rational Compassion* (New York: Ecco, 2016).

45 **discredit him as anti-Semitic:** Andrew Sullivan, "How Should We Talk About the Israel Lobby's Power?" *New York,* March 8, 2019.

46 **genetically predetermined:** Fernando Racimo (FerRacimo), tweet, April 4, 2018, https://twitter.com/FerRacimo/status/981534568783253505.

46 **"when they are found":** David Reich, "How Genetics Is Changing Our Understanding of 'Race,'" *New York Times,* March 23, 2018.

46 **overlapping than he acknowledged:** Jonathan Kahn et al., "How Not to Talk About Race and Genetics," BuzzFeed News, March 30, 2018.

46 **same-sex sexual activity:** Pam Belluck, "Many Genes Influence Same-Sex Sexuality, Not a Single 'Gay Gene,'" *New York Times,* August 29, 2019.

47 **"set you free":** Andrew Solomon, "As I wrote earlier, this study will be controversial," Facebook, September 6, 2019.

Chapter 4: Defend the Right to Voice Unpopular Speech

49 **Evelyn Beatrice Hall:** Marjorie Garber, *Quotation Marks* (New York: Routledge, 2003), 20.

50 **"too easily offended these days":** Joanna Piacenza et al., "PC and Prejudice: Gauging Divides in America's Culture War," Morning Consult, April 24, 2019.

50   *justifiably be silenced:* John Stuart Mill, *On Liberty* (Indianapolis: Hackett, 1978), 15.

50   *"offensive or shocking to others":* Nani Jansen Reventlow, "The Right to 'Offend, Shock, or Disturb,' or the Importance of Protecting Unpleasant Speech," Berkman Klein Center, August 13, 2017.

51   *"these rights are guaranteed":* Jacob Mchangama, "We Need to Defend the Right to Offend," *National Review,* February 14, 2015.

51   *deemed blasphemous:* Patricia Bauer et al, "Satanic Verses," *Encyclopaedia Britannica,* 2019.

51   *acts of lethal violence:* Richard Bernstein, "Passages in Defense of a Colleague: Writers Read and Speak for Rushdie," *New York Times,* February 23, 1989.

52   *"targets of such attacks":* Barack Obama, "Remarks by the President at National Prayer Breakfast," National Prayer Breakfast, February 5, 2015, Washington Hilton, Washington, D.C.

52   *hateful speech is vital:* David Bernstein, "No, President Obama, 'We'—and Especially You—Are Not Obligated to Condemn Insults to Religion at All, Much Less Do So with Same Vigor We—And Especially You—Must Defend Freedom of Speech," *Washington Post,* February 6, 2015.

52   *"freedom of thought becomes impossible":* Salman Rushdie, "Democracy Is No Polite Tea Party," *Los Angeles Times,* February 7, 2005.

53   *"we'll even discipline him":* Des Bieler, "Adam Silver Says China Asked NBA to Fire Rockets' Daryl Morey," *Washington Post,* October 17, 2019.

53   *"provocative or, yes, offensive?":* Anemona Hartocollis, "Yale Lecturer Resigns After Email on Halloween Costumes," *New York Times,* December 7, 2015.

54   *their residential roles:* Libby Nelson, "Yale's Big Fight over Sensitivity and Free Speech, Explained," Vox, November 7, 2015.

54   *resigned from teaching at Yale:* Anemona Hartocollis, "Yale Professor and Wife, Targets of Protests, Resign as College Heads," *New York Times,* May 26, 2016.

54   *bigotry by Yale fraternities:* PEN America, "And Campus for All: Diversity, Inclusion, and Freedom of Speech at U.S. Universities," New York, PEN America, 2016.

54   *"exactly right":* David Shimer, "Admins Speak Out on Racial Tensions," *Yale Daily News,* November 6, 2015.

55   *can and must do both:* Monica Wang and Victor Wang, "Salovey, Holloway Affirm Support for Christakises," *Yale Daily News,* November 18, 2015, https://yaledailynews.com/blog/2015/11/18/salovey-holloway-affirm-support-for-christakises/

55   *"injured the community":* Erika Christakis, "My Halloween Email Led to a Campus Firestorm—And a Troubling Lesson about Self-Censorship," *Washington Post,* October 28, 2016.

55   *"Byyyeeeeeee":* Chris Bell, "A Professor Spoke Ill of the Dead. What Happened Next?" BBC, July 29, 2019.

56   *reprisals for speech:* Cleve R. Wootson Jr. and Herman Wong, "After Calling Barbara Bush an 'Amazing Racist,' a Professor Taunts Critics: 'I Will Never Be Fired,'" *Gazette,* April 19, 2018.

56   *position was secure:* Scott Jaschik, "Fresno State Won't Punish Professor for Tweets," Inside Higher Ed, April 25, 2018.

56   *"reflect our ambition":* Conor Friedersdorf, "A Dissent Concerning Kevin Williamson," *The Atlantic,* April 8, 2018.

56   *"premeditated homicide":* Jordan Weissmann, "Why Would the Atlantic Hire Kevin Williamson?" Slate, March 27, 2018.

56   *"opportunity to change":* Ibid.

56   *outcry became too furious:* Michael M. Grynbaum, "The Atlantic Cuts Ties with Conservative Writer Kevin Williamson," *New York Times,* April 5, 2018.

57   *"language of my harassers":* Andrew Sullivan, "When Racism Is Fit to Print," *New York,* August 3, 2018.

57   *controversial and unpopular speech:* Aja Romano, "The 'Controversy' over Journalist Sarah Jeong Joining the *New York Times,* Explained," Vox, August 3, 2018.

58   *"lecture espousing phrenology":* Jelani Cobb, "The Mistake the Berkeley Protesters Made about Milo Yiannopoulos," *The New Yorker,* February 15, 2017.

59   *commitment to free speech:* Thomas Fuller and Christopher Mele: "Berkeley Cancels Milo Yiannopoulos Speech, and Donald Trump Tweets Outrage," *New York Times,* February 1, 2017.

59   *"with vigor":* University of California, Berkeley Public Affairs, "Chancellor Christ: Free Speech Is Who We Are," UC Berkeley News, August 23, 2017.

59   *"cancelled the event":* Carol Christ, "Chancellor Christ: Our Authentic and Ever-Changing Story," UC Berkeley News, September 27, 2018.

59   *less than twenty minutes:* Kimberly Veklerov et al., "Milo Yiannopoulos' Brief Visit was 'Most Expensive Photo Op' in Cal History," *SFGate,* September 24, 2017.

60   *"adequate emotional support staff":* Office of the President, "A Message from President Bradley," Vassar Office of the President, October 24, 2017.

60   *objected to his visit:* Paul Mansour, "Alum Critiques Bradley's Jacobson Response," *Miscellany News,* November 29, 2017.

60   *rising global authoritarianism:* Suzanne Nossel, "Not All Campus Speakers Are Created Equal (Especially When They're from the German Far Right)," *Washington Post,* October 31, 2017.

60   *"Jongen and the AfD":* Andrew Arato et al., "An Open Letter to the Hannah Arendt Center at Bard College," *Chronicle of Higher Education,* October 23, 2017.

60   *"reject these arguments":* Roger Berkowitz, "'Against the Tyranny of Intellectual Mobs,'" *Chronicle of Higher Education,* October 24, 2017.

60   *"the public denouncements of the Soviet era":* Leon Botstein, "An Open Letter to the Hannah Arendt Center: A Response by Leon Botstein," Medium, October 24, 2017.

61 *"part of their education":* Francine Prose, "My Students Heard a Far-Right Politician on Campus. Here's What They Learned," *Guardian,* October 31, 2017.

61 *book him on their shows:* David Boddiger, "Here's an Idea: Stop Inviting Rudy Giuliani on Your Show," Splinter, December 16, 2018.

61 *committed an impeachable offense:* Paul LeBlanc, "Rudy Giuliani Denies Asking Ukraine to Investigate Biden—Before Admitting It," CNN, September 19, 2019.

62 *right to exchange ideas:* PEN America, "United States Government Must Explain Decision to Deny Entry to Activist Author Omar Barghouti," April 11, 2019.

Chapter 5: Apologize When You've Said Something Wrong

63 *"apology tour":* Edward-Isaac Dover, "Obama's Apology Complex," Politico, May 22, 2016.

63 *"his regret for what she endured":* Alison Durkee, "Anita Hill Eviscerates Joe Biden's 'Apology' in Scathing Interview," *Vanity Fair,* April 25, 2019.

63 *"so don't do it":* Jonathan Allen, "Does Being Donald Trump Still Mean Never Having to Say You're Sorry?" NBC News, December 31, 2018.

65 *"sometimes with [his] help":* Eric Bradner, "Beto O'Rourke Apologizes for Jokes about Wife, Says He Has Benefited from 'White Privilege,'" CNN, March 17, 2019.

65 *benefit of their male partners:* Eric Bradner et al., "Beto O'Rourke's Launch: Big Promises, Apologies, and Unanswered Questions," CNN, March 17, 2019.

65 *benefits he enjoys as a white man:* Ibid.

65 *conditionality, minimization, and sidestepping:* Aaron Lazare, *On Apology* (Oxford: Oxford University Press, 2005), 8.

66 *"It's about my fear":* Jonah Weiner, "Kevin Hart's Funny Business," *Rolling Stone,* July 29, 2015.

67 *his previous apologies:* Megh Wright, "Where Are Kevin Hart's Past Apologies? An Investigation," Vulture, January 4, 2019.

67 *"sometimes deadly homophobia":* Justin Carissimo, "Don Lemon Urges Kevin Hart to Be an Ally to LGBT Community," CBS News, January 5, 2019.

67 *Jackson's moonwalk:* Alan Blinder, "Was That Ralph Northam in Blackface? An Inquiry Ends Without Answers," *New York Times,* May 22, 2019.

68 *"shouldn't have done":* Ramsey Touchberry, "Justin Trudeau Says He's Been 'More Enthusiastic About Costumes' Than Appropriate Amid Brownface Scandal," *Newsweek,* September 19, 2019.

68 *crediting or endorsing it:* Denny Bonavita, "Unintentional Hurt: Apology, No, Regret, Yes," *Courier Express,* May 28, 2019.

69 *stop using the word:* David Raban, "Racism Thrives at the Law School," *Chicago Maroon,* March 5, 2019.

69 *anecdote in class:* Matthew Pinna, "U. of C. Professor Heeds Critics and Drops Racist Anecdote from His Lecture," *Hyde Park Herald,* March 7, 2019.

Chapter 6: Consider Intent and Context When Reacting to Speech

74 ***leave us craving more:*** Kelly McSweeney, "This Is Your Brain on Instagram: Effects of Social Media on the Brain," Now, March 17, 2019.

75 ***Obama called to apologize:*** William Saletan, "The Lynching of Shirley Sherrod," Slate, July 21, 2010; Ashley Hayes, "Former USDA Employee Sues Conservative Blogger over Video Posting," CNN, February 15, 2011.

76 ***her job as well:*** Jon Ronson, "How One Stupid Tweet Blew Up Justine Sacco's Life," *New York Times,* February 12, 2015.

76 ***criticism and threats:*** Gabriella Paiella, "New Yorker Fact-Checker Resigns After Fallout Over ICE Tweet," The Cut, June 25, 2018; Lloyd Grove, "Fox News Called Talia Lavin and Lauren Duca 'Little Journo Terrorists.' Now They're Facing Death Threats," Daily Beast, March 25, 2019.

77 ***CNN likewise apologized:*** Oliver Darcy, "Media Outlets Take Trump Out of Context to Suggest He Called Undocumented Immigrants 'Animals,'" CNN, May 17, 2018.

77 ***Hebdo's alleged racism:*** Kachka, "How and Why 35 Writers Denounced PEN Over Charlie Hebdo," Vulture, April 29, 2015.

78 ***far-right's naked racism:*** Zack Beauchamp, "A New Website Explains Charlie Hebdo Cartoons for Americans," Vox, January 14, 2015.

79 ***understood what it meant:*** FreakTheory, "Christiane Taubira's Tribute to Tignous—with English Subtitles," YouTube, posted May 2015.

79 ***"just below the surface":*** Caleb Crain, "Charlie Hebdo and the Previous Question," Steamthing, April 30, 2015.

80 ***liability faults the builder:*** Suzanne Nossel, "We Cannot Continue to Treat All Offensive Speech Acts—Intentional or Not—as Equally Blameworthy," *Los Angeles Times,* March 7, 2018.

80 ***"when conflicts arise":*** Jonathan Mahler, "Watch What You Say," *New York Times,* September 5, 2018.

80 ***"scintilla of evidence":*** Leslie Brody, "Teacher at Quaker School Gets His Job Back," *Wall Street Journal,* October 1, 2018.

81 ***cancellation of his entire course:*** Colleen Flaherty, "Ending a Course Over the N-Word," Inside Higher Ed, February 14, 2018.

81 ***"use-mention distinction":*** Colleen Flaherty, "Too Taboo for Class?" Inside Higher Ed, February 1, 2019.

81 ***reinforce racial divides:*** Daniel Smith, "That Word," *The Atlantic,* January 2002.

82 ***unacceptable:*** Wyman King et al., "Who Has the 'Right' to Use the N-Word? A Survey of Attitudes about the Acceptability of Using the N-Word and Its Derivatives," *International Journal of Society, Culture & Language* 6, no. 2 (2018): 47–58.

Chapter 7: Call Out with Caution

86   *"I deserve to die":* Mari Uyehara, "The Perpetual Foreigners," *GQ,* February 19, 2018.

86   *evicted him from his office:* Deepti Hajela, "N.Y. Lawyer Who Ranted at Span-
ish Speakers Faces Eviction, Complaint—and a Mariachi Band," *USA Today,* May
18, 2018; Debra Cassens Weiss, "Lawyer's Viral Video Rant Amounted to Malpractice, Ex-Clint Alleges in Lawsuit," *ABA Journal,* January 9, 2019.

86   *"proving my point":* Suzanne Nossel, "Sometimes More Speech Isn't the Solution
to Offensive Speech," *Washington Post,* May 29, 2018.

86   *who accepted the apology:* Alix Spiegel, "The Callout," *Invisiblia,* podcast audio,
April 13, 2018.

87   *costing Sacco her job:* Jon Ronson, *So You've Been Publicly Shamed* (New York:
Riverhead Books, 2015), 68.

89   *"guardians of political purity":* Loretta Ross, "I'm a Black Feminist. I Think
Call-Out Culture Is Toxic," *New York Times,* August 17, 2019.

89   *Stanford, Princeton, and the Massachusetts Institute of Technology:* Romano,
"Harvard President Resigns."

91   *"Just learn and breathe":* Christine Teigen (chrissyteigen), "It's called perpetual
otherism or perpetual foreigner syndrome," tweet, February 12, 2018.

91   *"promote their work":* Tom Williams, "Cancel Culture May Have Peaked, but
the Backlash to It Hasn't," Medium, October 5, 2019.

93   *resigned under pressure:* Cara Buckley, *"New York Review of Books* Editor Is Out
Amid Uproar Over #MeToo Essay," *New York Times,* September 19, 2018.

93   *fear of antagonizing readers:* Ibid.; Boris Kachka, "The Backlash to the Backlash
at *The New York Review of Books," New York,* September 27, 2018.

94   *"Public disgrace is open-ended":* Ian Buruma, "Editing in an Age of Outrage,"
Financial Times, March 29, 2019.

94   *"hurtful or problematic":* Garnett Achieng', "The Problem with 'Cancel Culture,'" Women's Media Center FBOMB, December 19, 2018.

94   *begun to publish again:* Buruma, "Editing in an Age of Outrage."

Chapter 8: Fight Hateful Speech and Hate Crimes

98   *"there to stop you":* Alexander Mallin, "'I am Talking Directly to You: US Attorney Delivers Powerful Rebuke to White Nationalists," ABC News, August 29, 2019.

99   *conflating more than it clarifies:* Suzanne Nossel, "To Fight 'Hate Speech,' Stop
Talking about It," *Washington Post,* June 3, 2016.

100   *"gender identity":* FBI, "What We Investigate: Hate Crimes."

100   *"no crime would occur at all":* Michael Lieberman and Steven M. Friedman,
"Confronting Violent Bigotry: Hate Crimes Laws and Legislation," in *The Psychol-
ogy of Hate Crimes as Domestic Terrorism: U.S. and Global Issues,* ed. Edward W.
Dubar et al. (New York: Praeger, 2017), 44.

100   *"other civil liberties":* FBI, "What We Investigate: Hate Crimes."

100   *race, ethnicity, identity, or beliefs:* Wisconsin v. Mitchell, 508 U.S. 476 (1993).

100   *xenophobic Facebook posts in 2018:* Amanda Taub and Max Fisher, "Facebook Fueled Anti-Refugee Attacks in Germany, New Research Suggests," *New York Times,* August 21, 2018.

101   *white supremacist dogma online:* Mark Berman, "Prosecutors Say Dylann Roof 'Self-Radicalized' Online, Wrote Another Manifesto in Jail," *Washington Post,* August 22, 2018.

101   *espousing anti-Semitic theories:* Louis Beckett, "Pittsburgh Shooter Was Fringe Figure in Online World of White Supremacist Rage," *Guardian,* October 30, 2018.

101   *shootings earlier that year:* Don Rowe, "How Christchurch Became a 'High Score' for the El Paso Shooter to Aspire to," The Spinoff, August 5, 2019.

101   *commonplace after the 2016:* Southern Poverty Law Center, "The Trump Effect: The Impact of The 2016 Presidential Election on Our Nation's Schools," November 28, 2016.

101   *for the third straight year:* LEAD Fund, "Report on the Uncivil, Hate and Bias Incidents On Campus Survey," 2018.

101   *same period:* Dan Bauman, "Hate Crimes on Campuses Are Rising, New FBI Data Show," *Chronicle of Higher Education,* November 14, 2018; Anti-Defamation League, "White Supremacists Continue to Spread Hate on American Campuses," June 27, 2019.

102   *"even when controlling for alternative explanations":* Griffin Sims Edwards and Stephen Rushin, "The Effect of President Trump's Election on Hate Crimes," January 14, 2018.

102   *lone actors in terrorist incidents:* National Consortium for the Study of Terrorism and Responses to Terrorism, "The Use of Social Media by United States Extremists," July 2018.

102   *religiously aggravated crimes:* Hate Lab, "Online Hate Speech Predicts Hate Crimes on the Streets," https://hatelab.net/2019/10/14/online-hate-speech-predicts-hate-crimes-on-the-streets/.

103   *"message with which one disagrees":* Nadine Strossen, *Hate Speech: Why We Should Resist It with Free Speech, Not Censorship* (Oxford: Oxford University Press, 2018), xxii.

103   *"more flexible and responsive" than censorship:* Jamie Bartlett and Alex Krasodomski-Jones, "Counter-Speech on Facebook," September 2016, https://demos.co.uk/project/counter-speech-on-facebook-phase-2.

103   *counterspeech run amok:* Nadine Strossen, "Counterspeech in Response to Changing Notions of Free Speech," *American Bar Association* 43, no. 4.

104   *"lasting change in beliefs":* Dangerous Speech Project, "Counterspeech on Twitter: A Field Study," October 14, 2016.

105   *"resolving their grievances":* Ibid.

106   *while deploring bigotry:* Jeremey Bauer-Wolf, "Lessons from Spencer's Florida Speech," Inside Higher Ed, October 23, 2017.

106 ***could not have conveyed:*** Maya Rhodan, "Obama Delivers Powerful Eulogy to Slain Charleston Pastor: Watch President Obama Sing 'Amazing Grace' at Slain Pastor's Funeral," *Time,* June 26, 2015.

107 ***denounced his plans:*** *Week* staff, "Florida's 'Suspended' Koran-Burning," *The Week,* September 10, 2010.

107 ***sexual harassment and stalking:*** Anti-Defamation League, "Online Hate and Harassment: The American Experience," https://www.adl.org/onlineharassment.

107 ***harassment or threats:*** PEN America, "Online Harassment Field Manual," https://onlineharassmentfieldmanual.pen.org/.

108 ***a health problem:*** Allison Klein, "A Sexist Troll Attacked Sarah Silverman. She Responded by Helping Him with His Problems," *Washington Post,* January 8, 2018.

108 ***response to bias incidents:*** Anti-Defamation League, "What Is Anti-Bias Education?" https://www.adl.org/education/resources/glossary-terms/what-is-anti-bias-education.

109 ***"political rights among immigrants":*** Per Adman and Per Strömblad, "Time for Tolerance: Exploring the Influence of Learning Institutions on the Recognition of Political Rights among Immigrants," *Comparative Migration Studies* 6, no. 1 (2018): 34.

109 ***interreligious tolerance in Indonesia:*** Christopher Roth and Sumarto Sudarno, "Does Education Increase Interethnic and Interreligious Tolerance? Evidence from a Natural Experiment," MPRA Paper 64558, 2015.

109 ***accepting attitudes among students:*** T. A. Baklashova et al., "The Effects of Education on Tolerance: Research of Students' Social and Ethnic Attitudes," *Mediterranean Journal of Social Sciences* 6, no. 1 (2015): 335–40.

109 ***notoriously underreported:*** Frank S. Pezzella et al., "The Dark Figure of Hate Crime Underreporting," *American Behavioral Scientist,* January 28, 2019.

109 ***prevalence of hate crimes:*** Yanqi Xu, "Explaining the Numbers behind the Rise in Reported Hate Crimes," April 3, 2019.

110 ***how to alert authorities:*** Rue Landau, "Hate Crimes and Bias Incidents," November 28, 2018, https://www.phila.gov/2018-11-28-hate-crimes-and-bias-incidents/.

110 ***mandated data collection:*** "Anti-Defamation League State Hate Crime Statutory Provisions," https://www.adl.org/media/12210/download.

110 ***prosecutors, and community organizations:*** International Association of Chiefs of Police and Lawyers' Committee for Civil Rights Under Law, "Action Agenda for Community Organizations and Law Enforcement to Enhance the Response to Hate Crimes," April 2019.

Chapter 9: Protesting Without Silencing

114 ***"heckler's veto":*** Patrick Schmidt, "Heckler's Veto," *First Amendment Encyclopedia.*

114 ***"before it starts":*** Nat Hentoff, "Mugging the Minutemen," *Village Voice,* November 8, 2006.

115   ***his or her message*:** Erwin Chemerinsky, "UC Irvine's Free Speech Debate," *Los Angeles Times,* February 18, 2010.

115   ***shout down their representatives:*** Clare Foran, "Republican Lawmakers Face Hostile Town-Hall Crowds," *The Atlantic,* February 23, 2017.

115   ***to hear the discussion:*** Liam Adams, "Pro-Trump Protesters Shout Down Democrat's Speech at Whittier College," *Chronicle of Higher Education,* October 16, 2017.

115   ***crossed the line into violence:*** Taylor Gee, "How the Middlebury Riot Really Went Down," Politico, May 28, 2017.

115   ***interfere with the performance:*** Michael Cooper, "Gay Rights Protest Greets Opening Night at the Met," *New York Times,* September 23, 2013; Jennifer Smith, "Protests Take Center Stage," *Wall Street Journal,* January 30, 2015.

116   ***after her remarks:*** Olivia Cheng, "More than 100 Penn Students Protest Heather Mac Donald for Discriminatory Speech at Event," *Daily Pennsylvanian,* February 8, 2019.

116   ***Pence's remarks:*** Liam Stack, "Notre Dame Students Walk Out of Mike Pence Commencement Address," *New York Times,* May 21, 2017.

116   ***"Students Are Not For Sale":*** Sameer Rao, "Harvard Students Protest Betsy DeVos with 'White Supremacist' Sign, Raised Fists," Color Lines, September 29, 2017.

116   ***escorted from the room:*** Valerie Strauss, "When DeVos Spoke at Harvard, Guests Were Told They Would Be Escorted Out If Disruptive. Some Protested Anyway," *Washington Post,* September 28, 2017.

118   ***for fear of reprisals:*** Conor Friedersdorf, "Camille Paglia Can't Say That," *The Atlantic,* May 1, 2019.

120   ***simply stood idly by:*** Martin Luther King Jr. Research and Education Institute, "Freedom Rides," https://kinginstitute.stanford.edu/encyclopedia/freedom-rides.

120   ***"And if so who?":*** Kenan Malik, "Do I Want People to Shut Up?" Pandamonium, December 5, 2014.

121   ***Times' own editorial board:*** Editorial Board, "A Rising Tide of Anti-Semitism," *New York Times,* April 30, 2019.

121   ***U.S. edition years prior:*** Steve Lohr, "*New York Times*'s Global Edition Is Ending Daily Political Cartoons," *New York Times,* June 10, 2019.

121   ***"political conversation over time":*** PEN America, "International *New York Times* Retiring Cartoons, In Effort to Avoid Future Lapses, Shuts Down Channel of Potent Political Commentary," June 12, 2019.

Chapter 10: Consider When to Forgive Speech-Related Transgressions

123   ***"hate our enemies":*** Martin Luther King Jr., *A Gift of Love: Sermons from Strength to Love and Other Preachings* (Boston: Beacon Press, 1963), 46.

124   ***hurtful actions:*** M. E. McCullough, E. L. Worthington Jr., and K. C. Rachal, "Interpersonal Forgiving in Close Relationships," *Journal of Personality and Social Psychology* 73, no. 2 (1997): 321–36.

125 *"I conducted myself then":* Borys Kit, "James Gunn Fired as Director of 'Guardians of the Galaxy Vol. 3,'" *Hollywood Reporter,* July 20, 2018.

126 *"hurt another person":* Kyle Buchanan, "Tina Fey Calls Tracy Morgan's Homophobic Rant 'Disturbing,'" Vulture, June 10, 2011.

126 *RehireJamesGunn.com:* Karen Han, "The *Guardians of the Galaxy* Cast Is Defending James Gunn against 'Mob Mentality,'" Vox, July 30, 2018; Ross A. Lincoln, "Fans Pay for 'Rehire James Gunn' Billboard Near Disneyland," The Wrap, October 30, 2018.

126 *made fun of his apology:* Dave Itzkoff, "'30 Rock' Seeks to Close a Controversial Chapter with Comedy," *New York Times,* January 20, 2012.

127 *no longer toxic:* Sheila Marikar, "Can Kathy Griffin Come Back from the Dead?" *The New Yorker,* March 18, 2019.

127 *before announcing it publicly:* Brooks Barnes, "James Gunn Is Hired Back to Helm 'Guardians of the Galaxy 3,'" *New York Times,* March 15, 2019.

127 *"severed our business relationship with him":* Brooks Barnes, "Disney Fires 'Guardians of the Galaxy' Director Over Offensive Tweets," *New York Times,* July 20, 2018.

127 *"will not be tolerated":* Sofia M. Fernandez, "Tina Fey, NBC Apologize for Tracy Morgan Anti-Gay Comments," *Hollywood Reporter,* June 10, 2011.

128 *"help us learn faster":* Bryn Elise Sandberg, "Netflix Fires PR Chief After Use of N-Word in Meeting (Exclusive)," *Hollywood Reporter,* June 22, 2018.

128 *the customs as racist:* Philip Weiss, "NAACP: Academic Magnet Football Coach Apologized, Did Not See Celebrations as Racially Insensitive," Live 5 WCSC News, October 22, 2014.

128 *racial or ethnic issues:* Amanda Kerr, "Magnet Coach Gets His Job Back," *Post and Courier,* October 21, 2014.

Chapter 11: Understand the Harms of Speech

134 *focusing on reputation:* Strossen, *Hate Speech,* 54.

135 *meet these tests:* Richard Parker, "Clear and Present Danger Test," *First Amendment Encyclopedia,* https://www.mtsu.edu/first-amendment/article/898/clear-and-present-danger-test.

135 *hate crimes between 2016 and 2017:* Jessica Schneider, "Hate Crimes Increased by 17% in 2017, FBI Report Finds," CNN, December 11, 2018.

135 *compared to similar counties:* David Choi, "Hate Crimes Increased 226% in Places Trump Held a Campaign Rally in 2016, Study Claims," Business Insider, March 22, 2019.

135 *other security precautions:* Emily Birnbaum, "TV Networks Boost Security for Reporters at Trump Rallies," The Hill, August 19, 2018.

135 *minority groups that Trump has denigrated:* Khaled Rahman, "Muslim Family Says 'Trump Supporter' Harassed Them in TJ Maxx Store, Yelled 'Go Back to Your Country,'" *Newsweek,* October 21, 2019.

135 *"Hispanic invasion" of Texas:* Peter Baker and Michael D. Shear, "El Paso Shooting Suspect's Manifesto Echoes Trump's Language," *New York Times,* August 4, 2019.

135 *legal in the United States:* Gordon Darroch, "Geert Wilders Found Guilty of Inciting Discrimination," *Guardian,* December 9, 2016.

137 *thoughts of suicide:* Victoria M. O'Keefe et al., "Seemingly Harmless Racial Communications Are Not So Harmless: Racial Microaggressions Lead to Suicidal Ideation by Way of Depression Symptoms," *Suicide and Life-Threatening Behavior* 45, no. 5 (2015): 567–76.

137 *"turmoil stayed with them":* Sue et al., "Racial Microaggressions against Black Americans: Implications for Counseling," *Journal of Counseling and Development* 86, no. 3 (2008): 330–38.

137 *"persistent and pervasive":* University of California, San Francisco Stress Center, "Stigma, Discrimination, and Vigilance for Bias," https://stresscenter.ucsf .edu/measures/stigma-discrimination-and-vigilance-bias.

138 *"slights and insults":* Derald Wing Sue et al., "Racial Microaggressions in Everyday Life: Implications for Clinical Practice," *American Psychologist* 62, no. 4 (2007): 271–86.

138 *impact on mental and even physical health:* Scott O. Lilienfeld, "Microaggressions: Strong Claims, Inadequate Evidence," *Perspectives on Psychological Science* 12, no. 1 (2017): 138–69.

138 *compared to peers:* Maureen D. Connolly, "The Mental Health of Transgender Youth: Advances in Understanding," *Journal of Adolescent Health* 59, no. 5 (2016): 489–95.

138 *being a transgender youth:* Deborah Temkin, "Research Shows the Risk of Misgendering Transgender Youth," Child Trends, October 23, 2018.

139 *"student survivors":* Becca Pachl, "Title IX Protects Those Who Emily Yoffe and Wellesley College Disempower," *Wellesley News,* November 13, 2018.

139 *opting not to see the movie:* Jake New, "Film and Free Speech," Inside Higher Ed, April 9, 2015.

139 *"our 'fragile' psyches":* Steven Glick, "ASPC Gets Madd," *Claremont Independent,* September 25, 2015.

140 *"moral identity is threatened":* Zachary K. Rothschile and Lucas A. Keefer, "A Cleansing Fire: Moral Outrage Alleviates Guilt and Buffers Threats to One's Moral Identity," *Motivation and Emotion* 41, no. 2 (2017): 209–29.

Chapter 12: Don't Equate Speech with Violence

141 *some persistent questioning:* Julia Carrie Wong, "Greg Gianforte to Plead Guilty for Assaulting *Guardian* Reporter," *Guardian,* June 9, 2017.

141 *taking photographs and video:* Zack Beauchamp, "The Assault on Conservative Journalist Andy Ngo, Explained," Vox, July 3, 2019.

141 *Trump rally in Minneapolis:* Mike Mullen, "Trump Supporter Pointed Gun at Downtown Minneapolis Protestors," *City Pages,* October 12, 2019.

141   *rule of law, chill speech:* Max Weber, *The Vocation Lectures,* translated by Rodney Livingstone, edited by David Owen and Tracy Strong (Indianapolis: Hackett, 2004).

142   *"menace and subjugation":* Toni Morrison, "Nobel Lecture," December 7, 1993.

142   *"costs of free speech":* David Cole, "The ACLU's Longstanding Commitment to Defending Speech We Hate," ACLU, June 23, 2018.

143   *lifeblood of democracy:* Lisa Feldman Barrett, "When Is Speech Violence?" *New York Times,* July 14, 2017.

144   *"a form of violence":* William F. Buckley Jr. Program at Yale, "30% of Students Believe That Physical Violence Can Be Justified to Prevent Someone from Using Hate Speech," October 16, 2017.

144   *"real form of violence":* Erika Morris, "Microaggressions Are a Form of Violence," *The Link,* March 6, 2017.

144   *"violence is changed," she wrote:* Anni Liu, "No, You're Not Imagining It: 3 Ways Racial Microaggressions Sneak into Our Lives," Everyday Feminism, February 25, 2015.

144   *deleterious force:* Jesse Singal, "Stop Telling Students Free Speech Is Traumatizing Them," *New York,* July 18, 2017.

144   *"it is in reality":* Daniel Nesbitt, "Speech, Whether Wrong or Right, Is Not Violence," *Trinity Tripod,* November 5, 2018.

145   *legitimate response to speech:* Eugene Volokh, "UC Santa Barbara Professor Steals Young Anti-Abortion Protestor's Sign, Apparently Assaults Protestors," *Washington Post,* March 20, 2014.

145   *not assure her safety:* Thomas Fuller, "Berkeley Cancels Ann Coulter Speech Over Safety Fears," *New York Times,* April 19, 2017.

145   *park instead:* Drew Mikkelsen, "Professor Told He's Not Safe on Campus After College Protests," K5 News, May 26, 2017.

146   *ensure his safety:* "Another Speaker Unable to Appear at Middlebury," Inside Higher Ed, April 19, 2019.

146   *only after the fact:* Riley Board et al., "Legutko Still Speaks to Politics Class After Administration Cancels Public Lecture," *Middlebury Campus,* April 17, 2019.

146   *transgender individuals:* Sam Riedel, "Deadnaming a Trans Person Is Violence— So Why Does the Media Do It Anyway?" The Establishment, March 17, 2017.

Chapter 13: Don't Politicize Free Speech

150   *"weaponizing" speech rights: Janus v. AFSCME* 585 U.S. __ (2018) (Kagan, dissent).

151   *conservative in content:* Lee Epstein, "Do Justices Defend the Speech They Hate?" *Journal of Law and Courts* (2018): 237–62.

151   *free speech cases to hear:* Adam Liptak, "How Conservatives Weaponized the First Amendment," *New York Times,* June 30, 2018.

151   *"any other modern Court":* Lee Epstein, "6+ Decades of Freedom of Expres-

sion in the U.S. Supreme Court," June 30, 2018, http://epstein.wustl.edu/research
/FreedomOfExpression.html.

151 *free speech jurisprudence:* Ibid.

151 *"meant for better things":* Dave Jamieson, "Justice Elena Kagan Says the Supreme Court Turned the First Amendment 'Into a Sword,'" Huffington Post, June
27, 2018.

152 *commitment to the same freedoms:* Joshua J. Dyck et al., "Citizen Attitudes
About Democratic Values and American Democracy," Center for Public Opinion,
https://www.uml.edu/docs/CPOR-Democratic%20Values-TOPLINE_tcm18
-278478.pdf.

152 *universities skew liberal:* Samuel J. Abrams, "One of the Most Liberal Groups
in America," Inside Higher Ed, November 8, 2018; Mitchell Langbert et al., "Faculty Voter Registration in Economics, History, Journalism, Law, and Psychology,"
Character Issues 13, no. 3 (2016): 422–51.

152 *"might find them offensive":* Emily Ekins, "The State of Free Speech and Tolerance in America," Cato Institute, October 31, 2017.

153 *during the national anthem:* Ashley Johnson, "KSU Cheerleaders Who Knelt
During National Anthem Cut from Squad," 11 Alive, August 22, 2018.

153 *whose side he is on:* Donald Trump, "Remarks by President Trump at Signing of
Executive Order, 'Improving Free Inquiry, Transparency, and Accountability at
Colleges and Universities,'" March 21, 2019, East Room, White House, Washing-
ton, D.C.

153 *First Amendment advocates:* Erwin Chemerinsky and Howard Gillman,
"Trump's Executive Order on Free Speech Is Unconstitutional," *Los Angeles Times,*
March 22, 2019.

153 *risk deepening divides:* PEN America, "Wrong Answer: How Good Faith Attempts to Address Free Speech and Anti-Semitism on Campus Could Backfire,"
https://pen.org/research-resources/wrong-answer/.

153 *"not protected by the First Amendment":* Eugene Volokh, "Howard Dean Dou-
bles Down on Support for UC Berkeley Excluding Ann Coulter," *Washington Post,*
April 25, 2017.

154 *speech with which they disagree:* Suzanne Nossel and Summer Lopez, "Kamala
Harris Wants to Boot Trump from Twitter. It Wouldn't Work," *Washington Post,*
October 4, 2019.

154 *50 percent by 2017:* Julie Voorhes and Marc Lendler, "Student Opinion on
Campus Speech Rights: A Longitudinal Study," August 27, 2018.

154 *those age 35 to 69:* Jacob Poushter, "40% of Millennials OK with Limiting Speech
Offensive to Minorities," Pew Research Center, November 20, 2015.

155 *leftists, liberals, and conservatives:* Scott Jaschik, "Should Bill Maher Be Commencement Speaker?" Inside Higher Ed, October 28, 2014.

156 *"shut your ears off":* Barack Obama, remarks by the president at commencement
address at Rutgers, the State University of New Jersey, May 15, 2016, New Bruns-
wick, New Jersey.

Chapter 14: Don't Caricature the Arguments For and Against Free Speech

158   *"filter bubble":* Eli Pariser, *The Filter Bubble: How the New Personalized Web Is Changing What We Read and How We Think* (New York: Penguin, 2012).

159   *book of the same name:* Jonathan Haidt and Greg Lukianoff, "The Coddling of the American Mind," *The Atlantic,* September; Jonathan Haidt and Greg Lukianoff, *The Coddling of the American Mind: How Good Intentions and Bad Ideas Are Setting Up a Generation for Failure* (New York: Penguin, 2018).

159   *"cause discomfort or give offense":* Haidt and Lukianoff, "The Coddling of the American Mind."

160   *experience it that way:* Ibid.

160   *take a joke:* Haidt and Lukianoff, *The Coddling of the American Mind,* 48.

160   *harassment, and sexism:* Ibid., 15.

161   *lives of black Americans:* German Lopez, "Why You Should Stop Saying 'All Lives Matter,' Explained in 9 Different Ways," Vox, July 11, 2016.

161   *reframe their consternation:* Haidt and Lukianoff, *The Coddling of the American Mind,* 253–62.

161   *interrupt these thought patterns:* Ibid., 46.

162   *safety pin:* Todd Starnes, "University President Rebukes 'Self-Absorbed, Narcissistic' Students," Fox News, November 30, 2015.

162   *self-centered:* Jim Dunn, "This Is Not a Day Care," *Washington Post,* November 30, 2015.

162   *"precious snowflakes":* Pam Key, "Conway: Millennials Protesting Trump Acting Like 'Precious Snowflakes,'" Breitbart, November 17, 2016.

162   *"political correctness":* Dana Kampa, "Conservative Pundit Ben Shapiro Lectures to Turbulent Crowd on Safe Spaces, Freedom of Speech," *Badger Herald,* November 17, 2016.

162   *"Boohoo":* Amanda Hess, "How 'Snowflake' Became America's Inescapable Tough-Guy Taunt," *New York Times,* June 13, 2017.

163   *snowflake, too:* Robby Soave, "Bret Stephens Is Not a Bedbug. He's a Delicate Snowflake," *Reason,* August 27, 2018.

164   *racial slur on a sculpture:* Kelly Nelson, "Law Professors Discuss Hate Crime at Campus Forum," *Mizzou Weekly,* February 24, 2011.

164   *"vast majority of Americans":* P. E. Moskowitz, *The Case Against Free Speech* (New York: Hachette, 2019).

164   *obscures the rot beneath:* Ibid., 208.

165   *"software update":* Jelani Cobb, "Race and the Free-Speech Diversion," *The New Yorker,* November 10, 2015.

166   *"as being 'uncivil'":* Reshmi Dutt-Ballerstadt, "When Free Speech Dismantles Diversity Initiatives," *CounterPunch,* October 31, 2017.

166   *"itself deeply suspect":* Jeannie Suk Gersen, "Donald Trump, the A.C.L.U., and the Ongoing Battle Over the Legitimacy of Free Speech," *The New Yorker,* April 23, 2019.

166   **other forms of justice:** Joe Palazzolo, "ACLU Will No Longer Defend Hate Groups Protesting with Firearms," *Wall Street Journal*, August 17, 2017; *Wall Street Journal*, "ACLU Case Selection Guidelines: Conflicts Between Competing Values or Priorities," June 21, 2018.

Chapter 15: Prevent Free Speech from Reinforcing Inequality

170   **that pervade society:** Ibram X. Kendi, *How to Be an Antiracist* (New York: Random House, 2019).

171   **"weapon of the powerful":** Catharine A. MacKinnon, "The First Amendment: An Equality Reading," in *The Free Speech Century*, edited by Geoffrey R. Stone and Lee C. Bollinger (Oxford: Oxford Universirty Press, 2019), 140.

171   **sidelined such considerations:** Ibid.

172   **"on his own merits":** *Beauharnais v. Illinois*, 343 U.S. 250 (1952).

172   **a few years later:** *Dennis v. United States*, 341 U.S. 494 (1951).

172   **only reinforces inequity:** *New York Times Co. v. Sullivan*, 376 U.S. 254 (1964); *R.A.V. v. City of St. Paul*, 505 U.S. 377 (1992).

172   **rights of corporations:** *Citizens United v. Federal Election Commission*, 558 U.S. 310 (2010).

172   **abortion rights:** *Janus v. AFSCME* 585 U.S. ___ (2018); *NIFLA v. Becerra* 585 U.S. ___ (2018).

173   **better address online hate:** Tim Wu, "Is the First Amendment Obsolete?" *Michigan Law Review* 117, no. 3 (2018): 547–81.

173   **make a legal comeback:** James Loeffler, "An Abandoned Weapon in the Fight Against Hate Speech," *The Atlantic*, June 16, 2019.

173   **take their words less seriously:** Miranda Fricker, *Epistemic Injustice: Power and the Ethics of Knowing* (Oxford: Clarendon Press, 2007), 1.

173   **full participants in society:** Anna J. Cooper, *A Voice from the South* (Aldine Printing House, 1892); Sojourner Truth, speech in the *Anti-Slavery Bugle*, June 21, 1851, *Chronicling America: Historic American Newspapers*, Library of Congress, https://chroniclingamerica.loc.gov/lccn/sn83035487/1851-06-21/ed-1/seq-4/.

174   **"very White sounding name":** Marianne Bertrand and Sendhil Mullainathan, "Are Emily and Greg More Employable than Lakisha and Jamal? A Field Experiment on Labor Market Discrimination," NBER Working Paper No. 9873, July 2003.

174   **same prejudices undoubtedly operate:** Lincoln Quillian et al., "Meta-Analysis of Field Experiments Shows No Change in Racial Discrimination in Hiring Over Time," *Proceedings of the National Academy of Sciences of the United States of America*, September 12, 2017.

174   **"Progressive stacking":** Jake Wright, "In Defense of the Progressive Stack: A Strategy for Prioritizing Marginalized Voices during In-Class Discussion," *Teaching Philosophy* 41, no. 4, (2018): 407–28.

175   **classroom participation:** Alex Rabin, "A Penn TA is Under National Scrutiny

for Using Progressive Stacking. But What is It?" *Daily Pennsylvanian,* October 28, 2017.

175   ***chance to take the floor:*** James Kierstead, "'Progressive Stacking' Leads to a Wobbly Form of Equality," *Times Higher Education,* May 24, 2018.

175   ***other subcultures depart:*** Center for the Study of White American Culture Inc., "Decentering Whiteness," https://www.cswac.org/; Jamie Utt, "A Case for Decentering Whiteness in Education: How Eurocentric Social Studies Curriculum Acts as a Form of White/Western Studies," *Ethnic Studies Review* 41, nos. 1–2 (2018): 19–34; Abigail Murrish, "De-Centering Whiteness in Our Conversations (PTM 221)," The Witness, October 8, 2018.

176   ***conferences and symposia:*** Saara Särmä, "Congrats, You Have an All-Male Panel," https://allmalepanels.tumblr.com/.

176   ***backgrounds and identities were included:*** Francis S. Collins, "Time to End the Manel Tradition," National Institutes of Health, June 12, 2019.

176   ***"someone else to take her place":*** Owen Barder, "The Pledge," https://www.owen .org/pledge/.

176   ***"touch my hair":*** Lilly Workneh, "Meet April Reign, the Activist Who Created #OscarsSoWhite," Huffington Post, February 27, 2016.

176   ***had been snubbed:*** David Carr, "Why the Oscars' Omission of 'Selma' Matters," *New York Times,* January 18, 2015.

176   ***"reflect our nation":*** Dominic Patten and Patrick Hipes, "Oscars Slammed by Congressman Over 'Lack Of Diversity' & Studio Bosses CC'd," Deadline, February 17, 2015.

176   ***"worse than last year":*** Brandon Griggs, "Once Again, #OscarsSoWhite," CNN, January 14, 2016.

176   ***joined the campaign:*** Patrick Ryan, "#OscarsSoWhite Controversy: What You Need to Know," *USA Today,* February 2, 2016.

176   ***75 percent male:*** Gregg Kilday, "Film Academy Invites a Record 683 New Members: 46 Percent Female and 41 Percent People of Color," *Hollywood Reporter,* June 29, 2016.

177   ***first time in four years:*** April Reign, "#OscarsSoWhite Is Still Relevant This Year," *Vanity Fair,* March 2, 2018.

177   ***both on and off-screen:*** Joseph Harker, "Green Book's Oscar Shows Hollywood Still Doesn't Get Race," *Guardian,* February 25, 2019.

177   ***"39 percent minority":*** Peregrine Frissell et al., "Missed Deadline: The Delayed Promise of Newsroom Diversity," Voices, July 25, 2017.

178   ***outdated language:*** Jelani Cobb, "When Newsrooms Are Dominated by White People, They Miss Crucial Facts," *Guardian,* November 5, 2018.

178   ***organizations into addressing it:*** Farai Chideya, "'This Deepening Division Is Not Inevitable': The Failing Diversity Efforts of Newsrooms," *Columbia Journalism Review,* May 22, 2018.

Chapter 16: Know the Legal Limits of Free Speech

183   *"breach of the peace":* Chaplinsky v. New Hampshire, 315 U.S. 568 (1942).

183   *"true threats":* United States v. Stevens, 559 U.S. 460, 468 (2010); *Virginia v. Black,* 538 U.S. 343, 359 (2003).

184   *"produce such action":* Brandenburg v. Ohio, 395 U.S. 444 (1969).

185   *right to prevent:* Schenck v. United States, 249 U.S. 47 (1919).

185   **Abrams v. United States:** Abrams v. United States, 250 U.S. 616 (1919).

185   *protections for political speech:* Thomas Healy, *The Great Dissent: How Oliver Wendell Holmes Changed His Mind—and Changed the History of Free Speech in America* (New York: Metropolitan Books, 2013).

185   *"counsels to time":* Abrams v. United States, 250 U.S. 616 (1919).

185   *"opinions that we loathe":* Andrew Cohen, "The Most Powerful Dissent in American History," *The Atlantic,* August 10, 2013.

186   *"imminent lawless action":* Brent Kendall, "Appeals Court Tosses Lawsuit Arguing Trump Incited Violence at Rally," *Wall Street Journal,* September 11, 2018.

186   *1942 decision in* **Chaplinsky:** Kathleen M. Sullivan and Gerald Gunther, *First Amendment Law,* 4th ed. (New York: Thomson Reuters/Foundation Press, 2010).

187   *First Amendment:* Alexia Fernández Campbell, "The Limits of Free Speech for White Supremacists Marching at Unite the Right 2, Explained," Vox, August 12, 2018.

187   *"invitation to a brawl":* John Hart Ely: *Democracy and Distrust: A Theory of Judicial Review* (Cambridge, MA: Harvard University Press, 1981), 114.

187   *"choke you to death":* Gooding v. Wilson, 405 U.S. 518 (1972).

187   *average citizen:* Lewis v. City of New Orleans, 415 U.S. 130, 135 (1974).

187   *"exchange fisticuffs":* Texas v. Johnson, 491 U.S. 397 (1989).

188   *"squeamish among us":* Cohen v. California, 403 U.S. 15 (1971).

188   *"stirs people to anger":* Terminiello v. City of Chicago, 337 U.S. 1 (1949).

188   *message they conveyed:* R. A. V. v. St. Paul, 505 U.S. 377 (1992).

189   *constitutional scrutiny:* David L. Hudson Jr., "When Do Rants Exceed First Amendment Boundaries and Become True Threats?" *ABA Journal,* August 1, 2018.

189   *purpose of intimidation:* Virginia v. Black, 538 U.S. 343, 359 (2003).

189   *no protection to "true threats":* Roberts v. United States Jaycees, 468 U.S. 609, 628, 104 S. Ct. 3244, 3255, 82 L. Ed. 2d 462 (1984); *Hishon v. King & Spalding,* 467 U.S. 69, 78, 104 S. Ct. 2229, 2235, 81 L. Ed. 2d 59 (1984).

190   *"violence is not":* Henry Weinstein, "Abortion Foes Are Ruled a Threat," *Los Angeles Times,* May 17, 2002.

190   *Civil Rights Act:* Meritor Savings Bank v. Vinson, 477 U.S. 57 (1986).

190   *can be barred or punished:* Roberts v. United States Jaycees, 468 U.S. 609, 628, 104 S. Ct. 3244, 3255, 82 L. Ed. 2d 462 (1984).

191   *"opportunity or benefit":* U.S. Supreme Court, "Davis v. Monroe County Bd. of Ed.," 526 U.S. 629 (1999).

191 **An American Tragedy**: Charles Rembar, *The End of Obscenity* (New York: Open Road Media, 2015).

192 *"sensitive readers"*: Rodney A. Smolla and Melville B. Nimmer, *Smolla and Nimmer on Freedom of Speech: A Treatise on the First Amendment*, 1994, § 7.01(2)(b).

192 *speech and the press: Roth v. United States*, 354 U.S. 476 (1957).

192 *"when I see it": Jacobellis v. Ohio*, 378 U.S. 184 (1964).

192 *scientific value: Miller v. California*, 413 U.S. 15 (1973).

192 *artistic value:* Isable Wilkerson, "Cincinnati Jury Acquits Museum in Mapplethorpe Obscenity Case," *New York Times*, October 6, 1990.

192 *"light and composition":* Ellen Goodman, "A Warning from the Mapplethorpe Trial," *Washington Post*, October 9, 1990.

193 *artistic merit: Luke Records, Inc. v. Navarro*, 960 F.2d 134 (11th Cir.).

193 *"violence into obscenity": Brown v. Entertainment Merchants Association*, 564 U.S. 786 (2011).

193 *spoken statements:* Digital Media Law Project, "Defamation," http://www.dmlp .org/legal-guide/defamation.

183 *free speech and reputational protection: McKee v. U.S.*, 586 U.S. ___ (2019).

194 *awarded him $500,000: New York Times Co. v. Sullivan*, 376 U.S. 254 (1964).

195 *communication of the information: Clark v. Commun. for Nonviolence*, 468 U.S. 288 (1984).

195 *requirement for public assemblies:* Andrew M. Winston, "Right to Peaceful Assembly: United States," Library of Congress Law, October 2014.

195 *First Amendment assembly rights:* Ibid.

195 *likely to be tested constitutionally:* International Center for Not-For-Profit Law, U.S. Protest Law Tracker, http://www.icnl.org/usprotestlawtracker/.

Chapter 17: Beware Expanded Government Controls on Speech

199 *fired for being subversive:* Robert M. Lichtman, *The Supreme Court and McCarthy-Era Repression: One Hundred Decisions* (Urbana: University of Illinois Press, 2015).

199 *jurisdictions throughout the world:* Tom Ginsburg, *Freedom of Expression Abroad: The State of Play in Bollinger and Stone's* The Free Speech Century (Oxford: Oxford University Press, 2019).

199 *white supremacist vitriol:* Jeremy Waldron, *The Harm in Hate Speech* (Cambridge, MA: Harvard University Press, 2014).

199 *what strictures should apply:* Andrew Marantz, "Free Speech Is Killing Us," *New York Times*, October 4, 2019.

199 *considered a political ad:* Mark Zuckerberg, "Mark Zuckerberg: The Internet Needs New Rules. Let's Start in These Four Areas," *Washington Post*, March 30, 2019.

200 *boycotts of U. S. allies:* Adam Steinbaugh, "New York Considers Israel-Related 'Hate Speech' Bill a Fourth Time. It's Still Unconstitutional," FIRE, June 20, 2019; PEN America, "Wrong Answer," https://pen.org/research-resources/wrong -answer/.

200 ***"democracies in the world":*** Laura Beth Nielsen, "Op-Ed: The Case for Restrict-
     ing Hate Speech," *Los Angeles Times,* June 21, 2017.

201 ***jailed for their work:*** Committee to Protect Journalists, "251 Journalists Jailed
     Worldwide; Third Worst Year on Record," December 13, 2018.

201 ***crime of expressing themselves:*** Academic Freedom Monitoring Project, "Free-
     dom to Think," October 2018, https://www.scholarsatrisk.org/wp-content/up
     loads/2018/10/Free-to-Think-2018.pdf.

202 ***without interference:*** Congressional-Executive Commission on China, "Judicial
     Independence in the PRC," https://www.cecc.gov/judicial-independence-in-the-prc.

202 ***platforms are unavailable:*** Paige Leskin, "Here Are All the Major US Tech
     Companies Blocked behind China's 'Great Firewall,'" Business Insider, October
     10, 2019.

202 ***should be covered:*** Freedom House, "China," 2019, https://freedomhouse.org
     /report/freedom-world/2019/china.

202 ***political or religious expression:*** Ibid.

202 ***dare raise them:*** PEN America, "Forbidden Feeds: Government Controls on
     Social Media in China," https://pen.org/research-resources/forbidden-feeds/.

202 ***domestic audience:*** Congressional-Executive Commission on China, "Freedom
     of Expression in China: A Privilege, Not a Right," https://www.cecc.gov/freedom
     -of-expression-in-china-a-privilege-not-a-right.

203 ***the firm complied:*** Marc Tracy, "In China, a Reuters Partner Blocks Articles on
     the Tiananmen Square Massacre," *New York Times,* June 4, 2019.

203 ***mobilize across borders:*** Adam Segal, "Year in Review: Chinese Cyber Sover-
     eignty in Action," Council on Foreign Relations, January 8, 2018, https://www
     .cfr.org/blog/year-review-chinese-cyber-sovereignty-action.

203 ***days or weeks:*** Internet Society, "Policy Brief: Shutdowns," November 13, 2017.

204 ***"prohibited by law":*** Office of the United Nations High Commissioner for
     Human Rights, "International Covenant on Civil and Political Rights," Decem-
     ber 16, 1966.

204 ***legitimate public interest:*** Centre for Law and Democracy, "Restrictions on
     Freedom of Expression," Briefing Note Series on Freedom of Expression, February
     2015.

205 ***compensation through the courts:*** Article 19, "Responding to 'Hate Speech':
     Comparative Overview of Six EU Countries," March 2018, https://www.article19
     .org/wp-content/uploads/2018/03/ECA-hate-speech-compilation-report_March
     -2018.pdf.

205 ***using the word "homophobic":*** Nico Lang, "French Hate Crime Ruling Sets a
     Dangerous Precedent for LGBT People: It's Now Illegal to Call Someone a 'Ho-
     mophobe' in France," Salon, November 8, 2016.

205 ***did not deny making:*** Aurelian Breeden, "French #MeToo Movement's Founder
     Loses Defamation Case," *New York Times,* September 25, 2019.

205 ***a boycott of Israel:*** Ali Abunimah, "Woman Arrested in France for T-shirt Criti-
     cal of Israel," Electronic Intifada, March 11, 2016.

206 ***those in the know:*** Brian Palmer, "White Supremacists by the Numbers," Slate, October 29, 2008.

206 ***speech related to Muslims was permitted:*** UN Watch, "OIC Defends 'Defamation of Religion' Proposal in Letter to UN," November 12, 2009.

206 ***punish left-wing activists:*** Glenn Greenwald, "In Europe, Hate Speech Laws Are Often Used to Suppress and Punish Left-Wing Viewpoints," The Intercept, August 29, 2017.

206 ***anti-Semitic sentiment and activity:*** Eva Cossé, "The Alarming Rise of Anti-Semitism in Europe," Human Rights Watch, June 4, 2019.

207 ***treatment of women in Islam:*** Nadine Strossen, *Hate Speech: Why We Should Resist It with Free Speech, Not Censorship* (Oxford: Oxford University Press, 2018), 96.

207 ***"dissent and minority speakers":*** Ibid., 104.

207 ***European Court of Human Rights:*** David Kaye, "Report of the Special Rapporteur on the Promotion and Protection of the Right to Freedom of Opinion and Expression," U.N. DOC. A/74/48050 (October 9, 2019).

207 ***one and the same:*** Jacob Mchangama, "Censorship as 'Tolerance,'" *National Review,* July 14, 2010.

207 ***Liverpool airport:*** Yascha Mounk, "Verboten," *The New Republic,* April 3, 2018.

207 ***the spread of extremist ideologies:*** Joanna Plucinska, "Hate Speech Thrives Underground," Politico, February 7, 2018; Renee Barnes, "8chan's Demise Is a Win Against Hate, but Could Drive Extremists to the Dark Web," The Conversation, https://theconversation.com/8chans-demise-is-a-win-against-hate-but-could-drive-extremists-to-the-dark-web-121521.

207 ***"other German Jews":*** Mounk, "Verboten."

207 ***victims of censorship:*** Ibid.

208 ***"argument for it":*** "Copenhagen, Speech, and Violence," *The New Yorker,* February 14, 2015.

209 ***cast themselves as martyrs:*** Phillip Oltermann, "Tough New German Law Puts Tech Firms and Free Speech in Spotlight," *Guardian,* January 5, 2018.

209 ***fighting it:*** "Twitter Suspends Jewish Newspaper, SPD Politician for Anti-AfD Tweets," DW, May 13, 2019.

209 ***substantial amounts of content:*** "The Network Enforcement Act Apparently Leads to Excessive Blocking of Content," Reporters Without Borders, August 3, 2018.

209 ***extremist content from their platforms:*** Henry Cooke, "Christchurch Call: Tech Companies, 17 Governments Sign New Zealand–Led Pledge—but Not the US," Stuff, May 16, 2019.

209 ***free expression under its terms:*** Graeme Wood, "Trump Was Right Not to Sign the Christchurch Call," *The Atlantic,* May 22, 2019.

210 ***remove such content:*** Daniel Funke, "Singapore's Anti-Misinformation Law Is Among the Most Comprehensive in the World. Here's Why that's Problematic," Poynter, June 13, 2019.

210 ***recorded in the United States:*** "Germany: Anti-Semitic and Xenophobic Crimes Rose in 2018," DW, May 14, 2019.

210   ***France, the United Kingdom, and Canada:*** David Chazan, "Hate Crimes
       Against Muslims and Jews Soar in France," *Telegraph,* December 30, 2015; Carol
       Kuruvilla, "Religious Hate Crimes in England and Wales Mostly Target People
       Thought to Be Muslim," Huffington Post, October 16, 2018; François Rihouay,
       "Canada Sees Worrying Rise in Hate Crimes," France24, March 15, 2019.
211   ***interference that occurred:*** Zach Montellaro, "The Honest Ads Act Returns,"
       Politico, May 9, 2019.
211   ***motives behind messages:*** Institute for Free Speech Staff, "Analysis: 'Honest Ads
       Act' Targets Americans, not Foreign Actors," Institute for Free Speech, Novem-
       ber 1, 2017.

Chapter 18: Beware Expanded Corporate Controls on Speech

214   ***apply equally online:*** Wendy Zeldin, "U.N. Human Rights Council: First Reso-
       lution on Internet Free Speech," Law Library of Congress Global Legal Monitor,
       July 12, 2012.
214   ***incendiary and extreme messages:*** Christopher Lane, "Flaws in the Algo: How
       Social Media Fuel Political Extremism" *Psychology Today,* February 9, 2018.
216   ***"done by the government":*** *Marsh v. Alabama,* 326 U.S. 501 (1946).
217   ***"speak and listen":*** *Packingham v. North Carolina,* 582 U.S. ___ (2017).
217   ***white supremacist content on YouTube:*** Elizabeth Dwoskin, "YouTube Will
       Remove More White Supremacist and Hoax Videos," *Washington Post,* June 5, 2019.
217   ***platform's guidelines:*** Paris Martineau, "Twitter Will Quarantine Politicians'
       Tweets if They Violate Rules—Finally," *Wired,* June 27, 2019.
217   ***health-related content:*** Travis Yeh, "Addressing Sensational Health Claims,"
       Facebook Newsroom, July 2, 2019.
217   ***political ideology over another:*** Makena Kelly, "Internet Giants Must Stay Un-
       biased to Keep Their Biggest Legal Shield, Senator Proposes," The Verge, June 19,
       2019.
218   ***until it did so:*** Kara Swisher, "Rules Won't Save Twitter. Values Will," *New York
       Times,* August 8, 2018.
218   ***"dangerously weaponizing" the medium:*** Swisher, "Trump Is Too Dangerous for
       Twitter," *New York Times,* October 1, 2019.
218   ***"news on the planet":*** Swisher, "Nancy Pelosi and Fakebook's Dirty Tricks," *New
       York Times,* May 26, 2019.
218   ***"Responsibility for the Chaos":*** Swisher, "'If You've Built a Chaos Factory, You
       Can't Dodge Responsibility for the Chaos,'" *New York Times,* June 19, 2019.
218   ***suppress more content:*** Daphne Keller, "Facebook Restricts Speech by Popular
       Demand," *The Atlantic,* September 22, 2019.
220   ***YouTube each day:*** "37 Mind Blowing YouTube Facts, Figures and
       Statistics—2019," Merchdope, July 29, 2019.
220   ***tweets per day:*** "Twitter Usage Statistics," https://www.internetlivestats.com/twit
       ter-statistics/.

220   *were by bots:* Nicholas Sakelaris, "About 20% of Election Posts on Twitter Last
        Fall Were 'Bots,' Study Says," UPI, February 5, 2019.

220   *are fake:* Andrew Hutchinson, "Facebook Outlines the Number of Fake Accounts
        on Their Platform in New Report," Social Media Today, May 16, 2018.

220   *contentious content:* Facebook, "Community Standards," https://www.facebook
        .com/communitystandards/; YouTube, "Policies and Safety," https://www.you
        tube.com/intl/en-GB/about/policies/#community-guidelines; Twitter, "The Twit-
        ter Rules," https://help.twitter.com/en/rules-and-policies/twitter-rules.

221   *fight back:* Jillian C. York, "Facebook and Twitter Are Getting Rich by Building
        a Culture of Snitching," QZ, July 14, 2016.

221   *ability to mobilize:* David Kaye, *Speech Police: The Global Struggle to Govern the
        Internet* (New York: Columbia Global Reports, 2019).

221   *average Facebook worker:* Casey Newton, "Bodies in Seats," The Verge, June 19,
        2019.

221   *companies offer them:* Sarah T. Roberts, *Behind the Screen: Content Moderation
        in the Shadows of Social Media* (New Haven, CT: Yale University Press, 2019).

221   *"individual cases":* Newton, "The Trauma Floor," The Verge, February 15, 2019.

222   *matter of seconds:* Brian Amerige, "Facebook Has a Right to Block 'Hate
        Speech'—but Here's Why It Shouldn't," Quillette, February 7, 2019.

222   *content it takes down:* Simon Van Zuylen-Wood, "'Men Are Scum': Inside Face-
        book's War on Hate Speech," *Vanity Fair,* February 26, 2019; Guy Rosen, "An
        Update on How We Are Doing at Enforcing Our Community Standards," Face-
        book Newsroom, May 23, 2019, https://newsroom.fb.com/news/2019/05/enforc
        ing-our-community-standards-3/.

222   *strict nondisclosure contracts:* Newton, "The Trauma Floor."

222   *individual moderators:* Ibid.

222   *fall short:* Max Fisher, "Inside Facebook's Secret Rulebook for Global Political
        Speech," *New York Times,* December 27, 2018.

222   *stonewalling the project:* Davey Alba, "Ahead of 2020, Facebook Falls Short on
        Plan to Share Data on Disinformation," *New York Times,* September 29, 2019.

223   *do anything about it:* Facebook, "Help Community," https://www.facebook.com
        /help/community/topics/.

223   *was removed:* Julia Angwin and Hannes Grassegger, "Facebook's Secret Censor-
        ship Rules Protect White Men from Hate Speech but Not Black Children," Pro-
        Publica, June 28, 2017.

224   *the president's supporters:* Steven Overly and Alexandra S. Levine, "Trump
        Draws Public into Bias Feud with Social Media Firms," Politico, May 15, 2019.

224   *discretionary decisions:* Newton, "The Real Bias on Social Networks Isn't
        Against Conservatives," The Verge, April 11, 2019; Michael Nunez, "Former
        Facebook Workers: We Routinely Suppressed Conservative News," Gizmodo,
        March 9, 2016; Amerige, "Facebook Has a Right to Block 'Hate Speech'—but
        Here's Why It Shouldn't."

224   *Palo Alto homes:* Natasha Bertrand and Daniel Lippman, "Inside Mark Zuck-

erberg's Private Meetings with Conservative Pundits," Politico, October 14, 2019.

225 ***often powerless:*** Angwin and Grassegger, "Facebook's Secret Censorship Rules Protect White Men from Hate Speech but Not Black Children."

225 ***little disruption:*** J. M. Berger, "Nazis vs. ISIS on Twitter: A Comparative Study of White Nationalist and ISIS Online Social Media Networks," GW Program on Extremism, September 2016.

225 ***removed en masse:*** Nitasha Tiku, "Tech Platforms Treat White Nationalism Different from Islamic Terrorism," *Wired,* March 20, 2019.

225 ***"improve our detection systems":*** YouTube (YouTubeInsider) Tweet, March 18, 2019, https://twitter.com/YouTubeInsider/status/1107646034958794753.

225 ***"blowback from the right":*** Tiku, "Tech Platforms Treat White Nationalism Different from Islamic Terrorism."

226 ***a good fight:*** Jack M. Balkin, "Free Speech Is a Triangle," *Columbia Law Review* 118, no. 7 (2018): 2011–56.

226 ***tune out:*** Amerige, "Facebook Has a Right to Block 'Hate Speech'—but Here's Why It Shouldn't."

226 ***misleading information:*** Robinson Meyer, "The Grim Conclusions of the Largest-Ever Study of Fake News," *The Atlantic,* March 8, 2018.

226 ***pulling ads from the platform:*** Van Zuylen-Wood, "'Men Are Scum': Inside Facebook's War on Hate Speech."

226 ***insulting the monarch:*** Angwin and Grassegger, "Facebook's Secret Censorship Rules Protect White Men from Hate Speech but Not Black Children."

227 ***expunge it from their outlets:*** Stuart Macdonald, "How Tech Companies Are Trying to Disrupt Terrorist Social Media Activity," *Scientific American,* June 26, 2018.

227 ***"reporting and analyzing it":*** Suhauna Hussain and Samantha Masunaga, "YouTube's Purge of White Supremacist Videos Also Hits Anti-Racism Channels," *San Francisco Chronicle,* June 7, 2019.

227 ***"animals to fight":*** Paige Leskin, "YouTube Criticized after Removing Videos of Robot Fights for Showing 'The Deliberate Infliction of Animal Suffering,'" Business Insider, August 21, 2019.

227 ***no human being even involved:*** Nick Feamster, "Artificial Intelligence and the Future of Online Content Moderation," Freedom to Tinker, March 21, 2018.

228 ***adjudicating the content itself:*** "Coordinated Inauthentic Behavior Explained," Facebook Newsroom, December 6, 2018.

228 ***"mislead users":*** Google, "How Google Fights Disinformation," February 2019, https://www.blog.google/documents/37/How_Google_Fights_Disinformation.pdf, 16.

230 ***"commercial speech":*** *Virginia State Pharmacy Board v. Virginia Citizens Consumer Council,* 425 U.S. 748 (1976).

230 ***affecting the company:*** *First National Bank of Boston v. Bellotti,* 435 U.S. 765 (1978).

230 ***"rights of these people":*** *Burwell v. Hobby Lobby,* 573 U.S. ___ (2014).

Chapter 19: Hold Tech Platforms Accountable for Their Influence on Public Discourse

233   ***basics of social media:*** Emily Stewart, "Lawmakers Seem Confused about What Facebook Does—and How to Fix It," Vox, April 10, 2018.

234   ***proportions are even higher:*** Pew Research Center, "Social Media Fact Sheet," June 12, 2019, https://www.pewinternet.org/fact-sheet/social-media/.

235   ***Social Media Revenues:*** Siva Vaidhyanathan, "Billion-Dollar Fines Can't Stop Google and Facebook. That's Peanuts for Them," *Guardian*, July 26, 2019; J. Clement, "Global Twitter Revenue 2010–2018," Statista, February 22, 2019, https://www.statista.com/statistics/204211/worldwide-twitter-revenue/.

235   ***3 percent of Alphabet's:*** Shobit Seth, "The World's Top 9 News Companies," Investopedia, November 22, 2018.

235   ***"sucked at it for years":*** Charlie Warzel, "'A Honeypot for Assholes': Inside Twitter's 10-Year Failure to Stop Harassment," BuzzFeed News, August 11, 2016.

235   ***ideological antagonists:*** PEN America, "Online Harassment Survey: Key Findings," https://pen.org/online-harassment-survey-key-findings/.

236   ***data, and security breaches:*** Michael Heller, "A Recent History of Facebook Security and Privacy Issues," Tech Target, April 30, 2019.

236   ***back to haunt them:*** PEN America, "Chilling Effects: NSA Surveillance Drives U.S. Writers to Self-Censor," https://pen.org/research-resources/chilling-effects/.

237   ***light of day:*** Nicolas Suzor, "What Do We Mean When We Talk about Transparency in Content Moderation?" Digital Social Contract, May 21, 2019; Spandana Singh, "Pressing Facebook for More Transparency and Accountability Around Content Moderation," New America, November 16, 2018.

238   ***bias toward the powerful:*** Santa Clara Principles, https://santaclaraprinciples.org/.

238   ***automated moderation:*** Kaye, "Report of the Special Rapporteur on the Promotion and Protection of the Right to Freedom of Opinion and Expression," 121–25.

239   ***create on their platform:*** Digital Media Law Project, "Immunity for Online Publishers Under the Communications Decency Act," http://www.dmlp.org/legal-guide/immunity-online-publishers-under-communications-decency-act.

240   ***offering users a free-for-all:*** Digital Media Law Project, "Immunity for Online Publishers Under the Communications Decency Act."

240   ***"third parties at all":*** Ibid.; Alina Selyukh, "Section 230: A Key Legal Shield for Facebook, Google Is About to Change," NPR, March 21, 2018.

240   ***violated the law:*** Electronic Frontier Foundation, "Section 230 of the Communications Decency Act," https://www.eff.org/issues/cda230.

241   ***content purveyor:*** John Bergmayer, "How to Go Beyond Section 230 without Crashing the Internet," Public Knowledge, May 21, 2019.

241   ***stripped of immunity:*** Danielle Keats Citron and Benjamin Wittes, "The Internet Will Not Break: Denying Bad Samaritans § 230 Immunity," *Fordham Law Review* 86, no. 2 (2017): 401–23.

241   *people of color:* Olivier Sylvain, "Intermediary Design Duties," *Connecticut Law Review* 50, no. 1 (2018): 203–77.

242   *serves the public interest:* Business & Human Rights Resource Centre, "UN Guiding Principles," https://www.business-humanrights.org/en/un-guiding-prin ciples.

242   *step in the right direction:* Kaye, "Report of the Special Rapporteur on the Promotion and Protection of the Right to Freedom of Opinion and Expression," 118–21.

243   *rooted in human rights law:* Jack Dorsey, "Agree w all of this. Our early values informed our rules. We likely over-rotated on one value, & then let the rules react to rapidly changing circumstances (some we helped create). . . ." Tweet, August 10, 2018, https://twitter.com/jack/status/1027962500438843397?lang=en.

243   *"human rights standards":* Monika Bickert, "Updating the Values That Inform Our Community Standards," Facebook Newsroom, September 12, 2019.

245   *content removal decisions:* Mark Zuckerberg, "A Blueprint for Content Governance and Enforcement," Facebook, November 15, 2018.

245   *"transparent and binding":* Kurt Wagner, "Facebook Is Building an Oversight Board. Can That Fix Its Problems?" Bloomberg, June 24, 2019.

246   *reversing the company's decisions:* Zuckerberg, "A Blueprint for Content Governance and Enforcement."

246   *reputation as feckless:* Facebook, "Oversight Board Charter," Facebook Newsroom Files, September 2019.

246   *the same purpose:* David Kaye, "The Clash Over Regulating Online Speech," Slate, June 6, 2019.

Chapter 20: Know the Case for Free Speech

250   *"no platforming":* Teresa M. Bejan, The Two Clashing Meanings of "Free Speech," *The Atlantic,* December 2, 2017.

250   *subject to the law:* Claire Breay and Julian Harrison, "Magna Carta: An Introduction," British Library, July 28, 2014, https://www.bl.uk/magna-carta/articles /magna-carta-an-introduction.

250   *bad ideas on their own:* John Milton, *Areopagitica and Other Prose Works* (New York: Dover, 2016).

250   *foster conflict:* Jack Miller Center, "John Locke: Toleration and Limited Government," https://jackmillercenter.org/cd-resources/john-locke-toleration-limited -government/.

250   *against fanaticism:* Steven Poole, "A Beginner's Guide to Voltaire, the Philosopher of Free Speech and Tolerance," *Guardian,* January 18, 2015.

251   *peaceful assembly, and association:* United Nations, "Universal Declaration of Human Rights" (1948).

251   *"free and open encounter?":* Milton, *Areopagitica and Other Prose Works,* 35.

252   *"competition of the market":* Abrams v. United States, 250 U.S. 616, 630 (1919).

252 *veracity and falsehood:* John Stuart Mill, *On Liberty* (London: Longman, Roberts & Green, 1869).

252 *"engine for advancing knowledge":* Frederick Schauer, *Free Speech: A Philosophical Enquiry* (Cambridge: Cambridge University Press, 1982).

253 *"responsibility to its constituents":* James Madison, *The Papers of James Madison,* vol. 17, *March 1797 through March 1801,* edited by David B. Mattern (Charlottesville: University Press of Virginia, 1991); Vincent Blasi, *Freedom of Speech in the History of Ideas: Landmark Cases, Historic Essays, and Recent Developments* (St. Paul, MN: Western Academic, 2015).

253 *"principle of the American government":* Whitney v. California, 274 U.S. 357 (1927).

253 *"silence its critics":* Harry Kalven Jr., "The New York Times Case: A Note on 'The Central Meaning of the First Amendment,'" *1964 Supreme Court Review* 64, 191–221.

253 *marketplace for political deliberation:* Nixon v. Shrink Missouri Government PAC, 528 U.S. 377.

254 *"confident, innovative citizenship":* Vincent Blasi, "The First Amendment and the Ideal of Civic Courage: The Brandeis Opinion in Whitney v. California," *William & Mary Law Review* 29, no. 4 (1988): 692.

254 *"challenge of threatening ideas":* Ibid., 694.

254 *"bondage of irrational fears":* Whitney v. California, 274 U.S. 357 (1927).

255 *what you choose:* Martin H. Redish, "Value of Free Speech," *University of Pennsylvania Law Review* 130, no. 2 (1982): 591–645.

255 *dignity and self-fulfillment:* Liz Halloran, "Explaining Justice Kennedy: The Dignity Factor," NPR, June 28, 2013.

255 *"foundation of our freedom":* United States v. Alvarez, 567 U.S. 709 (2012).

255 *quest for knowledge:* Eileen Reeves, "Augustine and Galileo on Reading the Heavens," *Journal of the History of Ideas* 52, no. 3 (1991): 563–79.

256 *Galileo, and Darwin:* James R. Ferguson, "Scientific Inquiry and the First Amendment," *Cornell Law Review* 64, no. 4 (1979): 641.

256 *lowering returns:* Amartya Sen, "Press Freedom: What Is It Good For?" *Index on Censorship* 42, no. 3 (2013): 6–14; Amartya Sen, "Democracy as a Universal Value," *Journal of Democracy* 10, no. 3 (1999): 3–17.

257 *grounded in repression:* Sen, "Press Freedom: What Is It Good For?" and Sen, "Democracy as a Universal Value."

257 *"diffuse tension":* Edward J. Eberle, "Art as Speech," *University of Pennsylvania Journal of Law & Social Change* 11, no. 1 (2007): 4.

258 *"form of freedom":* Palko v. Connecticut 302 U.S. 319 (1937).

258 *against their conscience:* West Virginia State Board of Education v. Barnette, 319 U.S. 624 (1943).

258 *Vietnam War:* Tinker v. Des Moines Independent Community School District, 393 U.S. 503 (1969).

258 *birth control illegal:* Griswold v. Connecticut, 381 U.S. 479 (1965).

258 *could not be prohibited:* Texas v. Johnson, 491 U.S. 397 (1989).

INDEX

ABOUT THE AUTHOR

SUZANNE NOSSEL is the CEO of PEN America, the foremost organization working to protect and advance human rights, free expression, and literature. She has also served as the chief operating officer of Human Rights Watch and as executive director of Amnesty International USA and held senior State Department positions in the Clinton and Obama administrations. A graduate of Harvard College and Harvard Law School, Nossel frequently writes op-eds for the *New York Times,* the *Washington Post,* and other publications, as well as a regular column for *Foreign Policy* magazine. She lives in New York City.